MONOGRAPHS OF THE
SOCIETY FOR RESEARCH IN
CHILD DEVELOPMENT

Serial No. 228, Vol. 57, No. 4, 1992

OVERREGULARIZATION IN LANGUAGE ACQUISITION

Gary F. Marcus
Steven Pinker
Michael Ullman
Michelle Hollander
T. John Rosen
Fei Xu

WITH COMMENTARY BY
Harald Clahsen

MONOGRAPHS OF THE SOCIETY FOR RESEARCH IN CHILD DEVELOPMENT
Serial No. 228, Vol. 57, No. 4, 1992

CONTENTS

ABSTRACT

MARCUS, GARY F.; PINKER, STEVEN; ULLMAN, MICHAEL; HOLLANDER, MICHELLE; ROSEN, T. JOHN; and XU, FEI. Overregularization in Language Acquisition. With Commentary by HARALD CLAHSEN. *Monographs of the Society for Research in Child Development,* 1992, **57**(4, Serial No. 228).

Children extend regular grammatical patterns to irregular words, resulting in overregularizations like *comed,* often after a period of correct performance ("U-shaped development"). The errors seem paradigmatic of rule use, hence bear on central issues in the psychology of rules: how creative rule application interacts with memorized exceptions in development, how overgeneral rules are unlearned in the absence of parental feedback, and whether cognitive processes involve explicit rules or parallel distributed processing (connectionist) networks. We remedy the lack of quantitative data on overregularization by analyzing 11,521 irregular past tense utterances in the spontaneous speech of 83 children. Our findings are as follows. (1) Overregularization errors are relatively rare (median 2.5% of irregular past tense forms), suggesting that there is no qualitative defect in children's grammars that must be unlearned. (2) Overregularization occurs at a roughly constant low rate from the 2s into the school-age years, affecting most irregular verbs. (3) Although overregularization errors never predominate, one aspect of their purported U-shaped development was confirmed quantitatively: an extended period of correct performance precedes the first error. (4) Overregularization does not correlate with increases in the number or proportion of regular verbs in parental speech, children's speech, or children's vocabularies. Thus, the traditional account in which memory operates before rules cannot be replaced by a connectionist alternative in which a single network displays rotelike or rulelike behavior in response to changes in input statistics. (5) Overregularizations first appear when children begin to mark regular verbs for tense reliably (i.e., when they stop saying *Yesterday I walk*). (6) The more often a parent uses an irregular form, the less often the child overregularizes it. (7) Verbs are protected from overregularization by similar-sounding irregulars, but they are not attracted to overregularization by similar-sounding regulars, suggesting that irregular patterns are stored in an associative memory with connectionist properties, but that regulars are not. We propose a simple explanation. Children, like adults, mark tense using memory (for irregulars) and an affixation rule that can generate a regular past tense form for any verb. Retrieval of an irregular blocks the rule, but children's memory traces are not strong enough to guarantee perfect retrieval. When retrieval fails, the rule is applied, and overregularization results.

I. INTRODUCTION

Overregularizations like *comed* and *foots* are among the most conspicuous grammatical errors in child language, and they have been commented on for as long as language development has been studied (Bateman, 1916; Brown, 1973; Brown & Bellugi, 1964; Bybee & Slobin, 1982a; Carlton, 1947; Carroll, 1961; Cazden, 1968; Chamberlain, 1906; Ervin, 1964; Ervin & Miller, 1963; Guillaume, 1927; Kuczaj, 1977a, 1981; Menyuk, 1963; Miller & Ervin, 1964; Slobin, 1971, 1978; Smith, 1933; see also Edwards, 1970). These errors are made possible by the fact that English has two ways of creating inflected forms. Most verbs add the suffix *-ed* to their stems to form the past tense, but about 180 exceptional or "irregular" verbs form their past tenses in idiosyncratic ways such as a vowel change (*come-came*), replacement of a final consonant or rhyme (*make-made, teach-taught*), substitution of another form (*go-went*), or no change at all (*cut-cut*). Overregularization errors consist of applying the regular pattern to an irregular stem. Since children do not hear these forms from their parents, the errors reveal the operation of a creative process, presumably corresponding to a mental operation implementing the *-ed*-suffixation rule posited by grammarians.

Past tense overregularization is just one kind of error in one peripheral aspect of one component of the grammar of one language. Nonetheless, it has assumed a surprising prominence in cognitive science over the past several decades. Overregularization has been offered as the quintessential demonstration of the creative essence of human language (Chomsky, 1959) and of the necessity of explaining cognitive processes by rules and representations rather than by rote and reinforcement (e.g., Brown & Bellugi, 1964; Lenneberg, 1964; McNeill, 1966; Slobin, 1971; Smith, Langston, & Nisbett, in press).

Overregularization has also become famous because of its interesting developmental course, first noted by Ervin and Miller (1963; see also Cazden, 1968; Miller & Ervin, 1964; Pinker & Prince, 1988). The first overregularization errors seem to appear after a period in which, when children mark tense on irregular verbs at all, they do so correctly. Overregularization thus represents a decline in performance in overt tense marking, resulting in a U-shaped curve if the proportion of irregular past tense forms that are correct is plotted against age. The nonmonotonicity has been taken as evidence for successive "reorganizations" of the child's linguistic system, reflecting a tendency to ferret out generalizations and to prefer them to exceptional forms, which must later be reintegrated in some fashion. As an example of cognitive reorganization triggered by a fondness for regularity, overregularization has often been considered paradigmatic of language development (Bowerman, 1982a, 1982b; Slobin, 1973) and cognitive development (Bever, 1982; Strauss, 1982) in general. It has been used as a metaphor for psychological processes ranging from solving balance-beam problems (Karmiloff-Smith & Inhelder, 1974–1975) to learning computer-user interfaces (Grudin & Norman, 1991) to developing expertise in medical decision making (Patel & Groen, 1991).

Recently, explaining overregularization has become relevant to the very foundations of cognitive science. Virtually all discussions have implicitly assumed that overregularizations can be modeled in principle only by some explicit representation of a rule in the child's head. Rumelhart and McClelland (1986, 1987) showed this assumption to be false. They devised a computer simulation of an associative network that acquired hundreds of regular and irregular verbs and generalized properly to dozens of new verbs that it had not been trained on. More strikingly, the model appeared to go through a U-shaped developmental sequence, first producing irregular verb forms correctly and later overregularizing them, and it also seemed to manifest several other effects previously known to characterize children's behavior. But the model had no explicit representation of words, rules, or a distinction between regular and irregular systems; it simply mapped from features standing for the sounds of the verb stem to features standing for the sounds of the past tense form. The Rumelhart-McClelland model is a prominent representative of the parallel distributed processing (PDP), connectionist, or neural networks approach, in which cognitive processes are modeled as densely interconnected networks of simple neuronlike units. Its apparent success is commonly seen as a dramatic piece of support for the PDP approach in general and as posing a severe challenge to rule-based approaches to language and cognition (see, e.g., McClelland, Rumelhart, & Hinton, 1986; Rumelhart & McClelland, 1986; Smolensky, 1988). One reviewer (Sampson, 1987), writing in the *Times Literary Supplement,* called the potential implications of the Rumelhart-McClelland model for the study of language "awesome" because "to continue teaching [linguistics] in the orthodox style would be like keeping alchemy alive."

Lachter and Bever (1988) and Pinker and Prince (1988) have challenged the psychological reality of the Rumelhart-McClelland model on a variety of grounds. But they praised it for the unprecedented precision of its quantitative predictions about child language data. Indeed, Rumelhart and McClelland were far ahead of the field of developmental psycholinguistics in the quality and quantity of data required for proper tests of their hypotheses. As such they have underscored the absence of systematic quantitative reports of the developmental course of overregularization, its distribution across children, verbs, and time, its relation to the size of the child's vocabulary, and the lexical factors that cause some verbs to be overregularized more than others. This data gap has left many fundamental questions unanswered.

The phenomenon of overregularization itself is not in doubt, nor is the creative nature of the psychological processes that cause it, which reveals itself in other ways. Children frequently inflect their own invented verbs such as *speeched* (Chamberlain, 1906), *by-ed* (i.e., "went by"; Miller & Ervin, 1964); *eat lunched* (Kuczaj, 1977a), *broomed* (Clark, 1982), and *grained* (Pinker, Lebeaux, & Frost, 1987). In many experiments, beginning with Berko's (1958) classic "*wug* test," children are given a made-up verb and are then asked to use it in a past tense context, for example, *Here is a man who likes to rick. He did the same thing yesterday. Yesterday he* ———. The children readily produce appropriate forms such as *ricked* and, when provided with an existing irregular stem, frequently overregularize it (Anisfeld & Tucker, 1967; Berko, 1958; Bryant & Anisfeld, 1969; Cox, 1989; Derwing & Baker, 1979; Kim, Marcus, Hollander, & Pinker, 1991; Kuczaj, 1978; Marchman, 1988; Miller & Ervin, 1964; Pinker et al., 1987). In other experiments, children have been found to judge overregularizations (Kuczaj, 1978) or made-up forms resembling regularly inflected forms (Anisfeld, Barlow, & Frail, 1968; Anisfeld & Gordon, 1968) as acceptable.

Beyond the mere fact that children do more than memorize their parents' verb forms, however, not much is known about the details of overregularization. Nowhere in the literature can one find solid answers to such basic questions as, How often do children overregularize? (One percent of the opportunities? Fifty? One hundred?) At what age do they start? At what age do they stop? What is the developmental curve for irregular verbs, and does it really look like a U? Are all verbs overregularized, or only some, and what factors account for differences among verbs? How is overregularization related to other events in children's language development, such as their vocabulary growth, and the syntax of tense marking? Given how often overregularization has been used to explain other things, it is surprising how little about the phenomenon itself has been documented.

This *Monograph* is an attempt to fill these gaps. Using the large set of transcripts of children's spontaneous speech recently made available by the Child Language Data Exchange System (ChiLDES; MacWhinney & Snow, 1985, 1990), together with previously published tallies of children's vocabulary and new unpublished data, we document the process of overregularization in quantitative detail. With these data in hand, we will be in a position to evaluate explanations of the psychological processes causing overregularization.

Presumably children are not designed to overregularize per se; their errors are a temporary side effect of a mechanism designed to learn the language. Thus, our investigation of overregularization is organized by a research program that addresses the central question of language acquisition research: how children acquire the ability to produce and understand an infinite number of sentences of their native language from the finite sample of speech available in conversations with adults. The "learnability approach" to language development (see Pinker, 1979, 1984; Wexler & Culicover, 1980) seeks to characterize these learning mechanisms; it treats language acquisition as a difficult software engineering problem and attempts to understand how children solve it. The approach dictates the starting point for this *Monograph* (indeed, for any systematic study of language development). One must begin with an analysis of what is learned, what information is available to learn it, and what kind of computational mechanisms are capable of carrying out the learning task successfully. Such mechanisms define hypotheses about the psychology of the child, which can then be tested and refined against developmental and linguistic data. (As we shall see, overregularization is a prime example of one of the fundamental problems in understanding language learnability: how children avoid or unlearn errors in the absence of parental corrections.) Learnability is not a theory but a research problem, and as such it in no way presupposes the nature of the child's language learning mechanisms (e.g., whether they are symbolic rules or connectionist networks; whether they are specific to language or widely applicable across many cognitive domains). What it does is pick out the central empirical fact to be explained—that children, at some point, become capable speakers of a language—and it seeks an explanation in terms of explicit computational operations, not metaphors or impressionistic descriptions. As such, it attempts to characterize the innate mechanisms responsible for human linguistic abilities. This does not single out learnability research as a "nativist" approach because all explicit theories involving learning must at some point specify the innate mechanisms that do the learning if they are to avoid an infinite regress.

Chapter II, the first substantive chapter of the *Monograph,* then, lays out the logic of linguistic irregularity and overregularization and proposes a simple psychological hypothesis of how children could learn the irregular system and why they might produce errors while doing so. We outline behavioral predictions relevant to this hypothesis and the current state of the evidence concerning them.

After describing the subjects and methods in Chapter III, we present the vital statistics of overregularization in Chapter IV. We begin by estimating the overall rate of overregularization, a figure of obvious importance. As we shall see, one's explanation of children's behavior would be very different depending on whether they make overregularization errors almost none of the time or almost all the time. We then examine whether the rate of overregularization substantially varies across time, children, verbs, and combinations of these sampling units. For example, we test whether an overall steady overregularization curve for a child might actually be a composite of curves for individual verbs each overregularized intensively for a brief period. We also compare the rate of overregularization to the rate of inflecting regular verbs, and we define and search for U-shaped developmental sequences.

In Chapter V, we examine a hypothesis that underlies the surprising ability of the Rumelhart-McClelland model to display U-shaped development. This hypothesis is that overregularization is triggered by an increase in the proportion of regular verb forms that the child processes during development. We first discuss the complex issue of how exactly one should compare the behavior of network simulations and children. On the basis of this discussion, we correlate children's overregularization rates with changes in the number of regular verbs and the proportion of regular verbs among all verbs in the children's speech, the speech they hear from their parents, and the children's vocabularies. Measuring vocabulary size is a notoriously difficult problem in language development, and we present a novel technique, which we also compare to other estimates in the literature.

In Chapter VI, we examine evidence that points to the development of the entire productive tense marking system, rather than the balance of regular and irregular verbs among the vocabulary items feeding it, as the immediate cause of the onset of overregularization.

Chapter VII, the final empirical chapter, tests hypotheses about the causes of overregularization by focusing on inherent properties of different verbs that might cause them to be overregularized more or less often. We consider factors related to memory strength (the frequency of an item in parental speech and its similarity to related items in parental speech), the relatedness of a stem to its past form, and the complexity of the mapping from stem to irregular form. This chapter includes a test of a second hypothesis inspired by the Rumelhart-McClelland model, that regular and irregular marking are computed in a single pattern associator.

In the concluding chapter, we summarize the findings, integrate them within a simple theory, and discuss related theoretical issues.

II. THEORETICAL BACKGROUND

At first glance, the development of overregularization has a straightforward explanation. This traditional explanation, employed both within psycholinguistics and in the other branches of cognitive science that have used overregularization as a metaphor, relies on a dissociation between two psychological processes: rote memory and rule deployment. The rote process memorizes verb forms one by one, and the child can use it at the outset of language development: children hear their parents say *broke,* so they say *broke.* But the English regular past tense rule is not present at the outset of language development, and the child cannot deploy it until he or she has learned it, presumably by abstracting the regular pattern from a set of regular forms accumulated over time from parental speech and juxtaposed as past and stem forms of the same verb (*walk-walked, use-used, play-played,* etc.). The young child sticks to correct forms because they are available from rote memory and there is no machinery capable of overregularizing them yet; the older child, possessing the rule, can apply it to irregular stems, resulting in overregularization errors.

The explanation is inadequate. The problem is that it does not point to any difference between the rule-possessing child and the rule-possessing adult. But there is a difference: children say *comed,* and adults do not. If children say *comed* because they possess a regular rule, why do adults, who also possess the regular rule, not say it too? In fact, the standard explanation in terms of a progression between a rote-only child and a rote-plus-rule child does not make any predictions about overregularization appearing at all. It predicts that the younger, ruleless child would fail a *wug* test (where the child has to provide an inflected form for a novel word like *to wug*), whereas the older, rule-possessing child would pass one. For similar reasons it predicts that the young, ruleless child would inflect familiar irregular verbs correctly (e.g., *broke*) while leaving new ones unmarked (e.g., *stick*), whereas older children would inflect familiar irregular verbs correctly (e.g., *broke*) and overregularize new ones (e.g., *sticked*). But it does *not* predict that children who first use a given verb properly (e.g., *broke*) would later err on that very verb (e.g., *breaked*), which they do (Cazden, 1968; Ervin & Miller, 1963; the phenomenon is documented in more detail in Chap. IV, Sec. II*A*). Possessing a rule that can be applied to novel verbs and applying a rule to existing verbs that already have a past tense form and that do not allow the rule are two different things, and the traditional account does not distinguish between them.

For similar reasons, the rule-rote distinction sheds little light on the other arm of the U, the fact that *breaked* ultimately gives way to exclusive use of *broke*. Once children have developed a rule and are overapplying it, how and why do they curtail its use?

Clearly, understanding the developmental course of overregularization requires more than distinguishing between rule and rote. We must also examine how the regular rule interacts with irregular items. Specifically, to explain differences in the ways children and adults treat irregular verbs, we must first understand how adults treat irregular verbs. Then we can ask what children might be doing that adults are not. We must also examine the information about irregular verbs available from conversation with adults that the child's language learning process might feed on. With knowledge of what is learned and what information is available to learn it, we can develop a theory of how the learning works and why it might result in errors in intermediate stages.

In this chapter, we review the current state of knowledge on these issues (deferring discussion of the Rumelhart-McClelland model to Chap. V) and develop a hypothesis that appears adequate to account for both the development and the cessation of overregularization. The hypothesis is extremely simple, uniting a standard proposal from formal linguistics (that, in the human language system, irregular memorized items block the application of regular rules) and a standard proposal from cognitive psychology (that retrieval of items from memory is probabilistic and sensitive to frequency of exposure). According to this hypothesis, children's language system, like that of adults, is designed so that retrieval of an irregular form suppresses overregularization, but retrieval is imperfect, and when it fails, the regular rule applies as a default, leading to overregularization errors. The hypothesis will lead us to an equally simple empirical prediction: that, at all ages, evidence that the child's system is designed to suppress overregularization should be available in the form of low overall rates of overregularization in comparison to utterances containing the correct irregular form. We will then compare this prediction to competing ones in the literature. This will set the stage for our investigation of the basic quantitative facts of overregularization in the following chapters.

I. BLOCKING OF REGULARIZATION IN ADULTS

Let us begin with a deceptively simple question. Why are overregularizations "errors" at all? This is intended not as a prescriptive question about what one ought to say but as a descriptive question about what adults do say. Adults who speak the most common dialect of American English do not say *breaked,* and they judge it as sounding deviant or childlike (Pinker & Prince, 1988; Ullman & Pinker, 1990, 1992).

The answer is surely not that overregularizations are defective in terms of communicative function; the meaning of *breaked* is perfectly clear. In fact, any child who is willing to overregularize has a communicative advantage over adults. No-change verbs in the adult language like *cut* and *set* are ambiguous between past and nonpast tenses: *On Wednesday I cut the grass* could mean last Wednesday, next Wednesday, or every Wednesday; *On Wednesday I cutted the grass* could mean only a preceding Wednesday.

Another unsatisfactory answer is that adults do not say *breaked* and *cutted* because they have never heard other adults say them. It is unsatisfactory because it assumes that adults would fail a *wug* test, and clearly they do not; people do not stick conservatively to the past tense forms that they heard their parents use or that they currently hear other adults use. Adults are not reluctant to create or accept past tense forms of verbs they never encountered before, such as *John plipped* or *Yeltsin has finally out-Gorbachev'd Gorbachev* (Kim, Pinker, Prince, & Prasada, 1991; Prasada & Pinker, in press). Indeed, new verbs enter the language frequently, such as *snarf* (retrieve a computer file), *scarf* (devour), *frob* (randomly try out adjustments), and *mung* (render inoperable), and their past tense forms do not require separate introductions. In other words, one cannot explain why adults avoid *breaked* by saying that they have never heard anyone else say *breaked* because adults have never heard anyone else say *snarfed* either, but they do not avoid *snarfed.*

A. The Blocking Principle

The problem with overregularizations is not that they have never been heard before but that the irregular counterpart *has* been heard. Clearly, there is a psychological mechanism that causes the experience of hearing an irregular form to block the subsequent application of a regular process to that item. Thus, several linguists have defined this phenomenon in terms of a *blocking principle* (Aronoff, 1976; Kiparsky, 1982; see also Pinker, 1984, who called it the unique entry principle): an idiosyncratic form listed in the mental lexicon as corresponding to a particular grammatical modification of a word (past tense, in this case) blocks the application of a general rule that would effect the same grammatical modification. Thus, *broke,* listed as an idiosyncratic past tense form of *break,* blocks application of the regular past tense rule, preempting *breaked; geese,* listed as a plural of *goose,* blocks *gooses; better,* listed as a comparative of the adjective *good,* blocks *gooder.* Of course, some verbs do have two commonly heard past tense forms, for example, *dived* and *dove;* in these cases, the regular version, which is idiosyncratic precisely because it flouts the blocking principle, would be recorded from the speech input just as if it were an irregular (Pinker, 1984; Ullman & Pinker, 1990).

Now that we have a mechanism that causes overregularizations to be treated as deviant by adults, we can state the developmental problem more precisely. Children do not apply blocking in the same circumstances that adults do. The question now is, Why not? One obvious possibility is that children might have to learn the blocking principle and that overregularizations appear before they have done so. In the following section, we show that this hypothesis is probably wrong and that the source of children's overregularization errors must be sought elsewhere. Before doing so, however, we add a few remarks about the status of the blocking principle.

B. The Psycholinguistic Status of the Blocking Principle

Blocking is not just a restatement of the fact that overregularizations are deviant sounding, nor is it a general prohibition against synonyms. Rather, it is a principle specifically governing the relations among the inflected versions of a given stem. Every word in a language implicitly defines a matrix or "paradigm" of its grammatically modified forms (first person singular present, first person plural present, first person singular past, and so on; see Carstairs, 1987). Blocking dictates that any cell of the matrix for a given word that is filled with an unpredictable specific entry from the input may not also be filled by applying a general rule for that particular combination of grammatical features. It can therefore be interpreted as a psychological mechanism that suppresses the operation of the regular rule in these circumstances.[1]

Blocking thus differs from a pragmatic prohibition against synonymy, such as Clark's (1987, 1990) "principle of contrast" stating that "every two

[1] The blocking principle, in turn, might be reduced to Kiparsky's (1982) more general "elsewhere condition": if the conditions licensing one morphological process constitute a proper subset of the conditions licensing another morphological process, then whenever the conditions of both processes are met by some item, only the process with the more restrictive conditions may apply; the other process applies "elsewhere." In this case, an irregular form like *broke* applies in the conditions "past tense of the verb *break,*" and the regular rule applies in the more general condition "past tense of a verb," so the latter is preempted.

forms contrast in meaning." First, blocking rules out only competing morphological variants and is agnostic about synonyms in general (e.g., it does not rule out *couch* and *sofa;* for recent arguments that languages tolerate true synonyms, see Gathercole, 1987, 1989; for counterarguments, see Clark, 1988, 1990).

More important, there are empirical reasons why blocking per se, not contrast, is needed to explain the fact that irregular verbs cannot be regularized. Neither violations of blocking nor conformity to it can be predicted from the availability of contrasts in meaning. Members of variant pairs such as *leaped-leapt, dived-dove,* and *sneaked-snuck* do not differ reliably in meaning (or do so with near-imperceptible subtlety); they seem to be recorded by the learner in response to the brute fact of hearing them (later we discuss one reason why they arise to begin with). Conversely, verbs like *put, make, give, take, have, come, go,* and *throw* each have dozens of extremely distinct meanings, especially in combination with particles such as *out, up, off, in,* and *away.* Nonetheless, without exception, speakers are not tempted to use the regularized versions of these verbs to express the contrasting meanings; *taked the punishment stoically, gived away the answer, haved a ball, maked out,* and so on are always impossible. This shows that different past tense forms do not necessarily evoke different meanings and that different meanings do not systematically call for different past tense forms (for discussion, see Kim, Pinker, et al., 1991; Pinker & Prince, 1988; and Ullman & Pinker, 1990, 1992).

In addition, blocking just rules out certain kinds of forms in a specific level of grammatical representation; it does not guarantee that an alternative way of expressing a given notion exists, and thus it differs from a communicative principle like contrast that is designed to provide a speaker with exactly one way to express each notion. In fact, there are special circumstances where blocking applies but the irregular is ruled out for other reasons and the speaker is left with an expressibility gap. In particular, blocking applies at a specific level of the mental representation of word forms, not to entire words; roughly, it applies at the level of inflected stems. An entire word may consist of a stem plus a (noninflectional) prefix. For example, speakers of English intuitively perceive *forgo* as containing the stem *go.* Hence, they cannot say *forgoed* because *went,* the listed past tense form of the stem *go,* blocks the application of the regular rule to *go.* However, speakers' sense of the *familiarity* or naturalness of an irregular form is a phenomenon that takes place at the level of the entire word, not the stem.[2]

[2] By "irregular form" here we mean "completely irregular," including the meaning of the combination of the prefix and stem, as in *forgo,* whose meaning cannot be predicted from the combination of *for-* and *go.* This differentiates it from compositionally prefixed forms whose stems preserve their meanings, such as *retake* or *overdo.*

Forgo is a relatively uncommon word, and uses in the past tense are even rarer, so *forwent,* while not sounding grammatically impossible like *forgoed,* nonetheless sounds stilted and unnatural (Pinker & Prince, 1988; Ullman & Pinker, 1992). The verb thus has no perfectly usable past tense form. The regular past is ruled out by blocking (applying at the level of the stem); the irregular past is tainted by unfamiliarity (applying at the level of the entire word). This shows that blocking is a mechanism that operates on specific representations of the speaker's grammatical system.

II. BLOCKING AS A MEANS OF RECOVERING FROM CHILDHOOD ERRORS IN THE ABSENCE OF PARENTAL NEGATIVE FEEDBACK

Logically speaking, given the blocking principle, children could learn that forms such as *breaked* are not English; they would just have to hear their parents say *broke.* Conversely, given the knowledge that forms like *breaked* are not English, children could learn the blocking principle. (As we saw, not hearing one's parents say *breaked* is not enough because parents never say *wugged* either and it is admissible.) Are there any empirical reasons to choose between these possibilities? In this section, we suggest that it is unlikely that children acquire blocking from evidence about which forms are ungrammatical; it is far more likely that they determine which forms are ungrammatical using blocking. The problem stems from the concept "the knowledge that forms like *breaked* are not English" or, more generally, "evidence about which forms are ungrammatical."

A. Negative Evidence and Overregularization

A significant problem in explaining language acquisition is that children do not receive "negative evidence": feedback from parents indicating, for any string of words the child may utter, whether it is a grammatical sentence. Children are not corrected or misunderstood more often when they speak ungrammatically (Brown & Hanlon, 1970), and although it is occasionally suggested that there is weak statistical information about grammaticality in the differential likelihood of parents' repetitions, expansions, or topic changes, there is considerable doubt as to whether such information exists and whether it is necessary or even useful to the child (see Bowerman, 1987; Gordon, 1990; Grimshaw & Pinker, 1989; Pinker, 1989; the literature and issues are analyzed in detail by Marcus, 1992). A lack of negative evidence means that, if the child ever develops a linguistic system that generates a superset of the target language (all the grammatical forms in the target language plus some ungrammatical forms not in the target language), the parental input cannot tell the child that anything is wrong (Gold, 1967;

Osherson, Stob, & Weinstein, 1985; Pinker, 1979). To explain how the adult grammar is attained, then, one must explain either how children avoid generating supersets or, if they do, how they expunge their errors.

Overregularization errors in particular pose this problem. A child who is producing *breaked* and *broke* is speaking a superset of adult English in this domain, which allows only *broke.* And overregularization errors in particular do not reliably occasion negative parental feedback. Kuczaj (1977a, p. 599) noted that, in his investigation, the children (especially his son Abe, who was the main subject) were not systematically corrected for overregularization errors. The following typical chunk of dialogue, which we have found in transcripts of conversations between Kuczaj and Abe (MacWhinney & Snow, 1985), illustrates his observation:

> *Father.* Where is that big piece of paper I gave you yesterday?
> *Abe.* Remember? I writed on it.
> *Father.* Oh that's right don't you have any paper down here buddy?

Moreover, it seems unlikely that children attend to corrections, requests for clarification, recastings, and so on when they do occur. For example, in describing systematic overregularization of participles by his 4½-year-old daughter, Zwicky (1970) reports that "six subsequent months of frequent corrections by her parents had no noticeable effect." The following dialogue, from Cazden (1972), gives the flavor of such attempts:

> *Child.* My teacher holded the baby rabbits and we patted them.
> *Adult.* Did you say your teacher held the baby rabbits?
> *Child.* Yes.
> *Adult.* What did you say she did?
> *Child.* She holded the baby rabbits and we patted them.
> *Adult.* Did you say she held them tightly?
> *Child.* No, she holded them loosely.

More precisely, Morgan and Travis (1989) report a quantitative study on the availability of negative evidence about overregularizations and its relation to children's recovery from such errors. They tabulated the number of overregularization errors and errors in *wh*—— questions, and their correct alternative forms, in the speech of the children known as Adam, Eve, and Sarah (Brown, 1973) and cross-classified them in terms of whether the utterances were followed by parental expansions, exact imitations, partial imitations, clarification questions, confirmation questions, attempts to move the conversation on, and no response. No consistent contingency was found between errors and parental responses: for Adam expansions and clarification questions were more likely to follow his ungrammatical sentences; for

Eve it was expansions and partial imitations that occurred more frequently following her ungrammatical sentences; and for Sarah all five categories of parental response showed the opposite pattern, occurring more frequently after *well*-formed utterances. Unless a child can figure out the kind of parent he or she has (e.g., a grammatical sentence expander or an ungrammatical sentence expander), such feedback is useless (see Marcus, 1992). Moreover, Morgan and Travis showed that, as children get older, even this inconsistent feedback signal disappears. Since the errors continue after the parent has stopped supplying potential feedback, unlearning the errors must depend on some other information source.

B. *How Blocking Obviates the Need for Negative Evidence*

Presumably, this information source is a constraint endogenous to the child's language system. Blocking is just the right kind of constraint: children do not have to receive direct information that *breaked* is ungrammatical; they can infer it from hearing *broke*. In sum, because the input information needed to learn blocking—that forms like *breaked* are ungrammatical—is not available to children, it is unlikely to have been learned from the input, but it may be part of the machinery that does the learning.[3]

If children's language systems incorporated a mechanism implementing blocking (Pinker, 1984) or its equivalent (e.g., MacWhinney, 1978), we would have a straightforward explanation of how they recover from overregularizations in the absence of negative evidence, converging on the adult state. Each time an irregular past tense form is heard in parental speech, the child can record it in the lexicon, and the regular rule is thereafter blocked from applying to it. Thus, blocking is consistent with a developmental sequence progressing from overregularization to correct perfor-

[3] Some such assumption has proved unavoidable to many researchers devising explicit models of language learning, working in a variety of frameworks. For example, Anderson (1983) required a constraint similar to blocking when applying his symbol-processing model of cognition called ACT to the acquisition of morphology (although the principle was not specific to language acquisition but constrained his production-system architecture across all the tasks it was given). In their very different connectionist model, Rumelhart and McClelland (1986) also implemented machinery that carries out a version of blocking. As we shall see, in their supervised learning paradigm, a special input pathway was designed that presented a single "correct" past tense form representing the parental input, and an error-correcting learning procedure acted to suppress the tendency of the model to produce an output that deviated from it. Then a separate mechanism, the whole-string binding network, which contains explicit representations of correct and overregularized forms, sets them in competition with one another to select the form that best approximates the output of the network.

mance (the adult state) without negative evidence. Blocking would prevent children from ever generating a superset of English; they would progress from *breaked* to *broke,* never saying both at the same stage.

III. EVIDENCE RAISING DOUBTS ABOUT BLOCKING IN CHILDREN'S LANGUAGE DEVELOPMENT

Unfortunately, when we examine the full developmental sequence of inflection in children, we immediately run into a problem. Blocking of overregularizations explains monotonic improvement, not U-shaped development. That is, the principle tells us only how children might get out of an overregularization stage. It does not explain how they got into it; indeed, it seems to predict that the child should never get into it in the first place. A child who respects blocking should never allow the regular rule to apply to an irregular form; the irregular would win the competition from the start, and no U-shaped sequence should be seen. If children really go from correct irregulars to overregularizations back to correct irregulars, the hypothesis that blocking is inherent to children's language system is cast into doubt.

At first one might try to explain the full sequence as follows. Suppose blocking is just one manifestation of a more general principle stating only that one of two competing forms must be eliminated, not that the form witnessed in the input eliminates the one generated by rule. Such principles can be found in Clark's (1987) principle of contrast, Wexler and Culicover's (1980) uniqueness principle, and Slobin's (1973) operating principle of one-to-one mapping.[4] If the competition between regularized and irregular forms is two-way rather than one-way, then two successive replacements, each respecting the principle, would define a U-shaped developmental sequence. In the first arm of the U, the listed form is eliminated by the newly acquired rule (perhaps falling under the general phenomenon of "imperialism" of newly acquired inflectional rules discussed by Slobin, 1973, and MacWhinney, 1978). In the second, blocking per se, which requires that the form attested in the input always win out over the one generated by a rule, applies. Crucially, in this hypothesis, the child still avoids a superset of English at all stages: *broke* is replaced by *breaked,* which is in turn replaced by *broke;* at no time may the two forms co-occur.

But this solution is inadequate. Aside from the fact that the imperialism phenomenon (an across-the-board preference for a newly acquired rule) is itself unexplained, the empirical picture of U-shaped development that it

[4] Clark's principle of contrast acts more like blocking per se when it is combined with her principle of conventionality, which forces the child to use the form that is conventional in the speech community whenever competing alternatives arise.

assumes, in which the child actually *loses* early irregular forms, does not seem to be accurate given the (admittedly scanty) data available at present. All the authors that have actually recorded overregularization errors note that these errors coexist with, rather than replace, the early irregulars (Cazden, 1968; Ervin & Miller, 1963; Kuczaj, 1977a, 1981). This is exactly what all the principles dictating unique forms proscribe. Maratsos (1987) points to such coexistence, which can last for months or years, as a reason to doubt the existence of such principles. Children, it seems, do generate a superset of English (they use *break* and *broke* simultaneously), so if blocking is the explanation of how children eventually abandon this superset, it leaves it a puzzle why they adopted it to begin with and why they retain it for so long.[5]

IV. BLOCKING AND RETRIEVAL FAILURE: A SIMPLE EXPLANATION OF OVERREGULARIZATION ERRORS

We appear to be at an impasse. The mechanism required to explain adult language (blocking) seems to be systematically flouted by the child during a period in which correct and overregularized forms coexist. But the information necessary to learn blocking—negative evidence through parental feedback—does not exist. As a result, the processes causing the appearance and disappearance of overregularization have been shrouded in mystery, and it is tempting to treat it as a qualitative developmental stage that the child enters and exits, driven by some fundamental reorganization. But positing two qualitatively different kinds of machinery, one for children, one for adults, is not exactly parsimonious, especially since no account has been proposed of how the unknown changing machinery leads to the development of overregularization. Is there a simpler alternative?

One of them is proposed in MacWhinney (1978, pp. 6–7) and Pinker (1984, pp. 194–195). Say that children possess a correct irregular in lexical long-term memory and represent it as the past of the corresponding stem, but that either the content of the memory entry for the irregular or the link to the stem, or both, is not accessible 100% of the time. If an irregular past tense lexical entry is not retrieved, it obviously cannot block regularization. If the child intends to mark tense and possesses a process for inflecting

[5] Another possible solution, originally proposed by Kuczaj (1977a, 1981), is that children may fail to realize that a given irregular form corresponds to the past tense version of some stem. Rather, they may treat the irregular past as an independent verb, and blocking would not apply. Errors would cease when the two verbs were united, presumably when the child noticed that they were semantically identical except for pastness and (in most cases) were phonologically similar as well. We discuss this solution in Chap. VII, Sec. II.

arbitrary stems, the output will be an overregularization.[6] Similarly, if the content of a stored past tense form is retrieved, but without its "past tense" link or feature, overregularizations consisting of an affixed past stem would result, like *broked* or *wented.*[7]

The blocking-and-retrieval-failure hypothesis is appealing because it can be deduced from the very logic of irregularity, supplemented only by an uncontroversial fact about human memory known since Ebbinghaus. What is the past tense form of the verb *to shend,* meaning "to shame"? If you answered *shended,* then you have overregularized; the correct form is *shent* (Bybee & Slobin, 1982b). Of course, this "error" is not surprising. Irregular forms are not predictable (that is what "irregular" means), so the only way you could have produced *shent* was if you had previously heard it and remembered it. But you have heard it zero times, hence cannot have remembered it. Now, if in two years you were asked the question again and overregularized it once more, it would still not be surprising, because you would have heard it only once. Since memory storage and retrieval are probabilistic, with a higher probability of retrieval for items that have been presented to the learner more often, hearing an irregular a small number of times should be only somewhat better than not hearing it at all. Thus, low-frequency irregulars are inherently prone to overregularization (MacWhinney, 1978; Pinker, 1984; Slobin, 1971).

Children, by definition, have not lived as long as adults. Among the life experiences that one accumulates through the years is hearing the past tense forms of irregular verbs. Many verbs for a given child will be like *shent* for an adult: never heard; heard but not attended to; heard and attended to,

[6] The principal difference between MacWhinney's (1978) and Pinker's (1984) expositions is that Pinker takes the blocking principle, as it was explicated and justified by linguists to explain adult knowledge, and simply attributes it to the child, whereas MacWhinney introduced it as a specific new claim about the child's morphological acquisition system. Note that MacWhinney has since disavowed the claims that regularizations are produced by a rule and that they are suppressed by rote forms across the board. He has proposed instead that regularizations are produced by a propertywise generalization process like that of the Rumelhart-McClelland model and that overregularizations are suppressed by specific, individually learned inhibitions of each overregularized form by its irregular counterpart (MacWhinney, 1987, pp. 285, 295; see also MacWhinney & Leinbach, 1991; and Chap. VIII, Sec. III).

[7] Presumably, the fourth logically possible retrieval pattern can occur as well: the existence of a stored past tense form linked to a stem is registered, but its content cannot be recovered, a state like that studied in memory phenomena such as tip of the tongue (Brown & McNeill, 1966), feeling of knowing (Hart, 1965), and deep dyslexia (Coltheart, Patterson, & Marshall, 1980). In such cases, we would not see overregularization, because the activation of the irregular memory entry blocks the rule; nor would we see the correct irregular, because its content is temporarily unavailable. What would surface is the unmarked stem.

but not enough times to be able to recall on demand reliably. A child should overregularize these verbs, even with a grammatical system identical to adults'. If children's memory retrieval is noisier than adults', they should make these errors even more often, holding number of exposures constant. But regardless of whether there are quantitative differences between children and adults, there need be no qualitative differences; blocking of a regular rule by retrieval of an irregular stored in memory and a memory retrieval rate of less than 100% are sufficient to account for the phenomenon.

The retrieval failure hypothesis predicts that overregularization is not confined to childhood, and, indeed, it is not. Adults occasionally make overregularization errors in their spontaneous speech (Stemberger, 1982; see Chap. IV, Sec. II*B*). Errors occur even more often in experiments where adults must utter past tense forms under time pressure, and for some kinds of irregulars, the errors are more likely with the lower-frequency verbs (Bybee & Slobin, 1982a). Even unpressured language use shows the forces of overregularization on low-frequency verbs. About 35 irregular verbs admit regular past tense forms as more or less natural alternatives in casual American speech, for example, *dreamt-dreamed* and *dove-dived* (for a list, see Pinker & Prince, 1988; Ullman & Pinker, 1992). Stemberger (1989) and Ullman and Pinker (1990, 1992) have found that these "doublets" have lower average nonpast stem frequencies than verbs that are exclusively irregular. Moreover, within doublets, the frequency of the irregular past tense form correlates significantly with experimental subjects' ratings of the naturalness of the irregular versus the regularized past tense forms: low frequency forms like *slew, slunk, trod, rent,* and *strove* were likely to be preferred in regularized versions. Finally, the hypothesis is consistent with the fact that irregulars in general tend to be high in frequency in English and that lower-frequency irregular verbs in earlier stages of the language (e.g., *geld-gelt, cleave-clove, abide-abode*) were likely to become regular over time (Bybee, 1985).[8] Low-frequency past tense forms are always in danger of not being uniformly memorized in some generation; if so, the verbs, if they remain in the language at all, will become regular. Verbs that survive as irregulars are thus more likely to be high in frequency.

In sum, the hypothesis of blocking with occasional retrieval failure augments the traditional rule-rote distinction to explain the time course of overregularization errors as follows. Very young children have not yet

[8] Bybee examined 33 surviving verbs from three classes of strong verbs in Old English. Fifteen have come through in Modern English as irregular verbs; 18 have become regular. The surviving irregulars have a mean Francis and Kucera (1982) frequency of 515 over all their inflectional forms, 137 in the past tense; the regularized verbs have a mean frequency of 21 over all forms, five in the past tense.

learned that English obligatorily marks tense and that an *-ed* suffixation rule is available to do so. However, they can memorize past forms from their parents and occasionally use them; all past tense forms recorded from children will thus be correct ones. Overregularizations appear when the regular rule is acquired. But the previously acquired irregulars do not go anywhere, nor are they ever incapable of blocking overregularization: they just have to be retrieved to be able to do the blocking, and they are retrieved probabilistically. The cure for overregularization is living longer, hearing the irregulars more often, and consolidating them in memory, improving retrievability. Crucially, this account serves to demystify overregularization, requiring no qualitative difference between children and adults during the overregularization period.

V. PREDICTIONS ABOUT THE RATE OF OVERREGULARIZATION

One crucial datum about overregularization is its actual rate as a proportion of the child's opportunities to make such errors. If overregularization occurred at a rate of 0%, then blocking alone would explain everything. Obviously, the rate is not 0%. But, surprisingly, there are few hard data as to what it is, and this allows for an interesting empirical test.

A. *Predictions of the Blocking-and-Retrieval-Failure Hypothesis*

The blocking-and-retrieval-failure hypothesis predicts that the child's linguistic system is at all times designed to suppress regularization of verbs remembered to be irregular. This suppression of regularization cannot be perfect because the child's memory is not perfect, but it is as good as the child's memory retrieval process. If we assume that children's memory for words, although imperfect, is quite good (the child is, after all, successfully using thousands of words and acquiring them at a rate of approximately one per waking hour; Miller, 1977), then overregularization should be the exception, not the rule, representing the occasional breakdown of a system that is built to suppress the error. The overregularization rate, therefore, while not being 0%, should be as close to 0% as the child's rate of successful memory retrieval permits. Minimally, an observed overregularization rate that is systematically less than 50% and not attributable to any factor confounded with irregular forms would serve as evidence that the child's language system is biased against overregularization in favor of an irregular form when it is available. Blocking effects exactly that bias, and the lower the rate turns out to be (assuming that it is less than 50%), the less need we would have for any explanation other than blocking and retrieval failure.

Children's overall overregularization rate, of course, is a weighted average of rates for different verbs, which themselves are predicted to range from 100% (for a verb never heard or attended to in the past tense, like *shent* for adults) to 0% (for an overlearned verb). But the best-learned verbs are the ones children hear their parents use most frequently, and the verbs that parents use most frequently are also likely to be the ones that the child uses most frequently and hence should be better represented in samples of children's speech than the rarer, hence more poorly memorized, hence more overregularization-prone verbs. Thus, the design of the child's linguistic system to block regularization of irregular verbs should be apparent in pervasively low rates of overregularization in children's spontaneous speech samples.

B. Competing Predictions

Strictly speaking, there are no alternative theories of the learning process in the literature that can be said to make competing "predictions" about children's overregularization rate. (Rumelhart and McClelland do present an alternative theory, but we save it for Chaps. V–VII, because its critical predictions do not concern the rate of overregularization.) The relation between data and hypothesis has generally gone in the other direction: researchers have made rough assumptions about what the overregularization rate is and have drawn conclusions about the nature of the learning process from them. But because few of the researchers cite actual data on the overregularization rate, and because their idealizations of the data contradict one another, the researchers are in effect making competing predictions about what the rate should turn out to be in a large-scale quantitative study such as the one we are about to report. In this section, we treat these idealizations as predictions of the approaches they have been taken to support and compare them with the predictions of the blocking-and-retrieval-failure hypothesis.

A rate of 100% is by far the most common idealization of the empirical picture in the literature. Recall that it underlies the one-to-one mapping hypothesis, which explains the two phases of overregularization in terms of subsequent replacement of irregulars by overregularizations and overregularizations by irregulars. It also inspired the picture of the child as the exception-hating rule monger that was imported into other branches of developmental psychology. As such, the assumption of a 100% overregularization rate can be found everywhere from textbooks to technical articles to the popular press. Here are examples, respectively, of each:

> Interestingly, when the general rule is learned, children will often stop using the previously learned irregular form and instead produce

> a regularized version. Thus a child who had been using the correct past tense of *sing*—namely, *sang*—may start using the form *singed* . . . instead. Before the correct irregular form is again learned, some children have been known to produce forms that combine the irregular and the regular form. In the case of *sing*, this would be *sanged*. Thus children may proceed through as many as five steps in the acquisition of some inflections . . . No inflection, Adult Form, Overregularization, Transition, Adult Form. [Reich, 1986, p. 148]

> At this time [overregularization] the irregular forms that the child had used earlier fade out in favor of the overregularized forms. When the irregular forms later reassert themselves, they have a new status: they are no longer isolates operating independently from their uninflected counterparts and from regular inflected forms; rather, they are integrated into a system, as exceptions to it. [Bowerman, 1982a, p. 321]

> The errors [children] do make are actually logical overgeneralizations of rules. Instead of "He went," for instance, they may say "He goed"—to them, a perfectly reasonable past tense of "go." They reject irregularities. When they have learned phrases by rote like "It broke" and "two mice," they will toss them out once they become aware of past tenses and plurals, notes University of California psychologist Dan Slobin. Suddenly, they start using "It breaked" and "two mouses." Says Jill de Villiers, only half joking: "Leave children alone and they'd tidy up the English language." [Gelman, 1986, p. 85]

We find a subtly different idealization in the following, superficially similar statement of the facts, from Eve Clark's article arguing for the principle of contrast:

> Children are pattern-makers. And when they begin to acquire the inflections that mark tense, for instance, they typically take irregular verbs such as *break, bring,* and *go,* and *treat them as if they belonged to the regular paradigm* of *walk, open,* and *jump*. So the past tense of *break* is produced as *breaked, bring* as *bringed,* and *go* as *goed*. [Clark, 1987, p. 19; emphasis added]

Note that Clark is not claiming that irregular past forms are tossed out or even that they fade; she says only that irregulars are treated as regular verbs. Crucially, while they are overregularizing, most children do not successfully inflect *regular* verbs with *-ed* 100% of the time. Brown (1973) reports that none of the three children he studied were producing regulars more than 90% of the time for six consecutive hours of samples during the time they began to overregularize, although they achieved this criterion several months later. We examine these data in detail in Chapter VI; for now assume that children inflect regular verbs during the overregularization years with a success rate of 75%. In that case, Clark's statement would be consistent with children overregularizing 75% of the time (or whatever the actual rate of inflecting regular verbs turns out to be). Indeed, it is broadly consistent with children continuing to produce correct irregulars some proportion of the 25% of uses that are not overregularizations. That, in turn, would be literally consistent with the finding discussed earlier that children use both overregularized and correct versions of a verb during the overregularization stage, as long as the overregularization rate was always capped by the successful suffixation rate for regular verbs.

However, many writers have interpreted the finding of coexistence as showing a more extreme deviation from complete overregularization. For example, in reference to an aspect of the development of verb argument structure that did not consist of complete replacement of a correct form by an error, Bowerman (1982a, p. 342) amends her earlier summary of overregularization as follows:

> However, it has become clearer in recent years that overregularization is not the all-or-none phenomenon it was once taken to be: Irregular forms rarely drop out, but rather continue to compete with their overregularized counterparts throughout the period of error marking. . . . The relative strength of the irregular and overregularized forms in this competition reflects a complex interplay of factors, such as how long the irregular forms have been part of the child's repertoire before their role in a broader system is perceived, how frequently they have been said or heard, whether the "irregular" forms are truly mavericks or belong to minor patterns of their own, and whether the child routinely activates a newly grasped systematicity in the course of sentence construction or perceives it only more passively.

No clear value for the assumed overregularization rate is given, but "relative strength of irregular and overregularized forms" implies in context that for some verbs overregularizations predominate and that for others the correct form does. There is no reason to expect that overregularizations or correct irregulars are *systematically* preferred, and given the large number of different biasing factors at work over a large number of verbs and children, we might expect on statistical grounds that they would roughly even out. We can therefore read Bowerman as basing her theorizing here on the assumption that the overall overregularization rate does not deviate from 50% by an amount large enough to attribute to some pervasive single cause.

In a review article on language development, Maratsos (1983, p. 763) is more explicit about his assumptions about children's overregularization rate:

> Kuczaj (1977b) examined longitudinal samples for one subject, and 6-hour cross-sectional samples for 13 children of different levels of competence. Again, no evidence indicates that *-ed* overregularizations drove out irregular past forms. Instead, even within individual verbs, overregularized and irregular forms alternated, often for periods of months to years. Overregularization, in general, ranged in frequency from .20 to .60 of the children's uses.

It is not clear from Maratsos's chapter what the figures of "from .20 to .60 of the children's uses" (attributed to an unpublished talk by Kuczaj) refer to, as we shall see in Chapter IV. For now, it suffices to note that Maratsos is suggesting that the typical rate of overregularization is not far from 50% (the literal implication of "alternation"), perhaps 40% (the midpoint of the range he cites). It is also clear that these are the data he considers as a refutation of blocking. In his review of Pinker (1984), he writes,

> Yet empirically, children do not act as though they have such a solution [blocking], but may alternate between the overregularized *-ed* form and the irregular form for a period of months to years, using both *broke* and *breaked*. . . . It is clear that their analysis and resolution of such alternatives is a long-drawn-out tabulational process, not one which quickly seizes upon one or two properties of the language as heard. [Maratsos, 1987, p. 19]

Thus, the literature contains a range of idealizations of children's typical overregularization rate, and theories based on them, ranging from 100%, to the rate of regular affixation (say, 75%–95%), to some aggregate rate reflecting systemwide indifference (perhaps not too far from 50%, or some range of values that includes it such as 20%–60%). A rate of exactly 0% is of course never entertained; nor is a rate near 0%, or even greater than 0% but pervasively less than 50%, representing a systematic preference for irregulars. Since we have derived this very prediction from the blocking-and-retrieval-failure hypothesis, there are now clear competing predictions. Thus, the first empirical tests in this *Monograph* will involve quantitative analyses of large samples of children's speech in an attempt to estimate children's characteristic overregularization rate. The estimate will be compared with the various predictions and assumptions in the literature and thus will test the corresponding ideas about the psychology of overregularization.

VI. SUMMARY

The mere fact that children develop a regular rule cannot explain why they overapply it to irregular verbs. Adults block the application of regular rules to idiosyncratic memorized items; we suggest that children do, too, but their retrieval of idiosyncratic items from memory, especially low-frequency ones, is probabilistic, and overregularizations occur when it fails. The hypothesis explains how children unlearn their errors in the absence of negative parental feedback and does not make the dubious prediction that overregularizations replace correct irregulars in children's speech. It predicts that overregularizations should generally be rare in children's speech relative to correct irregular past tense forms, contrary to most current views about language development.

III. METHOD

I. SUBJECTS

To assess overall overregularization rates we wanted to examine as large and diverse a set of children as possible. Using the 1990 version of the ChiLDES data base and documentation (MacWhinney, 1990), we selected all the unimpaired English-speaking children who met the following criteria. (1) The children were known to speak Standard American English. (2) The transcripts were in CHAT format, the standard for ChiLDES transcripts, allowing efficient and accurate computer searches using the CLAN software package (MacWhinney, 1990). (3) The investigator did not include warnings that the transcripts were in a preliminary state and possibly dangerous to use. (4) Information was available about the subjects and the circumstances in which their speech was recorded. (5) The transcripts contained at least 10 irregular past tense forms per child (regardless of whether they were correct or overregularizations). Applying these criteria yielded a sample of 83 children, who produced 11,521 utterances containing past tense forms of irregular verbs. Table 1 shows the children, their ages, and their recording schedules. Among these 83 children we focus on the 10 represented by longitudinal samples and on the 15 with single samples from Hall, Nagy, and Linn (1984). The remaining 58 came from multichild data bases, and we used their data as a replication of the basic findings on overregularization rate obtained from the main sample.

Sarah was a child from a working-class background whose parents had high school degrees and whose father worked as a clerk; all the other individual children were from professional families. The children in the group data bases are all from middle-class, although not necessarily professional, backgrounds. Ten of the children were black (Adam and nine of the children in the Hall et al. sample). There were 5 boys and 5 girls among the children with individual data bases, 10 and 5 from Hall et al. (1984), 8 and 6 from Gathercole (1979), 14 and 10 from Gleason (1990), and 10 and 10 from Warren-Leubecker (1982).

TABLE 1

CHILDREN STUDIED

Child	Age	Source	Total Samples	Sampling Frequency
Abe	2-6–5-0	Kuczaj (1976)	210	Weekly
Adam	2-3–5-2	Brown (1973)	55	2–3/month
Allison	1-5–2-10	Bloom (1973)	6	Occasionally
April	1-10–2-11	Higginson (1985)	6	Occasionally
Eve	1-6–2-3	Brown (1973)	20	2–3/month
Naomi	1-3–4-9	Sachs (1983)	93	Weekly to monthly
Nat	2-8	Bohannon & Marquis (1977)	21	Within 1 month
Nathaniel	2-3–3-9	Snow (unpublished)[a]	30	Weekly
Peter	1-3–3-1	Bloom (1973)	20	Monthly
Sarah	2-3–5-1	Brown (1973)	139	Weekly
15 children	4-6–5-0	Hall et al. (1984)	30	2 days/child
24 children	2-1–5-2	Gleason (1980)	72	3 samples/child
20 children	1-6–6-2	Warren-Leubecker (1982)	20	1 sample/child
14 children	2-9–6-6	Gathercole (1979)	16	1–4 samples/child

[a] See MacWhinney and Snow (1985).

To answer questions about longitudinal development and vocabulary size, we need to focus on samples that began before the onset of overregularization and continued long enough for performance in tense marking to approach adult levels. Brown's (1973) Adam, Eve, and Sarah meet this criterion; overregularizations are absent from their early transcripts, and their later transcripts extend to Brown's "Stage V," in which most inflections are supplied in their correct forms more than 90% of the time.

There are also extensive longitudinal transcripts for Kuczaj's son Abe (Kuczaj, 1976, 1977a, 1978), but they begin later than those for Adam, Eve, and Sarah, and Abe was already overregularizing in the first, so questions about his onset of overregularization must remain unanswered. However, we examine other aspects of his development and take advantage of the prodigious numbers of overregularizations and correct irregulars in his transcripts when focusing on individual verbs and their developmental courses.

Finally, when examining the effects of lexical factors, we analyzed overregularization rates for individual verbs from all 19 children and correlated them with various properties of the verbs. Such analyses involve a trade-off. Individual children often supply too few errors to provide the wide range of overregularization rates and the wide range of predictor variable values needed for correlational analyses, but aggregate data are in danger of displaying averaging artifacts. Therefore, in the lexical analyses we seek converging results from 19 individual children who overregularized and, where possible, an aggregate measure that combines their overregularization rates.

II. PROCEDURE

We tabulated all past tense forms of irregular verbs, correct and overregularized, for all the children (for an exhaustive list of irregular verbs in present-day American English, sorted into subclasses, see the appendix of Pinker & Prince, 1988). Irregular verbs such as *dream* and *dive* admitting of a common regular alternative in adult speech were excluded. Overregularizations included stem + *ed* forms like *eated* and past + *ed* forms like *ated*. We did not search for other possible kinds of error involving the regular suffix such as *sweepened* or *brecked* (for *broke*); such errors, in any case, are quite rare. The actual tabulation procedure differed slightly for the different children.

For Abe, the data were gathered and tabulated by Kuczaj (1976), the boy's father. For each month from age 2-5 to age 5-0, Kuczaj recorded the number of times Abe used each of 70 irregular verbs, the number of times he produced the present stem of the verb with *-ed* appended (such as *goed* and *breaked* ["stem + *ed*" errors]), the number of times he produced doubly marked pasts in which *-ed* was added to the irregular past form (such as *wented* and *broked* ["past + *ed*" errors]), and the number of times he used the stem form in obligatory past tense contexts (such as *Yesterday we go out*). Kuczaj's tables also contain one occurrence of *beed,* but Kuczaj did not tally other uses of *be, was,* or *were,* presumably because they could also be forms of the auxiliary *be;* this would also account for why *have-has-had* and *do-did* are absent. Our analyses of Abe thus omit all three verbs. Kuczaj reported his data in two ways: in a table listing the number of correct and incorrect forms, summed over verbs, for each month (his table 18) and in an appendix listing how many times each individual verb, in each of its possible forms, was used each month (his app. G). Occasionally, there were discrepancies between these two tables that we could not resolve from the text of the thesis, so we relied on tallies of the raw data from Kuczaj's investigation, provided to us by Michael Maratsos. Data from the months 2-5–2-7 and for four no-change verbs were absent from these tallies; for them we used the thesis tables exclusively.

For Adam, Eve, and Sarah, verb usages were tallied on a DEC Microvax II running UNIX. Individual transcript files were combined into a single master file for each child. The FREQ program in the CLAN software package (MacWhinney, 1990; MacWhinney & Snow, 1990) counts the number of times every word is used in a particular transcript session, for a particular speaker, and it was run on the individual transcript files and the combined files. The combined frequency list for each child was then edited to include only words that the child may have used as a verb, including words that occur only infrequently as a verb (e.g., *fish, color, ground, milk*). For all such items (i.e., all words that are not exclusively verbs in the child's vocabulary), the UNIX utility FGREP, which finds matches of alphanumeric string patterns, extracted all the transcript lines they occurred in. Each of the resulting lines was checked by hand and excluded if the matched word turned out not to be used as a verb. If a word appeared in a single-word utterance, it was excluded; thus, *sleep* or *put* appearing alone were not counted as verbs, but *Adam sleep* or *put Mommy* were included. Verbs repeated in successive sentences such as *I falled down. I falled down, Momma* were counted separately since children are capable of saying both a correct and an overregularized version of a single verb in successive utterances, as in Abe's *Daddy comed and said "hey, what are you doing laying down?" And then a doctor came.*

For all instances of Adam, Eve, and Sarah's no-change verbs such as *cut* and *put,* past tense usages were distinguished from present and infinitival usages by hand; when the transcript did not provide information regarding the verb's tense, it was inferred from the context. Contractions such as *gimme, gonna, I'm, it's,* and *doesn't* were excluded, as were participles such as *broken* or *gone* and the quasi-modal *used to.* A very small number of mimicked utterances at early ages, regular participles, and irregular participles that are identical to past tense forms may have been included. Intentionally included were verbs that were not very clearly uttered but were clear enough for the transcriber to have made a reasonable guess; so were some slight phonetic variations such as *-in* for *-ing,* particularly for Sarah, whose samples were transcribed more narrowly than the others. Brown (1973) notes, however, that all three children's speech was carefully transcribed with regard to the presence or absence of phonetic material corresponding to inflections.

For Adam, Eve, and Sarah, *have, be,* and *do* were included only when they were used as main verbs (i.e., possessional *have, have to* unless transcribed as *hafta,* copula *be,* and pro-verb *do*), never when they were used as auxiliaries (i.e., perfect auxiliary *have,* progressive and passive auxiliary *be, do* used to form questions, negations, or emphatics). This is consistent with the criteria used by Brown (1973; Brown, Cazden, & de Villiers, 1971), Bybee and Slobin (1982a), and Slobin (1971).

For the other children, and for the Gleason, Warren-Leubecker, and Gathercole collections, we used a Sun Microsystems Sparcstation 4 running under UNIX to tabulate all irregular past tense utterances. Using the FREQ program, we extracted the number of occurrences for each uniquely irregular verb listed in the Pinker and Prince (1988) appendix, together with all forms ending in *-ed,* with the exception of the no-change verbs, *read* (which is orthographically a no-change verb), and all forms of *do, be,* and *have* (i.e., neither auxiliary nor main verb usages were counted). We then isolated all the overregularization errors from this list by removing regular verbs and other part of speech categories. Because we did not check this large collection by hand, we were unable to exclude overregularized participles such as in *the window was broked.* Since we did exclude correct participle forms if they were distinct from the past tense forms (about 60 irregular verbs have this property; see Pinker & Prince, 1988), this can result in an overestimate of overregularization rates, although it would be small. The word *seed* presented particular problems since most of its uses are as a noun rather than as an overregularization of *see;* these were eliminated by hand. Repetitions were counted separately, as with the Brown children.[9]

The verb *get* is complicated. When adults speaking the standard dialect use *got* in a stative possessional sense (as in *I've got an ice cream cone*), it is the perfect participle of *get* (meaning "obtain"), accompanied by some form of the auxiliary *have.* The meaning is possessional because of the semantics of perfect aspect in English: if the state resulting from obtaining something in the past currently holds, you possess it now (Bybee, 1985). However, if children do not attend to the auxiliary, it would be natural for them to reconstrue *got* as a present tense form meaning "possess," and there are numerous forms like *Look, I got an ice cream cone* that suggest that they do often use *got* as a present tense verb. For these usages we would erroneously credit the child with the correct past form of *get.* Kuczaj (1976) noted this problem and used the context to distinguish present from past usages of *got* in Abe's speech. For Adam, Eve, and Sarah, we excluded all forms that were clearly present tense statives. For the other children, our observed overregularization rates for *get* are probably underestimates, and since *get* is a frequent verb, the overall overregularization rates across verb tokens will be, too. As we shall see when the verb is excluded, however, the degree of underestimation is small.

To verify the accuracy of the machine-generated tabulations for the children other than Adam, Eve, Sarah, and Abe, we compared an exhaustive hand tabulation for these four children with machine-generated totals like those used for the other children. The hand-generated totals were calculated by (1) extracting all utterances containing irregulars and all utterances with forms containing *-ed,* not including *have, be, do,* and the no-change verbs, and (2) checking these utterances to remove all participles, nouns, and all other nonpast forms. The mean discrepancy between the two estimates of the overall overregularization rates for the four children

[9] Because the ChiLDES transcripts contain typographical errors and inconsistencies, a handful of past tense forms may have gone undetected by the automatic search procedure. For example, Michael Maratsos has called our attention to an overregularization rendered as *fell'd* in April's transcripts. We ascertained that such isolated misses are rare by checking for all words spelled with *'d* in the transcripts of Adam, Eve, Sarah, and Abe; none were overregularizations. To be consistent, we did not add April's *fell'd* to her overregularization total, because the transcripts from various children contain a small but unknown number of mistranscribed correct irregulars that our searches also missed, such as *gotalright* and *stucki'm.*

was less than 0.2 percentage points (maximum 1.2 percentage points), with the machine giving a higher estimate for two of the children and the human giving a higher estimate for the other two. We also compared the overregularization rates derived by the two methods across verb types. The two sets of estimates correlated fairly well: r = .98, .77, .91, and .82 for the four children, respectively, and the overregularization rates averaged over types were higher when estimated by machine for two of the children, lower for the other two (never by more than 2 percentage points). Most of the discrepancy can be attributed to small samples for some verbs, where disagreement over a single sentence can greatly affect the overregularization rate for that verb (e.g., if a verb was used twice, once correctly and once incorrectly, its estimated overregularization rate could change from 0% to 100% if one of the sentences is omitted or misclassified). For the children other than Adam, excluding verbs used fewer than 10 times brings the correlations between verbs' overregularization rates calculated by hand and by machine to .98 or greater. Thus, in several analyses in this *Monograph,* when it is important to exclude verbs that were produced too few times to yield reliable estimates of their overregularization rates, we use a criterion of a minimum of 10 tokens per verb per child.

For several analyses it is necessary to tabulate the frequency of use of past tense forms in the speech of the adults that habitually talked to the children. In all cases the same criteria for counting verbs were used for adults and children. Although we did not distinguish among the different adults talking to a given child (e.g., the mother, father, or psycholinguists, who came to be treated like family members), we did keep separate tallies for the sets of adults talking to each child, so each child has his or her own adult speech data.

III. CALCULATING OVERREGULARIZATION RATES

We defined the child's "overregularization rate" as the proportion of tokens of irregular past tense forms that are overregularizations:

$$\frac{\text{(No. of overregularization tokens)}}{\begin{array}{c}\text{[(No. of overregularization tokens)}\\ +\ \text{(No. of correct irregular past tokens)]}\end{array}}.$$

Overregularization tokens included both stem + *ed* and past + *ed* forms. Virtually all children's past tense forms are in past tense contexts (Brown, 1973; Kuczaj, 1976), so we need not take into account the semantic correctness of the tense marking. Overregularization rates were calculated over tokens for a given verb for a given child and over tokens of all verbs for a given child.

A. Rationale for Calculation of Overregularization Rates

Note that this measure of the overregularization rate excludes no-marking errors (stems in obligatory past tense contexts). This is because no-marking errors could be caused by a failure to try to mark the past tense at all (in which case the stem would be used because in English it is the most frequent and grammatically nonspecific form), and the issues at hand pertain to *how* tense is marked, on those occasions when the child decides to mark it at all, not to *whether* the child decides to mark tense, a logically independent question. For example, if overregularization were measured as a proportion of all forms in past tense contexts (by adding no-marking errors to the denominator), it would appear that young children's overregularization rates were low, but that could just be because they were usually not trying to mark tense at all, not that they were successfully suppressing errors. And if overregularizations were lumped together with no-marking errors to yield an overall error rate (by adding no-marking errors to the numerator), then overregularization errors themselves would be hidden from view; a given error rate could correspond to nothing but overregularization errors, nothing but bare stem errors, or anything in between. In particular, tests of a regression in development (the left arm of the U-shaped developmental sequence) would be impossible. Cazden (1968, p. 437) describes the sequence as "no use, followed by infrequent but invariably correct use, followed only later by evidence of productivity"; the distinction between "use" and "correct use" presupposes that correct forms are being considered as a proportion of total marked forms (irregulars plus overregularizations). Thus, Rumelhart and McClelland (1986), using the same rationale that we do, plot a quantity corresponding to our overregularization rate in their demonstration of how their model mimics U-shaped development, as shown in the graph that we reproduce below as Figure 17. That is, Rumelhart and McClelland assume that the past/nonpast tense distinction has been mastered independently of the computations performed by their model in deriving past tense forms, so they simply feed it correct stem-past pairs from the start.

Of course, the decision to count only overtly tense-marked forms because they are clear examples where the child has decided to mark tense does not imply that nonmarked stem forms exclusively represent the absence of a decision to mark tense. Rather, no-marking errors are highly ambiguous and can arise in at least four ways. First, as mentioned, they can represent a failure to attempt to mark past tense. Second, while attempting to mark tense, the child may retrieve the information that an irregular past form of a given verb exists but fail to retrieve its phonetic content (see n. 7 above); the past feature or pointer would block the regularization, but the child would not have the irregular form at hand either. Third, a child may fail both to retrieve the irregular and to block the regular and might thus feed the stem into the regular suffixation process, which ordinarily results in an overregularization. But the regular suffixation process does not succeed 100% of the time for regular verbs, so it may occasionally fail here too, yielding the unchanged stem. Finally, some irregular verbs actually show no change between stem and past (e.g., *hit, cut, put, set*), and the child might analogize the no-change pattern to similar irregular verbs.

During the early stages of language development, where stem forms are the great majority of forms uttered (Brown, 1973; Cazden, 1968; see also Chap. VI below), it is reasonable to assume that the absence of intention to mark is the usual or exclusive cause. Although tense and agreement are marked obligatorily in languages like English, the child cannot be born knowing this. Thus, it is not surprising that there might be an initial period in which children have not yet developed any mechanism for systematic marking of any specific inflectional feature. Indeed, bare stems constitute the great majority of young children's verb forms in English, not only in past tense contexts, but also in progressive and third person singular contexts (Brown, 1973). Thus, the simplest hypothesis is that most of these early stems represent failures to mark tense at all, not attempts that fail for the three possible reasons listed above.

During the later stages, when the child frequently marks tense on irregular verbs, it is plausible that some of the stem errors represent attempts to mark tense that end up unsuccessful. Luckily, we shall see in Chapter VI that, during the time when overregularization errors occur, stem errors become rare, so little hinges on whether or not one looks at an index that includes them. Where relevant, we discuss these possible effects.

IV. ESTIMATES OF NO-MARKING ERRORS (STEMS IN OBLIGATORY PAST TENSE CONTEXTS)

Although no-marking errors are not counted in the overregularization rate, we will require them in a number of other calculations, such as how often the past tense is overtly marked at all or how successful regular past tense marking is. Unfortunately, automatic computer searches cannot discriminate stems used in obligatory past tense contexts from stems used properly as infinitives, imperatives, and present tense forms. Thus, the relevant data must be tabulated by hand by a linguistically sophisticated scorer. This heroic task was beyond the scope of this study but has already been done for Adam, Eve, and Sarah by Courtney Cazden (Brown, 1973; Brown et al., 1971; Cazden, 1966, 1968), summarized in unpublished tables that she and Roger Brown have generously provided us. It has also been done for Abe by Stan Kuczaj, summarized in an appendix to his thesis (Kuczaj, 1976).

For certain analyses in Chapters IV and VI, we will need to combine data on the form of marking (correct irregular vs. overregularized) with data on the presence of marking (unmarked stem vs. correct irregular). For Abe this is straightforward because all token counts are provided in a single table in Kuczaj (1976). For Adam, Eve, and Sarah this cannot be done because Cazden did not count overregularizations at all (neither as irregular errors, as correct irregulars, nor as correct regulars) and counted fewer correct irregular past tokens than we did. The reason was that she needed a constant definition of *obligatory past context* across stems and correct forms, and many tokens occurred in contexts that were not unambiguously obligatory for past tense and thus could not be included.[10] In order to combine the data sets we adopted the assumption that overregularizations were not any more likely than correct irregulars to occur in "obligatory" contexts as opposed to "nonobligatory" contexts; the distinction, after all, is defined in terms of the knowledge of the observer, not the child. Therefore, we calculated what proportion of total irregular tokens (by our counts) Cazden listed and multiplied this proportion by the number of our overregularization tokens, yielding an estimate of the number of overregularization tokens occurring in obligatory past tense contexts (i.e., an estimate of the number of overregularizations that Cazden would have found had she looked for them among the contexts in which she counted correct irregulars and unmarked stems). These token estimates could then be meaningfully combined with Cazden's counts of irregular and stem tokens.

V. OTHER ERRORS RELATED TO OVERREGULARIZATION

Note finally that our study excludes two kinds of errors that are sometimes lumped with overregularization but that are logically distinct from it. In languages with richer inflectional systems than English, children often inflect a stem with an affix that is incorrect for some feature of the word, such as gender or animacy, or incorrect for some feature of the context, such as case or definiteness (Pinker, 1984; Slobin, 1973). Pluralizing mass nouns (e.g., *waters*) or extending the third person singular suffix to other persons or numbers (e.g., *we walks*) would be examples in English. Such errors are best characterized as *underdifferentiation*—an insensitivity to some

[10] Brown et al. (1971, p. 2) define obligatory contexts as including "adverbs like *yesterday*, marginal notations [comments by the transcriber], expansions [by adults], continuity of tense, etc."; attempts by the child to imitate adult sentences containing tensed forms were also counted.

systematic distinction relevant to inflection—rather than as overregularization, which involves idiosyncratic lexical exceptions to a systematic inflectional process.

Second, we are excluding overapplications of *irregular* patterns to inappropriate irregular verbs such as *tooken* or *brang*. Because irregular patterns, even when used productively, have qualitatively different properties than the regular suffix (reviewed in Chap. 8, Secs. I*B*, IV), they are logically distinct from overregularizations and should be tallied separately. Theories differ as to whether regular and irregular patterns are in fact handled by the same kind of mechanism; according to the particular hypothesis we are considering in this *Monograph,* they would represent competition between two irregular forms for one memory slot, not a competition between a stored irregular and the regular rule (for discussion, see Ullman & Pinker, 1990, 1992). These issues can be sidestepped in the present investigation; Bybee and Slobin (1982a) point out that over-irregularizations are extremely rare in preschool children's language, and there are very few in our samples. For Adam, Eve, and Sarah, Cazden (1966) reports only *beat-bate* and *hit-heet* for Adam and *beat-bet* for Sarah, to which we can add *bite-bat* for Adam. *Sweepened* was the only such form we happened to come across for Abe, although, because there is no mechanical way of searching for such errors, there may be others. Overextensions of irregular patterns to regular verbs appear to be even rarer; we are aware only of *trick-truck* from Adam.

IV. THE RATE OF OVERREGULARIZATION

In this chapter, we estimate children's typical overregularization rate in an attempt to resolve the empirical inconsistencies in the literature and to test possible explanations of the nature of overregularization.

As discussed in Chapter II, the most frequent characterization in the literature is that once children begin overregularizing they do so all the time, replacing correct irregulars altogether. Other characterizations have children varying freely between overregularized and correct irregular forms, either at a rate near the rate of tense-marking regular verbs (if irregulars are not being discriminated from regulars) or at a rate that is not markedly far from values that can be interpreted as representing systemwide indifference (if neither the irregular form nor the overregularized form of irregular verbs is systematically favored, but a panoply of factors settles a competition between them for each verb). In either case, a preference for the irregular would emerge slowly before culminating in adult performance. Such a stage of free variation would call into question any kind of blocking or uniqueness principle (Maratsos, 1987) and would leave unsolved the learnability problem of how children eliminate the incorrect forms.

The third possible empirical pattern is that overregularization errors are rare relative to correct irregulars. If so, there would be no qualitative difference between children and adults. Both would discriminate between regularized and irregular forms, presumably because application of their regularization mechanism to listed irregulars is blocked. Children's occasional overregularizations, like adults' speech errors and adults' uncertainty about low-frequency irregulars like *smote,* could be attributed to probabilistic imperfect retrieval from rote memory. Strictly speaking, it would suffice to show that the rate of regularizing irregular verbs is reliably less than 50% to demonstrate that children possess some mechanism that acts to give the irregular past tense form of a verb priority over the regularized form, contrary to the predictions of all hypotheses other than blocking. The claim that that mechanism in fact is blocking (which actively suppresses overregularization), as opposed to some weak statistical preference for the irregular for some other undiscovered reason, would be more convincing the lower the overregularization rate is, the more pervasive such a low rate turns out to be, and the more clearly it can be shown that irregularity per se, not some variable confounded with it, is associated with low rates of using the regular suffix.

Of course there is no single quantity that we can call "children's overregularization rate." Any estimate must aggregate over children, ages, and verbs, and the estimates will necessarily vary depending on which subsets one chooses to include. Therefore, after calculating some initial estimates of the overall rate, we will break down the data in a variety of ways, to ensure against various kinds of averaging artifact and sampling error. Ideally, the range of different estimates should not stray too far from one of the predicted values (near 100%, near the regular tense-marking rate, near 50%, near 0%) as one focuses on subsamples.

I. OVERALL OVERREGULARIZATION RATE

We first calculated overall overregularization rates. The median overregularization rate across the 25 children with individual transcripts was 2.5%. Table 2 shows the relevant data for the 25 individual children, whose distribution of overregularization rates is plotted in the histogram in Figure 1. The distribution is roughly exponential, with most children at the extreme low end; only two children, April and Abe, overregularized more than 10% of the time (13.0% and 24.0%, respectively). The average overregularization rate across the 25 children was 4.2%. The three group data bases replicate this figure, with rates ranging from 1.0% to 6.5% and a mean of 3.7%. After we have examined some of the factors that affect overregularization rates, we will be in a better position to speculate on why Abe's rate was so much higher than those of the other children (see Sec. VII below and also Chap. VI); some of the difference, we shall see, may be artifactual. But even Abe was very far from overregularizing 100% or even 50% of the time, and his is the highest rate we see. Thus, the global data suggest that overregularization is a relatively rare phenomenon; if they legitimately reflect children's tendencies, it would suggest that children's language systems, like adults', are strongly biased to suppress overregularization, contrary to common belief.

II. CHANGE IN THE OVERREGULARIZATION RATE OVER TIME

Of course, the surprisingly low rates obtained may be an averaging artifact: each child could go through a circumscribed U-shaped period of

TABLE 2

OVERREGULARIZATION RATES FOR INDIVIDUAL CHILDREN

Child	Correct	Stem + *ed*	Past + *ed*	Total	Overreg Rate
Abe	1,786	465	99	2,350	.240
Adam	2,444	44	4	2,492	.019
Allison	31	2	0	33	.061
April	47	6	1	54	.130
Eve	283	23	1	307	.078
Naomi	378	34	2	414	.087
Nat	52	0	0	52	0
Nathan	243	11	3	257	.054
Peter	853	17	4	874	.024
Sarah	1,717	61	4	1,782	.036
Hall et al. (1984):					
ANC	79	2	0	81	.025
BOM	112	1	0	113	.009
BRD	128	2	0	130	.015
CHJ	151	4	0	155	.026
DED	106	5	0	111	.045
GAT	159	10	0	169	.059
JOB	130	0	0	130	0
JUB	132	8	0	140	.057
KIF	100	0	0	100	0
MAA	105	2	0	107	.019
MIM	77	0	0	77	0
TOS	84	0	0	84	0
TRH	47	3	0	50	.060
VOH	64	1	0	65	.015
ZOR	98	0	0	98	0
Mean of individual children = .042					
Aggregate data bases:					
Gleason (1980)	472	32	1	505	.065
Gathercole (1979)	454	16	1	471	.036
Warren-Leubecker (1982)	317	3	0	320	.009
Mean of aggregate data bases = .037					

constant or indiscriminate overregularization, preceded and followed by many more months of near-perfect performance. For example, if there were a span of 33 months in which overregularization did not occur in 32 of the months but went up to 96% in the other one, the average overregularization rate for the span would be only 2.9%. This possibility is shown in Figure 2. (All our developmental graphs plot the proportion of past tense forms that are correct [100% minus the overregularization rate] rather than the proportion overregularized, so that regressions in development appear as U's, not inverted U's.)

Figures 3–6 plot monthly overregularization rates (pooled across two to four transcripts) for the children whose overregularization rates we tabulated longitudinally (Adam, Eve, Sarah, and Abe); the data are provided in Appendix Tables A1–A4. For all four children overregularization begins early in the span sampled and lasts for the rest of the period. Aside from

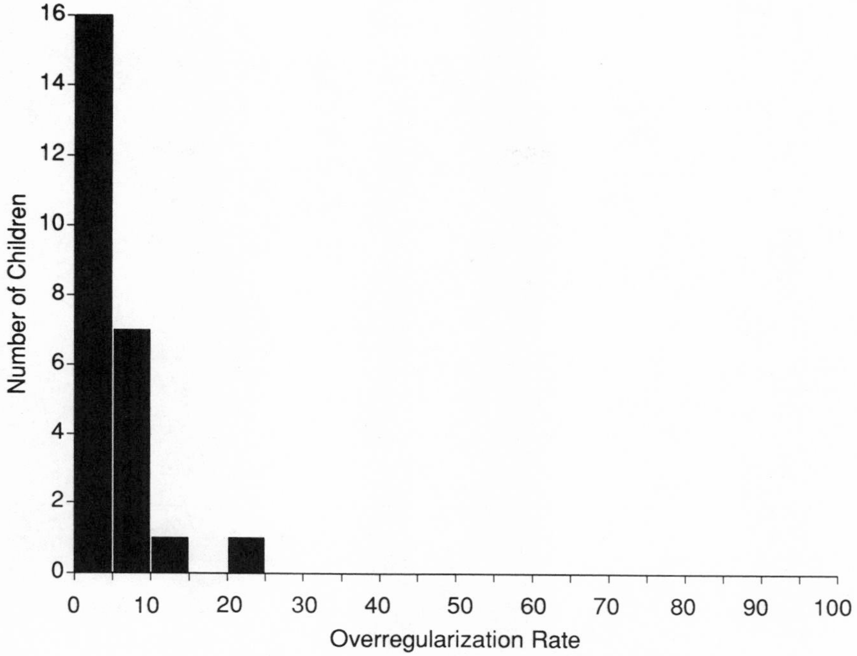

FIG. 1.—Histogram of overregularization rates across 25 children

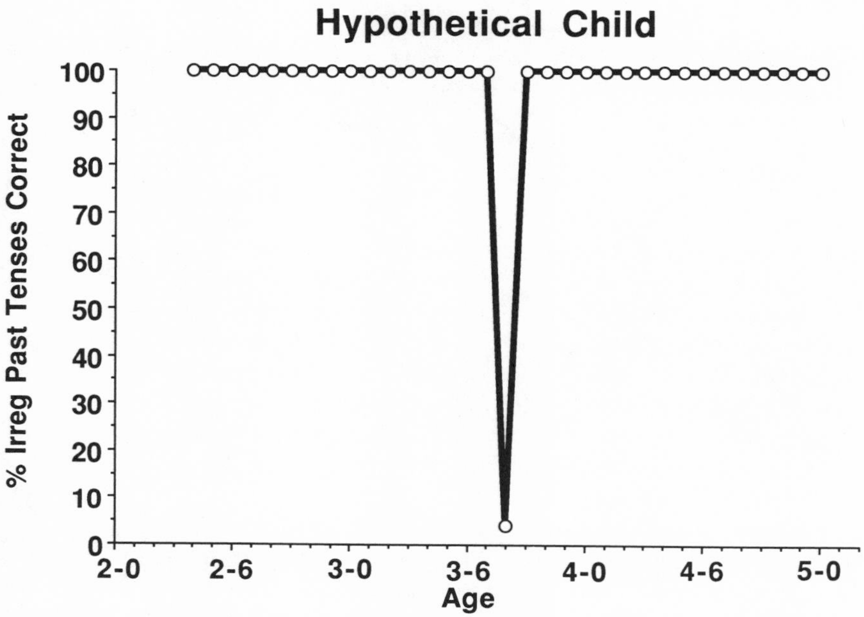

FIG. 2.—Hypothetical developmental sequence that would yield low overregularization rates as an averaging artifact.

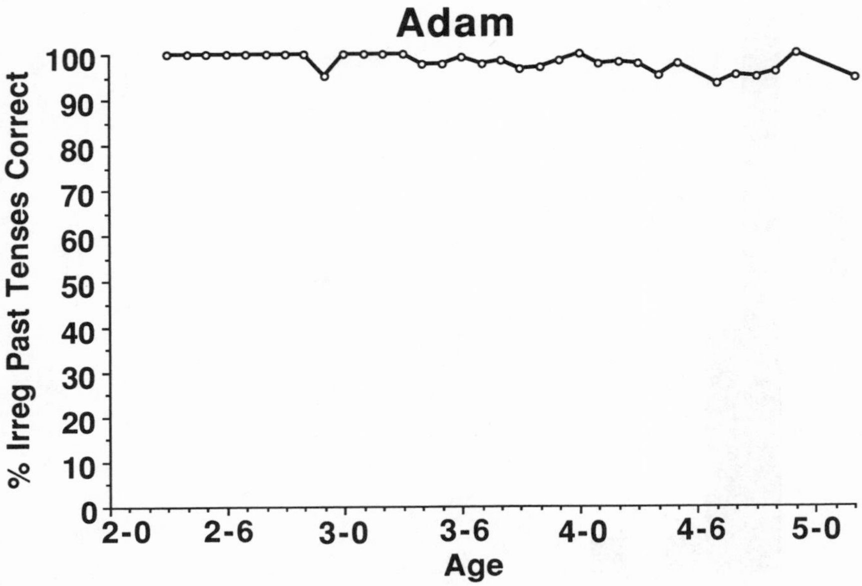

FIG. 3.—Percentage of Adam's irregular past tense forms that are correct (100% minus the overregularization rate).

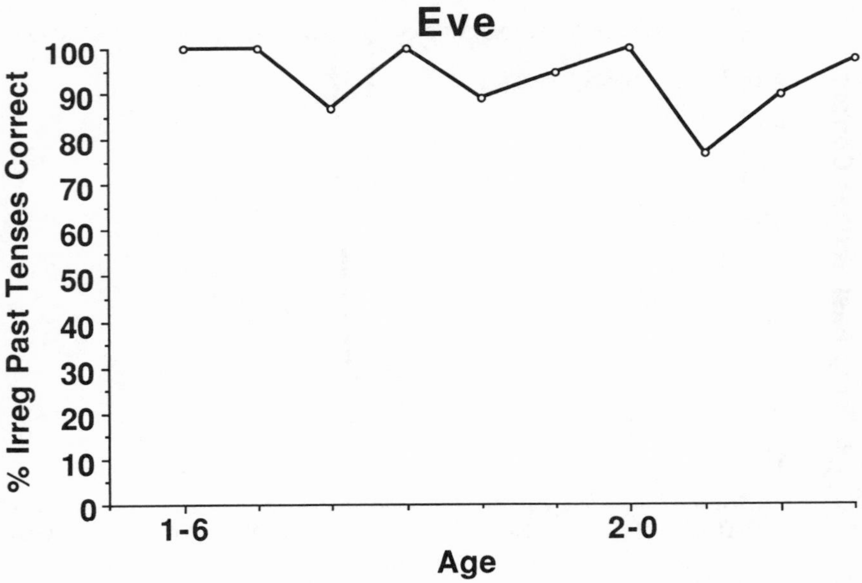

FIG. 4.—Percentage of Eve's irregular past tense forms that are correct (100% minus the overregularization rate).

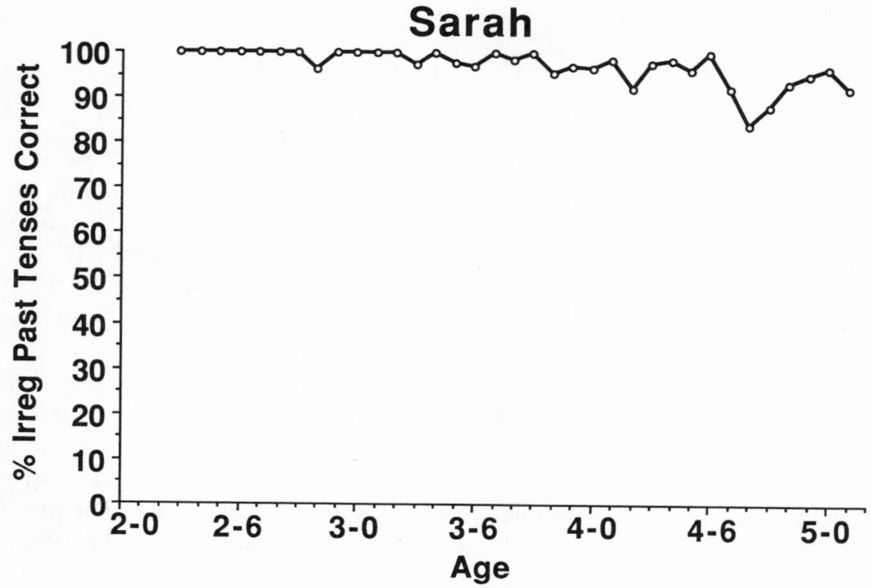

FIG. 5.—Percentage of Sarah's irregular past tense forms that are correct (100% minus the overregularization rate).

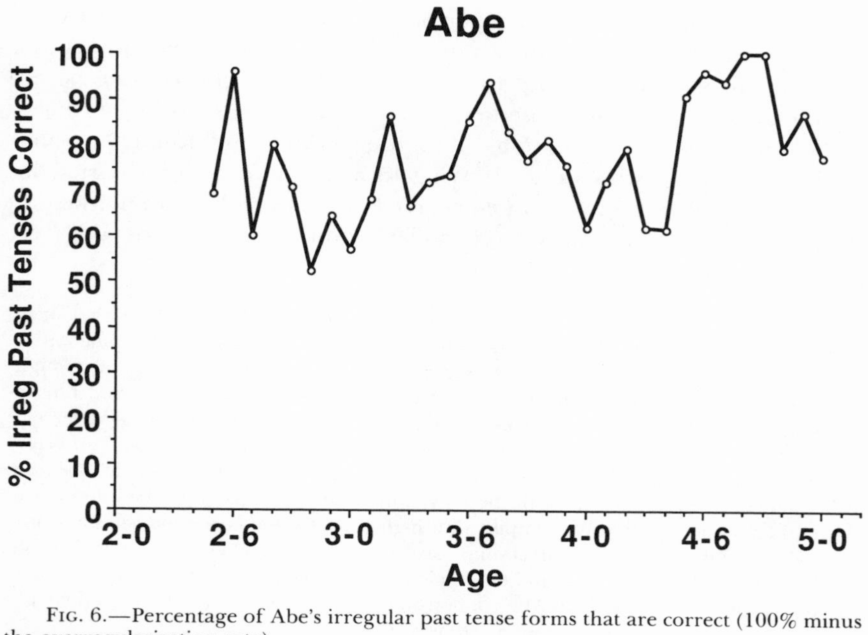

FIG. 6.—Percentage of Abe's irregular past tense forms that are correct (100% minus the overregularization rate).

Eve, whose samples end at 2-3, we see fairly steady overregularization from some time in the third year at least into the sixth year. Only for Abe is there any hint of a reduction in overregularization rate late in development.

The graphs demonstrate that low rates characterize the entire period of overregularization. Adam's highest monthly rate of overregularizing is only 6.8%; Eve's is 23.1% and Sarah's 15.8%. Even Abe, an outlier among the 25 children, displayed an overregularization rate of only 47.6% in his most extreme month (see Fig. 6); this is the highest rate we find among 109 monthly estimates from the four children who were examined longitudinally.[11]

A. *Is There a U-Shaped Developmental Sequence?*

The ubiquitous claim that children pass through a U-shaped developmental sequence in acquiring irregular verbs (in particular, that their performance declines at some point) is based on observations by Cazden (1968), Ervin and Miller (1963), and Miller and Ervin (1964) that a few irregular forms were often used correctly by the children before they started to overregularize. U-shaped development has never been documented quantitatively, however, and Marchman (1988) and Stemberger (1989) have questioned whether it exists. In this subsection, we define the phenomenon precisely and test for it in our data.

Many measures of children's performance that one plots against time will show some kind of dip, for a variety of reasons, and many others will not. Until one specifies with precision what a *U-shaped* sequence is supposed to refer to, one cannot test whether such a sequence exists or what causes it. We will follow the definitions of Cazden (1968) and Rumelhart and McClelland (1986), who were referring to a transition from a period in which past tense forms are marked correctly whenever they are marked at all to a period in which some overregularization errors occur as well (see

[11] Note that it would not even be sound to conclude that Abe went through a stage at which his overregularization rate was 47.6%, because of the statistical phenomenon of regression to the mean. This particular month was chosen post hoc *because* of its high rate. Any monthly estimate reflects a sum of the child's true overregularization rate (a psychological tendency that could be measured as how frequently the child would overregularize over a very large number of comparable opportunities at that age) and an error component (from sampling and other sources of noise independent of the true rate). By deliberately selecting the month with the maximum observed overregularization rate, we are simultaneously selecting for samples with high true overregularization rates and for samples with high noise in the direction of overregularization. The true rate, therefore, would be expected to be lower than the sampled rate in such months. For similar reasons it would not be sound to point to Abe's data from 4-8 and conclude that he went through a stage in which his overregularization rate was zero.

Chap. III, Sec. IV). The previous section showed that when overregularizations appear, they neither predominate nor alternate with the correct irregulars but are always a minority. However, one can still test whether a period of extremely accurate performance precedes the first overregularizations—in other words, whether children at some point in development get worse (even if they never get very bad).

Our sample includes nine children with extended longitudinal data. For two of them, Abe and Nathaniel, the first transcript contains an overregularization. If these transcripts happen to coincide exactly with the boys' very first uses of irregular past tense forms, the transcripts show that they did not undergo U-shaped development. But it is more likely that the transcripts began well after irregulars of one or both kinds were being produced, in which case the transcripts are uninformative. Note that, for the same reason, any set of transcripts that does not begin early enough in the child's language development is apt to underestimate the length of any overregularization-free sequence in which irregular pasts are used.

For the other seven children, one does see correct irregulars in the transcripts before the appearance of the first overregularization (not surprisingly, since three of them—Adam, Eve, and Sarah—were the ones studied by Cazden). However, the impression of a developmental change could be a sampling artifact. Since we now know that children's overall overregularization rate is low, their tendency to overregularize could be unchanged throughout development, but their early samples might simply be too small to contain any examples of overregularization. Imagine drawing playing cards from a deck with replacement, looking for a black king (whose frequency in the deck is approximately equal to children's overregularization rate). One might have to draw a large number of cards before the first one appears, even if the deck is complete and properly shuffled.

It is not legitimate to test for a change in rate by comparing overregularization rates before and after the first overregularization because the post hoc nature of the dividing line will inflate the chances of obtaining a spurious difference. One stringent test can be conducted as follows. If the child's overregularization rate is p, then, under the null hypothesis of no change in this rate over time, the chance that the first irregular verb form in the sample will be correct is $1 - p$. If the likelihood of a child overregularizing an utterance is unaffected by whether the child overregularized the previous past tense utterance (an assumption we will examine below), then the chance that the first two utterances will both be correct is $(1 - p)^2$, the chance that the first three will be correct is $(1 - p)^3$, and so on. One can test whether there is an improbable run of consecutive correct irregular past tenses at the beginning of a child's records by calculating $(1 - p)^n$, where n is the number of irregulars in the transcripts preceding the transcript containing the first overregularization. (Correct forms preceding the

TABLE 3

TESTS OF U-SHAPED DEVELOPMENT: CORRECT IRREGULARS PRECEDING THE SAMPLE WITH THE FIRST OVERREGULARIZATION

Child	First Overregularization		Consecutive Correct in Preceding Samples	Overregularization Rate	Probability
	Age	Sample			
Adam	2-11	18	381	.01926	.0006
Allison.	2-10	6	18	.06061	.3245
April	2-1	2	3	.12963	.6593
Eve	1-8	5	7	.07818	.5656
Naomi	1-11	20	15	.0870	.2555
Peter	2-6	14	275	.024027	.0012
Sarah.	2-10	33	231	.03648	.0002

first overregularization within that transcript would be excluded because including them would correspond to the rather implausible assumption that the child had brought the regular rule on line for the first time in the midst of that very session.)

Table 3 shows the results. For Adam, Sarah, and Peter, the probability of obtaining a string of correct utterances of the observed length or less if the early overregularization rate was the same as that for the entire corpus is very small (.0012 or less). For the other children considered individually, no conclusions about U-shaped development can be drawn: the first overregularization, although coming after a number of correct forms, does not appear substantially before it is expected to, given the children's overall overregularization rates. However, the seven children can be treated as a single sample in a meta-analysis, allowing us to assess the aggregate probability of observing such longer-than-expected strings of correct forms under the null hypothesis. Following Rosenthal (1984), we converted the children's individual probabilities to *z* scores, summed them, divided by the square root of the number of children (seven), and transformed the resulting *z* score back to probability values; pooling the children's probabilities, not their sentences, avoids an obvious averaging artifact. The overall probability of obtaining the data under the hypothesis of a constant overregularization rate is .000045.

These analyses crucially depend on the assumption that the probability of overregularizing is independent of whether the preceding irregular past tense utterance was correct or an overregularization. We tested the validity of the analyses in two ways. First, we estimated the validity of the assumption directly on a sample of data, namely, Abe from 3-3 to 3-4. His conditional probability of producing a correct irregular past (as opposed to an overregularization) given that his preceding irregular past tense form was correct was .58; his conditional probability of producing a correct irregular past given that his preceding irregular past tense form was an overregularization was .62. The difference is negligible and not in the direction that would compromise the probability analyses. Second, we tested the robustness of the conclusions under a pessimistic assumption of one kind of violation of independence: that every other correct verb form in a pre-overregularization string was completely determined by a perseveration effect from the preceding correct verb form. Under this assumption, each string of correct forms would be effectively half as long as originally measured, so we divided the number of initial consecutive error-free pasts in Table 3 by two. The probabilities of obtaining strings of correct forms of those lengths or greater, under the hypothesis of no change in underlying overregularization rates, remain less than .05 for Adam, Peter, and Sarah individually and less than .06 for the aggregate sample in the meta-analysis.

In sum, there is quantitative evidence that children's first overregularization follows an extended period in which their overtly tensed irregular verbs are all correct, and this effect can be demonstrated very strongly for some children. In this sense, children do get systematically worse as they get older.

Other senses of "U-shaped development."—Some discussions in the literature claim either that there is no such thing as U-shaped development of irregular tense marking or that connectionist models developed after Rumelhart and McClelland's can account for it better than their model did. These discussions, however, refer to very different phenomena than the one discussed by Ervin and Miller, Cazden, and Rumelhart and McClelland. We review these other senses of "U-shaped development" and point out the extent to which the corresponding empirical claim is supported in our data.

In the network model described by Plunkett and Marchman (1990), early acquired verbs were permanently resistant to overregularization; the so-called onset of overregularization in their model pertained to its performance on newly acquired verbs.[12] In actuality, once children begin to overregularize, they produce errors for many of the verbs that earlier they had produced correctly (i.e., the sequence does not consist of correct performance for some irregulars early and overregularization only for newly acquired verbs, with the early correct ones eternally protected). For Adam, 15 of his 23 overregularized types (65%) had been produced correctly at least once before. For Eve and Sarah, the respective figures were 3 of 9 (33%) and 15 of 26 (58%).

Stemberger (1989) suggested that Rumelhart and McClelland (1986)

[12] "Interestingly, however, the initial 20 verbs are likely to continue to be mapped correctly by the network, even in the presence of the other erroneous mappings" (Plunkett & Marchman, 1990, sec. 4, p. 32).

were misled by the psycholinguistics literature into trying to model a nonexistent phenomenon. He plotted data from Abe showing no signs of U-shaped development. However, Stemberger is simply discussing a different quantity than the one Ervin and Miller, Cazden, and Rumelhart and McClelland focused on. What Stemberger plotted was not overregularization rate but a different measure, overall correct performance, defined as one minus

$$\frac{[(\text{No. of overregularization tokens}) + (\text{No. of stems in past contexts})]}{[(\text{No. of overregularization tokens}) + (\text{No. of stems in past contexts}) + (\text{No. of correct irregular past tense tokens})]}.$$

The data in Appendix Tables A1–A4 confirm that the overall rate of correct performance does not decline notably with age for any of the children. But it is not clear that anyone in the psycholinguistics literature has ever claimed that it did, so the point of Stemberger's objection is unclear.

Plunkett and Marchman (1990, 1991) refer to yet another sense of the term "U-shaped development" in arguing for the psychological reality of their connectionist models. In Plunkett and Marchman (1991), the learning curves all start out at levels of performance far *less* than 100% and then increase; the authors call the small wiggles in this overall increasing curve "U-shaped development." Although all the children we examine show local ups and downs in their monthly measures of overregularization rates, there are many explanations of these blips, of which sampling error is the simplest.[13]

Finally, in Plunkett and Marchman (1990), any verb that is used once correctly and then once incorrectly is characterized as undergoing U-shaped development, which is misleading for a different reason: any stationary stochastic process (e.g., a string of coin flips) will produce local sequences with such patterns. Neither the fact that children produce such sequences nor the ability of their model to do so is surprising.

B. When Does Overregularization Cease?

There are no signs of overregularization going away or even decreasing in Adam's, Eve's, or Sarah's samples, which last through the early 5s for the former and the latter. Perhaps because Abe's overregularization rate is higher to begin with, one can discern a trend of gradual overall improve-

[13] Kruschke (1990, p. 61) makes the point a slightly different way: "The recent work of Plunkett and Marchman [1991] does *not* exhibit U-shaped learning, contrary to their claims. They showed that acquisition fluctuated depending on the particular training sequence, but they failed to mention that *on average* their model showed monotonic, not U-shaped, acquisition."

ment (the slope of the best-fitting straight line is +6.0 percentage points per year), superimposed on seemingly random fluctuations that leave many late months with higher overregularization rates than early ones. Clearly, overregularization diminishes extremely gradually. On the basis of a personal communication from Slobin, Kuczaj (1977a) notes that it is still present in school-age children of 9 or 10.

Two studies provide us with estimates of the overregularization rate in older children. Moe, Hopkins, and Rush (1982) report a sample of 10,530 irregular past tense utterances from over 329 first graders. The overregularization rate in their data is 2.8%. Carlton (1947) reports 2,196 past tense tokens among the speech of 96 fourth graders she recorded. These included 13 overregularizations. If approximately 75% of past tense tokens in speech are irregular (see Chap. V), the overregularization rate for this group is 0.8%.

Do overregularization errors ever completely disappear? Joseph Stemberger has kindly provided us with the full set of past tense overregularizations in his corpus of 7,500 adult speech errors. The list includes 25 past tense overregularizations (18 of the stem, 7 of the irregular past form); Stemberger (1989) suggests that the rate of adult speech errors might be about one error per 1,000 sentences. If we assume that all sentences contain verbs, that about 10% of verbs in casual speech are in the past tense (Adams, 1938; Smith, 1935), and that 75% of adults' verb tokens are irregular (Slobin, 1971; see Chap. V), we get a very crude estimate of adults' overregularization rate of .00004—three orders of magnitude lower than preschoolers' and two orders lower than fourth graders'.

So although in one sense both children and adults overregularize, there is also a dramatic difference in their rates of doing so. Perhaps the difference is just a consequence of hearing more tokens of each irregular verb as one lives longer, with more exposures leading to more reliably accessible memory traces. For example, a negative exponential learning curve with a time constant of one order of magnitude of improvement in retrieval probability for every 5 years' worth of irregular past tense tokens could handle the reported overregularization rates from the preschool years through adulthood comfortably. In the absence of more plentiful and finer-grained data, it is premature to claim that there is no qualitative difference between children and adults, but current evidence does not demand that there be a difference.

III. DIFFERENCES IN OVERREGULARIZATION RATE AMONG VERBS

Another possibly misleading effect of averaging could result from combining data on individual verbs: perhaps a few very commonly used verbs are never or rarely overregularized, but most verbs are overregularized most of the time or at least indiscriminately. Because these verbs may differ from one child to another, the question can be addressed only by examining overregularization rates for different verbs in individual children. The relevant data for Adam, Eve, Sarah, Abe, and the other children are presented in Appendix Tables A5–A9. Aggregate measures of overregularization rate, described in Chapter VII, are presented in Appendix Table A10.

It is important to note, however, that sampling error can make estimates of overregularization rates for particular verbs of particular children extremely misleading. In the extreme case, if a verb is used only once, its observed overregularization rate can only be 0% or 100%, regardless of the child's actual overregularization tendency. If it is used twice, the observed rate can be 0%, 50%, or 100%, and so on. Even with a low overall regularization rate and slightly larger samples, high estimates of overregularization rates for a given verb frequently will arise by chance. Histograms of the overregularization rates for all a child's verbs show spikes at values corresponding to ratios of small integers such as 0, 1/4, 1/2, 3/4, and 1. But if we restrict attention to only those irregular verbs that were used 10 times or more in the past tense (the cutoff suggested in Chap. III), we find that Adam did not overregularize any of his 32 verbs at a rate higher than 10%, Eve overregularized *fall* 8 out of 10 times but did not overregularize any of the other 9 more than 20%, and Sarah overregularized *throw* 7 out of 10 times but did not overregularize any of the other 26 more than 33%. Histograms of Adam, Eve, and Sarah's overregularization rates for verbs used a minimum of 10 times are displayed in Figures 7–9.

Even for Abe, the extreme overregularizer, most commonly used verbs fall at the low end of the distribution of overregularization rates (mode 10%–20%, median 30%, mean 32%). This is shown in Figure 10, a histogram of overregularization rates for Abe's verbs used 10 times or more.

It is clear that the overall low overregularization rate is not an artifact of averaging a few verbs that are never overregularized but used extremely frequently with a majority of verbs that are usually overregularized but used less often. Rather, low overregularization rates characterize most of children's commonly used verbs. Nonetheless, it is also quite clear (especially for Abe) that different verbs are overregularized at different rates, and estimates of overall overregularization rates must be qualified by examining different verbs. For Adam, Eve, Sarah, and Abe, chi-square tests amply show that overregularization rates differ among verbs used more than 10 times (all p's $< .001$). It is statistically permissible to perform such chi-square tests for four other children in our sample (GAT, Naomi, Nathan, and Peter); the tests are significant for all of them. Chapter VII is devoted to investigating properties of verbs that make them more or less likely to be overregularized. The most important, not surprisingly, is frequency: verbs that parents use in the past tense less often are more likely to be overregularized by their children.

It is important to note that the correlation between verb overregularization rate and verb frequency necessarily interacts with any cutoff designed to eliminate small samples. The verbs that parents use less often are also the verbs that their children use less often (see Chap. VII). Therefore, excluding verbs likely to give rise to sampling errors will also tend to exclude verbs with higher overregularization rates. Appendix Tables A5–A8 confirm that many infrequently used verbs yield high estimated overregularization rates. In fact, computing the unweighted mean of the overregularization rates of all verb types yields figures of 22% for Adam, 17% for Eve, 18% for Sarah, and 47% for Abe; the mean of the type means for all 25 children is 10.5%, the median 11%. One might wonder whether the relatively high type mean for Abe when it is calculated over all his verb types casts doubt on the conclusion that his grammatical system suppresses overregularization. Such doubts are not warranted. Means calculated over types do not reflect the functioning of the child's grammatical system because a verb used once is weighted exactly as strongly as a verb used a thousand times. Rather, what the typewise mean is capturing is the distribution of frequencies of the child's irregular verb vocabulary: the more low-frequency verbs a child uses, the higher the mean. In fact, although the theory invoking blocking and retrieval failure predicts low overregularization rates *overall,* it also predicts *high* overregularization rates for low-frequency verbs: 100% for verbs that have never been heard or attended to in the past tense form (like *shend* for adults), lower but still high rates for verbs that have been heard occasionally, and so on (see Chap. II). In a sense, a child's seldom-used verbs are misleading for two reasons: we cannot be confident about the actual overregularization rate of an irregular verb used once or twice, and a child cannot be confident that a verb is irregular if he or she had heard it used only once or twice.

Irregular verbs are, quite generally, overregularized at low rates, but the verbs themselves can be very different from one another. This suggests that the overall low overregularization rate reflects some phenomenon that suppresses overregularization globally across the irregulars (modulo frequency) and is unlikely to be attributable to any general bias of the child to favor correct irregulars because of some lexical property that many of them happen to possess. For example, it might be argued that children's grammatical systems allowed both overregularizations and correct irregulars but that they had a response bias in favor of producing irregulars because they tend to be shorter and simpler than overregularizations and that this is the cause of the measured overregularization rate being less than 50%. Such a counterexplanation can easily be ruled out. Among the irregular verbs that our subjects used, 14 have correct past tense forms that are the same length

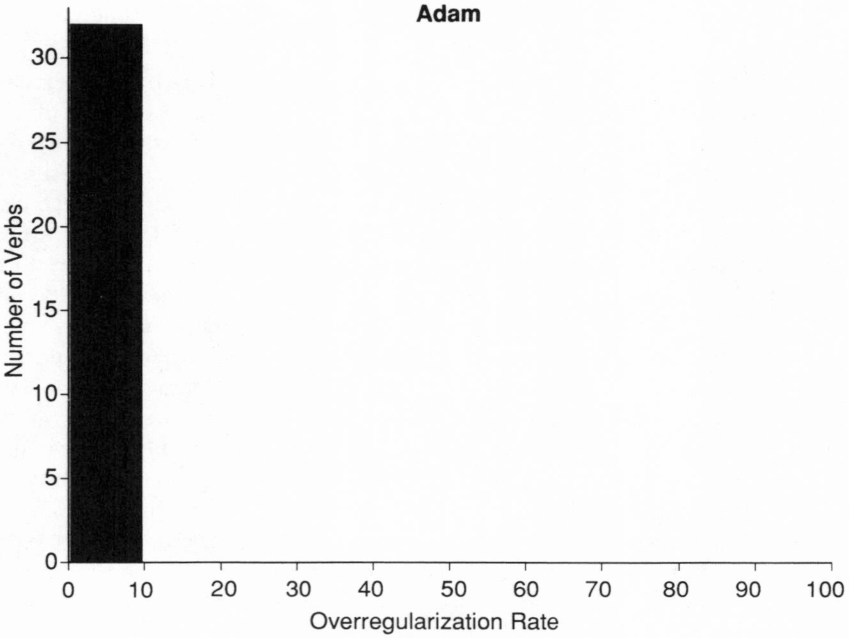

Fig. 7.—Histogram of overregularization rates of Adam's verbs (10 or more tokens per verb).

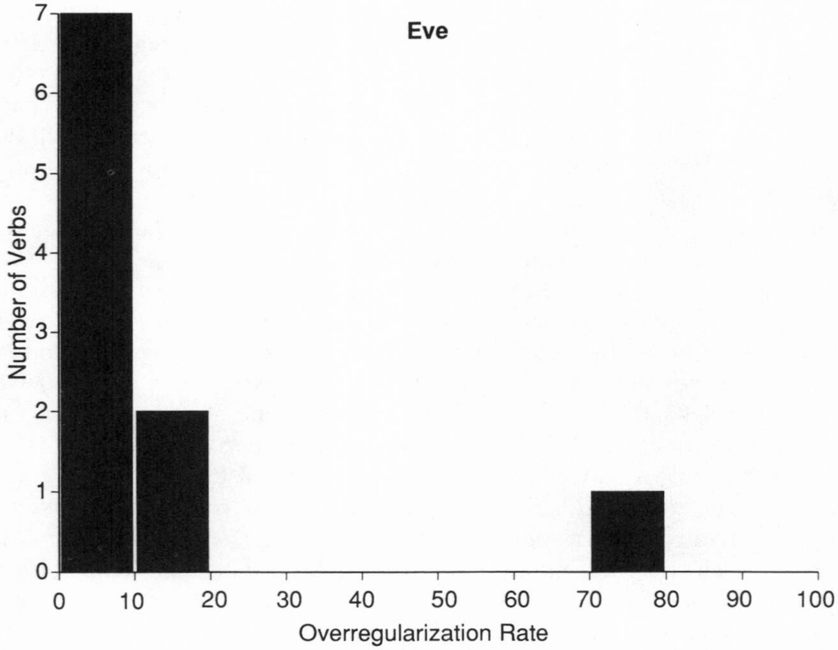

Fig. 8.—Histogram of overregularization rates of Eve's verbs (10 or more tokens per verb).

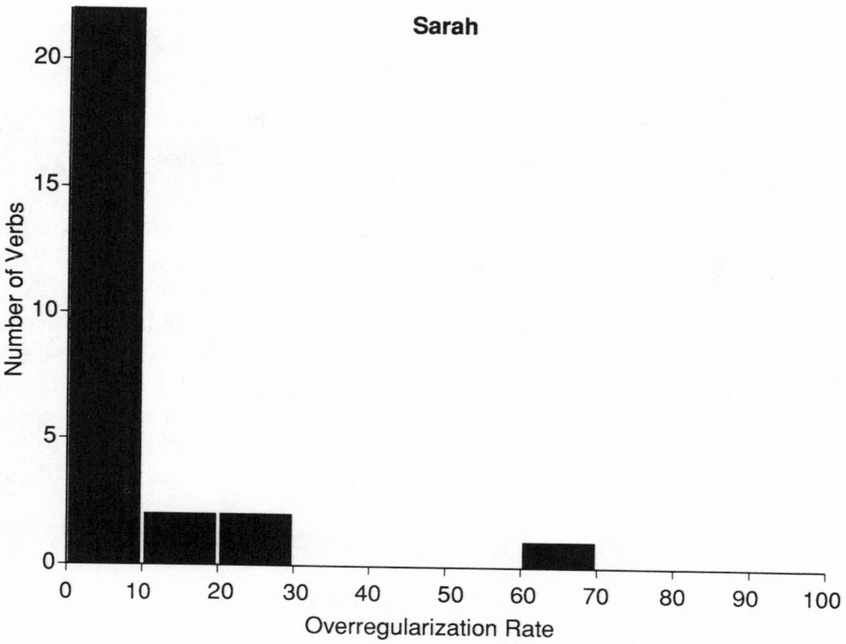

FIG. 9.—Histogram of overregularization rates of Sarah's verbs (10 or more tokens per verb).

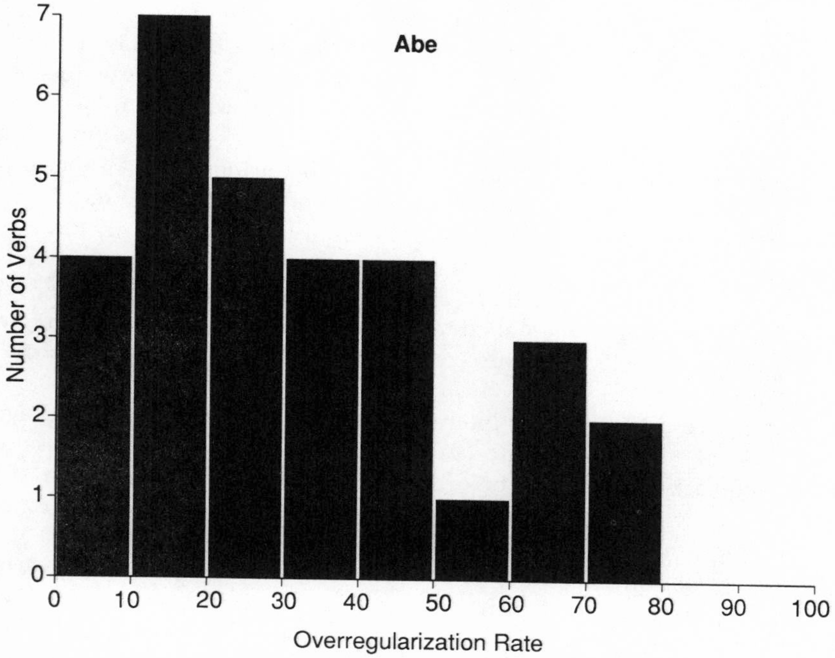

FIG. 10.—Histogram of overregularization rates of Abe's verbs (10 or more tokens per verb).

or shorter than their overregularized counterparts, usually with a similar phonological structure: *be, buy, do, feel, go, hear, keep, leave, lose, mean, say, sleep, sweep,* and *tell.* If simplicity, not irregularity, were responsible for the overall low overregularization rates, then these verbs, lacking that advantage, should show overregularization rates much closer to 50%. Instead, the overregularization rates for tokens of these verbs were 0.7% for Adam, 9.3% for Eve, 2.8% for Sarah, and 19.9% for Abe. The mean overregularization rates across these verb types were 18.3% for Adam, 5.25% for Eve, 5.0% for Sarah, 36.9% for Abe, and about 8% for the aggregate rates from all 19 children who overregularized at least once (see Chap. VII). Medians were far lower, usually 0%. All these figures are close to or lower than those obtained for the full set of irregular verbs. More generally, the data suggest that the only property of irregular past tense forms that is likely to account for children's strong tendency to prefer them to overregularizations is irregularity itself.

IV. CHANGES IN OVERREGULARIZATION RATES OVER TIME AMONG DIFFERENT VERBS

The most stringent test of the hypothesis that overregularization is a probabilistic and relatively rare event would look at the fate of individual irregular verbs for individual children as they grow older. This is independent of the overall level of overregularization for different verbs that we have just examined, just as the waveform of a sound wave is independent of its amplitude and its DC component. For example, it is possible that each child goes through a stage for each verb during which the verb is overregularized exclusively (see Fig. 11) or as often as it is produced correctly. If these stages are fairly brief and circumscribed, the steady low rate of regularization could be an averaging artifact of a sequence of deep narrow U's, one for each verb. If so, or if the verbs all follow some other set of out-of-phase developmental curves, the protracted period of overregularization would reflect a failure to apply blocking to different verbs at different times.

There are other possible interactions among children, verb, and age that would be noteworthy. One can determine whether any verbs cease to be overregularized altogether before the end of the period or, alternatively, whether a child begins to stop overregularizing all verbs at the same time; the latter finding would suggest that the child learns or develops the blocking principle only at that point. Another possibility is that various verbs follow different and largely unsystematic patterns, perhaps because, as we have suggested, overregularization is a quasi-random performance deficit.

Clearly, low rates of overregularization are not an artifact of a sequence

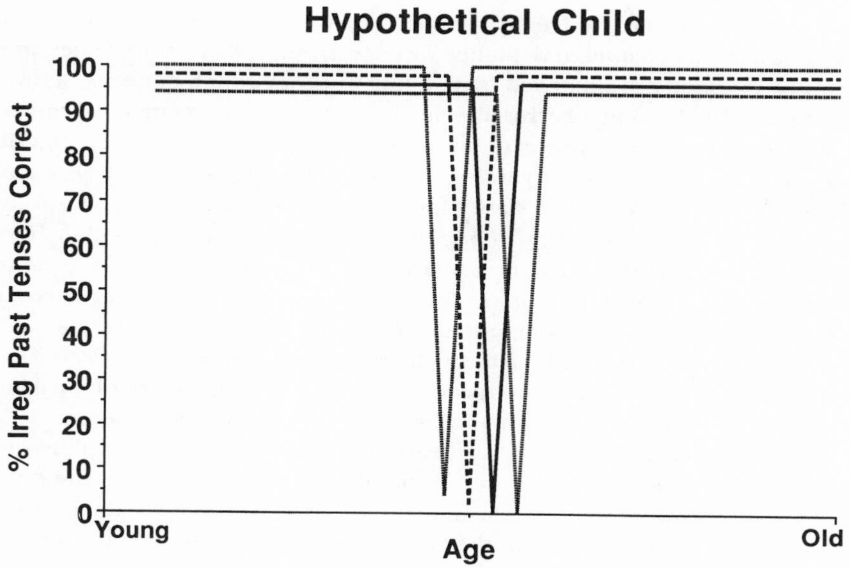

FIG. 11.—Hypothetical developmental sequence for different verbs that would yield low overregularization rates as an averaging artifact.

of transient overregularization stages, one for each verb: individual verbs can be overregularized across large spans of time. The very first verb that Adam overregularized was *feel* at 2-11; he also overregularized *feel* in his last sample at 5-2. Similarly, *throw* was overregularized at 3-4 and at 4-4, *make* at 3-5 and 5-2, and *fall* at 3-5 and 4-10. Sarah's first overregularization, *heared* at 2-10, appeared again at 4-11; *winned* and *maked* also made appearances in the samples separated by a year or more. Even the 9 months' worth of samples from Eve contain *falled* at 1-10 and again at 2-2. More than half of Abe's overregularized verbs (44) were overregularized over a span of 1 year or more; 32 were overregularized over a span of 2 or more years.

Unfortunately, when we turn away from the simple question of whether overregularizations of a given word reappear across long time spans and try to trace each one of a child's irregular verbs over time, we run up against severe sampling limitations. As mentioned, small samples yield inaccurate estimates of overregularization rates, and many of the samples of tokens of a given verb for a given child in a given month were very small. Thus, developmental curves for individual verbs with low token frequencies for the child can oscillate wildly among a few discrete values, revealing little about changes in the underlying true rates. With these caveats in mind, we now examine curves for individual verbs for Abe, the most prolific overregularizer.

For most of the 70 irregular verbs that Abe used, the curves can best be described as chaotic and highly variable from verb to verb. They are most conveniently summarized by pointing out four rough patterns, shown in Figures 12–15. Some verbs, like *eat* (Fig. 12), are overregularized in the earlier transcripts but appear to be completely mastered before the end of the sampling period. (Other verbs with this pattern include *cut, fall, go, make, think,* and *throw.*) A second class of verbs, such as *say* (Fig. 13), is rarely overregularized at any point. (*Find, forget, see,* and *tell* are others.) A few, such as *draw* (Fig. 14), are overregularized throughout the sample (*build* is similar); such verbs were used only rarely and might be overregularized because they are also rare in parental speech, although sampling error cannot be ruled out. But many verbs, such as *win* (Fig. 15), *bite, break, blow, buy, catch, come, feel, get, know, put,* and *shoot,* show no interpretable trend, oscillating between samples with high and low measured overregularization.

In sum, apart from haphazard variation (possibly due to sampling error) and overall low or high rates (to be discussed in Chap. VII), the only meaningful temporal pattern for individual verbs seen in Abe's data is that a few appear to be mastered in the late 4s, thereafter resisting overregularization completely.

V. HOW HIGH CAN ESTIMATES OF CHILDREN'S OVERREGULARIZATION RATE GO?

Given that the overregularization rate varies across verbs and, to a lesser extent, across children and ages, there is no absolute "overregularization rate"; the estimates will change somewhat with methodological decisions of which verbs, children, and ages to include. The low estimates in Section I above included all the samples meeting the criteria described in Chapter III, without any exclusions based on how the data came out. Still, it is conceivable that these criteria adventitiously included some samples of questionable representativeness, relevance, or accuracy. In this section, we will test the robustness of the low estimated overregularization rate, by eliminating all samples that could be challenged, for any plausible reason, as potentially deflating the measured overregularization rates. If these worst-case estimates continue to be low after steps are taken to bias them as high as possible, one can have more confidence that there is some real process causing them to be low and that the effect is not an artifact of the adoption of one selection criterion or another.

First, for some of the children the samples are small, and we may have caught them in conversations where few irregular verbs were used in the past tense, or perhaps only a small number of well-mastered ones. Hence, we can eliminate all children who contributed less than 100 irregular verb tokens to the overall sample.

Second, because of possible U-shaped developmental sequences, some of the youngest children sampled may not have entered the stage at which overregularization had begun. If so, it would be misleading to count their samples from the pre-overregularization period (with rates of 0%, by definition) because the psychological process of interest was not yet occurring. Moreover, even if overregularization had begun, it may not have reached its peak. So, following the suggestion of one of the referees of an earlier draft, one might question the inclusion of Allison, April, Nat, and Peter, none of whom were recorded any later than 3-1. These children could not have been excluded a priori because Abe had his *worst* month of overregularizing at 2-10 and Eve overregularized at 1-8. But let us assume that these four children were on the verge of overregularizing at high rates and exclude their data. We will continue to include Eve, even though she falls within the age range of the children excluded here for being too young; this decision renders overregularization estimates higher than they would be if she were excluded. The rationale might be that her language development was precocious and hence her true overregularization tendency was indeed manifested in the available samples.

Third, we might be sampling overregularization-shy children from the opposite arm of the U, where the errors have already disappeared. The Hall et al. (1984) children might be suspect for these reasons. (In fact, data from the children we analyzed in longitudinal detail—Adam, Sarah, and Abe—do not themselves call for such an exclusion because, while Abe showed an overall decline in the age range corresponding to the Hall et al. children, he was still overregularizing at rates from 0% to 22%, and Adam's and Sarah's overregularization rates *increased.*)

Turning now to the different samples within longitudinal records, we can consider the fact that there was a demonstrated overregularization-free period in the early months of Adam, Peter, and Sarah. So here we will exclude all correct forms in the transcripts preceding the transcript in which the first overregularization is found.

Fifth, perhaps not all verbs deserve to be included. *Get* could be problematic for children other than Abe, for whom Kuczaj (1976) carefully coded all forms as the past of *get* versus the present of *got.* For Adam, Eve, and Sarah, recall that we checked contexts and excluded present tense forms, but some cases counted as past forms could have been present forms. For the other children the computer counted all instances. We will report estimates that exclude all instances of *got* for children other than Abe.

Sixth, one might argue that *have, be,* and *do* (included only for Adam, Eve, and Sarah) are special. Even though we did not include any auxiliaries in our analyses, these verbs obviously share their morphemes with the auxil-

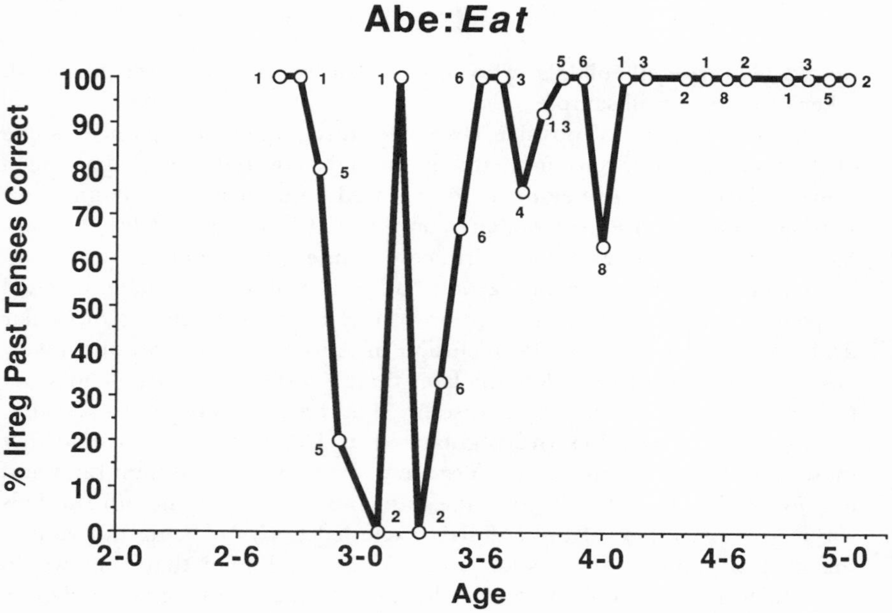

FIG. 12.—Example of a verb that resists overregularization as the child gets older

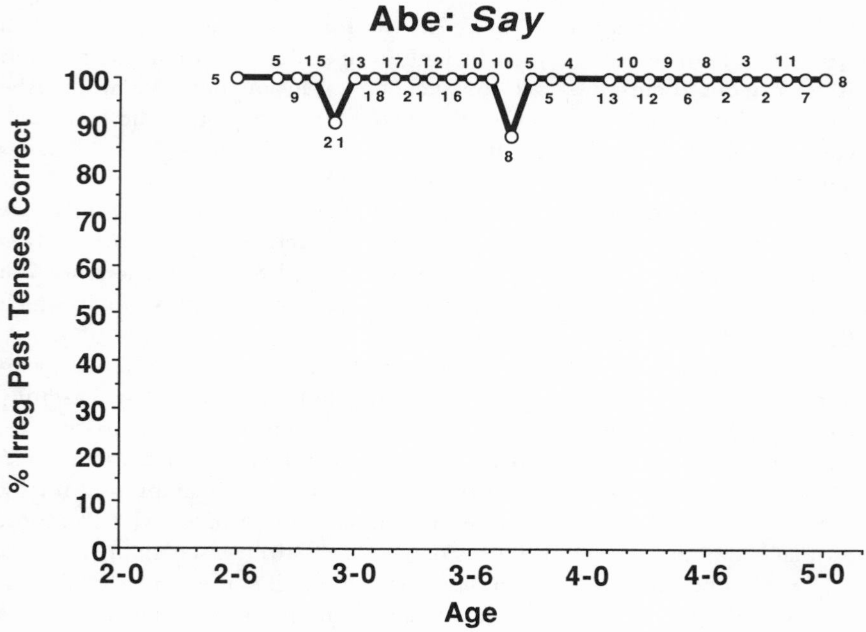

FIG. 13.—Example of a verb that is rarely overregularized at any age

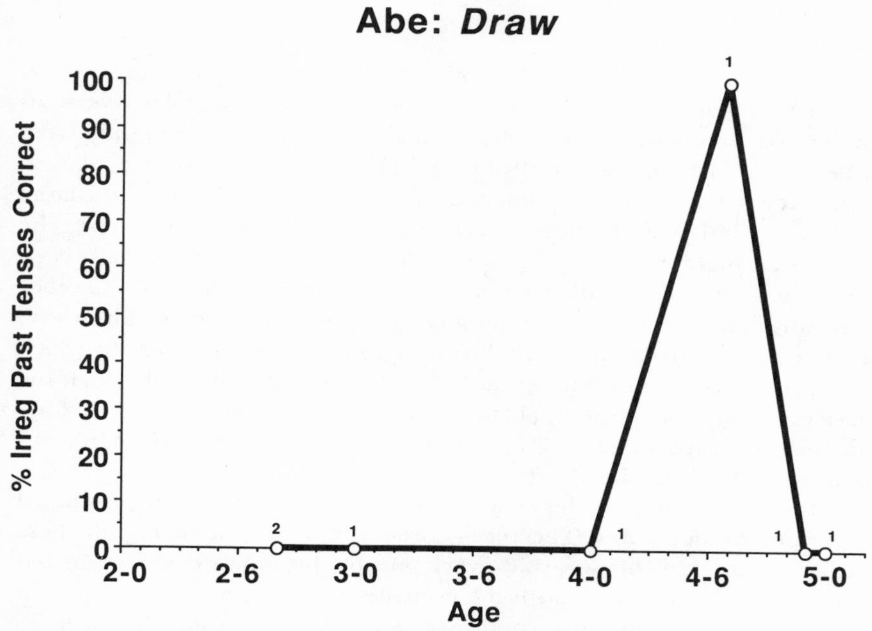

FIG. 14.—Example of a verb that is overregularized throughout development

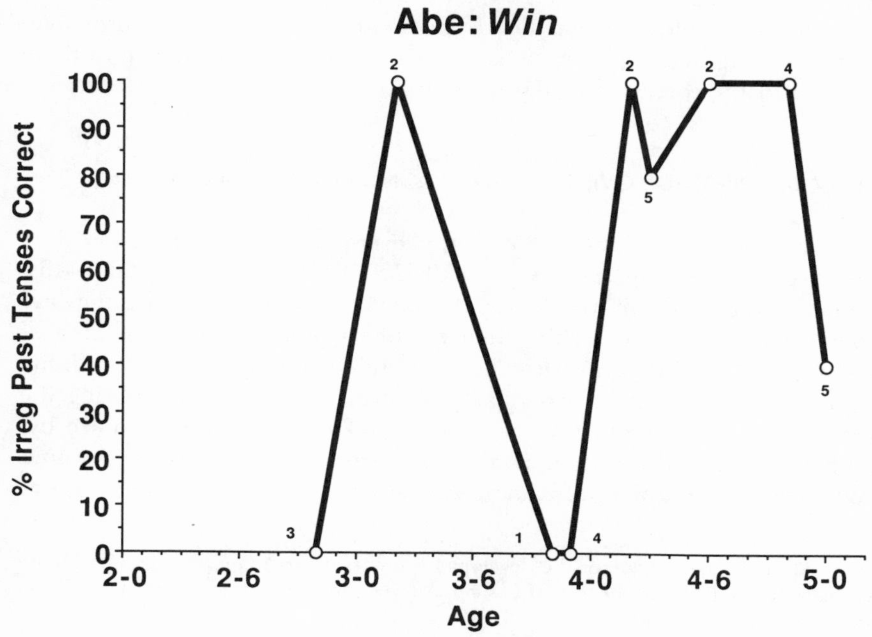

FIG. 15.—Example of a verb with a chaotic developmental pattern

iaries, and they are irregular not only in the past but in the third person singular present. Conceivably, the child might treat nonauxiliary versions of *have, be,* and *do* similarly to the auxiliary versions and differently from other verbs. Actually, when Stromswold (1990) examined overregularization rates for auxiliary and nonauxiliary forms of these verbs in a large sample of ChiLDES children overlapping with the one we use here, she found that the nonauxiliary versions—that is, the ones that we have been counting—were overregularized at rates comparable to those of the other verbs that we report here. Counting correct forms from the children who made overregularization errors during the developmental spans in which they made them (a procedure that yields slightly higher estimates than the ones we report), Stromswold obtained overregularization estimates of 2.5% for *have,* 4.3% for *be,* and 7.5% for *do* (see also App. Tables A5–A10). But again we will report the effects of excluding them.

Table 4 summarizes the results of various exclusions on the estimated overregularization rates. The results are clear. Even combining all these exclusions in an effort to avoid every possible bias toward low estimated rates, we are only able to push the estimate up to a mean across children of 9.8% and a median across children of 8.7%, ranging from 3.6% to Abe's 24.0% (which we will focus on below). These worst-case estimates are still far closer to 0% than they are to 100%, 50%, or, for the bulk of the children, even 25%. They are low enough that it seems difficult to avoid the conclusion that the child's grammatical system contains some mechanism that, while allowing overregularizations to occur, is strongly biased against them in favor of the correct irregular counterpart.[14]

VI. COMPARISON OF OVERREGULARIZATION WITH REGULARIZATION

The fact that the absolute rate of overregularization is quite low does not disprove the suggestion (e.g., in Clark, 1987) that children fail to discriminate regular from irregular verbs during the period in which they are overregularizing. Conceivably, children inflect *regular* verbs only 2.5% of the time during this period, leaving the regulars uninflected the remaining 97.5% of the time. If so, irregular past forms would not be blocking the regularization of irregular verbs, as the blocking-and-retrieval-failure hypothesis claims; instead, the low rate of overregularization would presumably mean that regular suffixation was an extremely error-prone process,

[14] Moreover, the shape of the developmental curves for Adam, Eve, and Sarah are virtually unchanged, and the tests of U-shaped development reported in Sec. IIA of Chap. IV all remain significant.

TABLE 4

Upper-Bound Estimates of Children's Overregularization Rates

A. Estimate of Overregularization Rate

Exclusion	Mean	Median	Range
Samples with fewer than 100 past tokens	.05	.03	.00–.24
Selected young children (Allison, April, Nat, Peter)	.04	.025	.00–.24
Hall et al. (1984) children	.07	.06	.00–.24
All three subsets	.09	.07	.02–.24
Adam, Eve, Sarah, and Peter before first overregularization	.05	.03	.00–.24
Combined with excluded children	.09	.07	.02–.24
got (other than Abe)	.05	.04	.00–.24
have, be, do (Adam, Eve, Sarah)	.05	.03	.00–.24
All four verbs	.05	.04	.00–.24
All exclusions combined	.10	.09	.04–.24

B. Upper Bounds for Individual Children, Following All Exclusions

Child	Correct	Stem + *ed*	Past + *ed*	Total	Overreg Rate
Abe	1,786	465	99	2,350	.240
Adam	1,276	43	4	1,323	.036
Eve	175	21	1	197	.112
Naomi	281	33	2	316	.111
Nathan	214	11	3	228	.061
Sarah	963	61	4	1,028	.063

failing most of the times it is invoked. Correct irregular forms would continue to be used, together with stems, in the circumstances in which the regularization process failed.

The data necessary to evaluate this suggestion consist of estimates of the rates of inflecting regular verbs in obligatory past tense contexts. These estimates are presented in full in Appendix Tables A1–A4. They clearly show that children are not failing to discriminate regular from irregular verbs. The rates of correctly affixing regular verbs in obligatory contexts in the months including and following the first recorded overregularization, summing over tokens, are 73% for Adam, 66% for Eve, 85% for Sarah, and 97% for Abe. These are way higher than the children's overregularization rates, and the difference can be seen in all 65 individual months for which data are available for the four children (for Adam, Eve, and Sarah, these are the months for which Cazden coded proportion of use in obligatory contexts, which do not extend to the end of the transcripts). More pertinently, we can compare the rate of marking tense on regular verbs in obligatory verbs with the rate of producing overregularizations as a proportion of all obligatory contexts, or

$$\frac{[\text{No. of overregularization tokens (in obligatory contexts)}]}{\{(\text{No. of overregularization tokens}) + (\text{No. of irregular past tokens}) + [\text{No. of stem tokens (in obligatory contexts)}]\}},$$

where our counts of the number of overregularization tokens are scaled to make them commensurable with Cazden's tallies, using the procedure explained in Chapter III. These overregularization rates were 0.6% for Adam, 4.5% for Eve, 1.1% for Sarah, and 23.2% for Abe, far lower than the rate of regular marking. Moreover, these rates were lower in all 65 individual months.

Although children clearly discriminate irregular from regular verbs in general, it is not clear that they discriminate them in the circumstances that lead to overregularization errors. We have suggested that overregularization is caused by a failure to retrieve an irregular past tense form, leading to the application of the regular rule to the stem. If retrieval is all or none, then, at the moment the child attempts to retrieve the irregular form but fails, the verb should be indistinguishable to the child from a regular form and should be overregularized by the same process that supplied the affix of a correct regular past tense form. Not all retrieval failures should lead to overregularization, just as not all regular verbs in obligatory past tense contexts are successfully marked for past tense. But among usages of irregular verbs that are not correct irregular past forms, the proportion that are overregularizations (as opposed to being left unmarked), which equals

$$\frac{[\text{No. of overregularization tokens (in obligatory contexts)}]}{\{(\text{No. of overregularization tokens}) + [\text{No. of stem tokens (in obligatory past contexts)}]\}},$$

should be identical to the proportion of regular verbs that are successfully affixed (as opposed to being left unmarked) in past tense contexts.

Stemberger (1989) compared these proportions on two of Abe's samples and found that the overregularization rate calculated as a proportion of nonirregular past tense attempts (overregularizations plus stems) was far lower than the rate of inflecting regular verbs correctly. (The rest of Abe's samples contain very few unmarked verbs in past tense contexts, either regular or irregular, so both marking rates are close to 100%; see App. Table A4.) We performed an analogous test on Adam, Eve, and Sarah, again after adjusting the number of overregularizations to be commensurable with Cazden's counts. Replicating Stemberger, we find that the overall rates of overregularization given nonuse of the irregular during the children's periods of overregularization (13.3% for Adam, 15.9% for Eve, and

10.4% for Sarah) were less than their rates of inflecting regular verbs (66%–97%) and that this was true for 32 of the 33 individual months available.

This analysis shows that when children fail to use an irregular past tense form in a past tense context, they do not treat it identically to a regular verb; they overregularize the irregular verb far less often than they correctly suffix a regular verb. In other words, irregular verbs tend to suppress application of the regular process even when they are not supplied in the correct irregular past tense form. Assuming that there is no consistent reason why children should decide to mark tense on irregular verbs less often than on regular ones, there are two plausible explanations for this difference. One is that the child is analogizing the no-change pattern seen in verbs like *cut* and *set* to other irregular verbs. Later, we review abundant evidence that verbs that end in *t* or *d* are particularly susceptible to this interference. Second, as mentioned in note 7 above, retrieval of an irregular may not be all or none. On some occasions, the child may not retrieve the content of an irregular entry (or may not retrieve enough of it to allow the form to be articulated) but might retrieve the information that a past tense entry exists (i.e., the child might retrieve only the pointer or tag to the entry). Since it is the existence of a past tense entry that ordinarily blocks regularization (rather than the particular phonetic content of any irregular form), such piecemeal retrieval would be sufficient to prevent an overregularization without actually supplying the correct irregular form.

VII. COMPARISON WITH PREVIOUS ESTIMATES IN SPONTANEOUS SPEECH

Given the stereotype that children go through a stage in which they always overregularize or even overregularize in free variation with correct irregular forms, our finding of a consistently low rate of overregularization across children, ages, and commonly used verbs comes as a surprise. Why has the low rate not been noted before?

One reason is that few investigators have counted the number of correct irregular past tense uses; typically, only a list of errors is reported. A second reason is that most summaries in the secondary literature, such as book chapters and textbooks, do not even try to provide empirical citations to document the overregularization rates they assume when discussing theoretical implications, as the quotations in Chapter II show.

Indeed, one source that does, Maratsos (1983), provides estimates that bear no obvious relation to the study he cites. Recall that Maratsos claimed that "overregularization, in general, ranged in frequency from .20 to .60 of the children's uses," based on an unpublished talk by Kuczaj (1977b). Maratsos is referring to the study Kuczaj reported in his thesis (Kuczaj, 1976) and in a published report (Kuczaj, 1977a), and these sources list a much lower range of overregularization rates calculated over uses: .01–.39 for different children and .12–.24 for different subclasses of verbs.[15] Breaking down the rates according to individual children's performance with different subclasses (many obviously with tiny sample sizes) gives a wider range, but the range runs from 0.00 to 1.00, not from .20 to .60. Maratsos (personal communication, October 1991) has explained to us that he in fact derived these estimates from Kuczaj's unpublished data by averaging overregularization rates over verb *types* for each month, not "uses," as his paper says; the range of monthly typewise means ran from .16 to .69, with the bulk of the months falling roughly within the .20–.60 range that he reports. As discussed in Section III above, averages over types should be systematically higher than the true overregularization rate because they overweight the rare and hence difficult verbs.

Let us now examine the actual data on overregularization rates in preschoolers in the original studies that report them. Bybee and Slobin (1982a) report figures from a pooled sample of 31 children; the rates are listed separately for different subclasses of irregular verbs. However, these figures are also averages over verb types, ranging from .1 to .8 for the different subclasses. The numbers of verb types and tokens in each class are not reported, so actual overregularization rates cannot be computed from the data. Fortunately, Slobin (1971) published actual token frequencies of individual verbs summed over 24 of these 31 children (those from the Miller & Ervin, 1964, samples). From his table one can calculate that the pooled children overregularized at a rate of 10.2%, far closer to our estimates.

Recently, Valian (1991) reported overregularization rates in a cross-sectional sample of 21 children, divided into four groups based on mean length of utterance (MLU), a measure that roughly correlates with grammatical development in English-speaking children (Brown, 1973). The mean ages of the four groups ranged from 2-0 to 2-7, and the mean MLUs ranged from 1.77 to 4.22, the range spanned by Adam and Sarah between 2-3 and 3-8 and by Eve between 1-6 and 2-3 (Brown, 1973). Valian included the main verb versions of *have, be,* and *do* and excluded their auxiliary versions. Using the individual subject data that Valian has kindly provided to us, we find that children in the first two groups (mean age 2-0 and 2-5) produced 67 correct irregular pasts and no overregularizations. The children in the third group (mean age 2-5, MLU 3.39) produced 109 correct

[15] These figures, taken from Kuczaj's (1977a) tables, refer to overregularizations as a proportion of total usages of irregular verbs in past tense contexts, including unmarked stems. Since most of the children's errors were overregularizations, not stems, the figures for overregularization rates as a proportion of overtly marked verbs are similar, ranging from .01 to .40.

irregular past tense forms and 9 overregularizations and had a mean overregularization rate of 8.4%. Of the three children in the fourth group (mean age 2-7, MLU 4.22), one child produced 15 overregularizations of a single verb, but the other 32 irregular past tokens were correct; the children's mean was 13.2%. The mean overregularization rate of the children in the study was 5.1%.

The ChiLDES archive contains a number of transcript sets that we excluded for the methodological reasons listed in Chapter III. However, it is of some interest to check whether they are consistent with the samples that we did report. Among the transcript sets that are from Standard American English–speaking children and in CHAT format, there were three sets of transcripts from individual children and six group transcripts, ranging in size from 5 to 1,596 irregular past tense tokens (median 54). The mean overregularization rate of the three individual children was 12.5% (range 5.1%–16.7%). The six group data bases showed overregularization rates ranging from 0% to 10.8%, with a mean of 3.25%.

The only partial anomaly in the empirical literature consists of the data reported by Kuczaj (1976, 1977a). Qualitatively, those data are consistent with our finding of a pervasive bias against overregularizing: neither the mean overregularization rate for the cross-sectional sample nor that for Abe comes close to the rates of 50% or higher that had been assumed in the literature. But there are quantitative differences. As we have seen, Abe is the outlier from among the 25 English-speaking children we studied in the ChiLDES data base. Kuczaj's cross-sectional sample (1977a) of 14 children from 2-6 to 5-6 includes six with overregularization rates comparable to those reported here (1.1%–8.33%), but for the other eight the rate ranged from 26.1% to 40.2%, with an average over all the children of 20.9%. Thus, neither Abe nor most of the 14 children in Kuczaj's cross-sectional sample appear to come from the distribution of unselected children we analyzed (most of whom had very similar backgrounds to Kuczaj's subjects). But Abe and the cross-sectional sample of children appear to come from the same distribution. What Abe and the sample have in common is that they were both studied by Kuczaj, as part of the only investigation we discuss that recorded children's speech expressly for the purpose of studying verbal inflection. Could there be some systematic factor in Kuczaj's methods that would push estimated overregularization rates upward?

According to his dissertation, Kuczaj (1976, p. 5) selected his 14 children from a larger sample of 23, according to the criteria of "(1) clarity of speech, (2) willingness to play games (in particular, to imitate model sentences when asked), and (3) willingness of the parents to aid the investigator by participating as experimenters (that is, by playing games with their child)." Among the ways that the parents aided Kuczaj were supplying the child with erroneous feedback, choosing the times to turn the tape recorder on and off, and asking the child to talk about specific events that took place in the past and about specific hypothetical events. (This was another attempt to elicit past tense forms because in English, as in many languages, the inflection called "past tense" is also used to express hypothetical events in certain contexts, as in *I wish I knew the answer* or *If I won the lottery*.) As Kuczaj points out, "The recorded conversations may then not be representative samples of normal conversation" (p. 8).

Kuczaj does not mention whether, in recording Abe, he tended to use the same manipulations that he instructed the parents of his cross-sectional sample to engage in. The transcripts themselves suggest that he may have. We tested for a conversational style involving a high degree of past tense elicitations in Abe's transcripts. Using the CLAN program COMBO, we searched for occurrences in Abe's parents' speech of three representative sequences of words that would tend to call for past tense forms in subsequent child utterances: *what did, what'd,* and *happened.* Abe's parents used these forms in 1.9% of their utterances, more frequently than 21 of the other 24 sets of adults in our samples, whose mean was 1.1%.[16]

It is unclear whether Kuczaj's selection criteria (or the parent's criteria for when to begin recording) adventitiously correlated with tendencies to overregularize. However, the instructions to parents to elicit past tense forms from their children could have elevated overregularization rates, for reasons we examine in the following section.

A. Discourse Patterns That Can Elevate Estimates of Overregularization Rates

There are three reasons to think that efforts to elicit past tense forms from children might cause them to overregularize more than they would in their spontaneous speech.

First, if children have any tendency to avoid forms in their spontaneous speech that they are uncertain of (in particular, the past tense form), then when the parent, rather than the child, chooses the verb, by asking a leading question, errors may be more likely. One example might be the following dialogue between Abe and his mother (from his 98th sample):

> *Mother.* And what did you choose to do?
> *Abe.* I choosed to make cookies.

Second, by eliciting descriptions of hypothetical and past tense events, the adult may be creating a discourse situation in which the child feels more

[16] Indeed, two of the children whose parents exceeded Abe's in past tense elicitations, Allison and Nat, were considerably younger, and younger children tend to be prompted more often in conversation than older children (see Marcus, 1992).

compelled on pragmatic grounds to mark tense than he would be otherwise. As we discuss in Chapter VI, Abe and Kuczaj's (1977a) cross-sectional sample had unusually high levels of compliance with the requirement of English syntax that past tense be marked in main clauses describing past or hypothetical events (i.e., they seldom used the stem form of verbs in obligatory past tense contexts), and overregularization tends to be accompanied by such high levels of past tense marking. The following bits of dialogue—from Abe's 34th and 144th transcripts, respectively—give a flavor of this possibility for past and hypothetical contexts:

Father. Abe do you remember what all you did yesterday? See if you can tell me what all you did yesterday.
Abe. We played the new games we fixed the wagon and we opened gifts.
Father. What did you do outside?
Abe. Hide. [Played hide and seek.]
Father. You hide? you hid?
Abe. Uhhuh and I count.
Father. You counted?
Abe. Uhhuh.
Mother. Abe was it . . . and he counted and came and looked for us.
Father. What happened then?
Abe. I finded Renee.

Father. What would have happened if they couldn't have found any water?
Abe. They gotted a hose.

Third, because of the syntax of English, questions without auxiliaries require insertion of *do* and the verb in stem form. If the child's representation of the stem form is primed by its appearance in a leading question, the stem could become unusually available for the regular inflection process and relatively less liable to being blocked by the irregular (for evidence that stem forms and regularly inflected forms prime each other, see Fowler, Napps, & Feldman, 1985; and Stanners, Neiser, Hernon, & Hall, 1979).[17] In contrast, spontaneous use of irregular past tense forms might involve activation of the entire lexical entry of a verb and the feature "past tense," directly indexing the stored past tense form, rather than first activating the

[17] Furthermore, providing the stem may have actively suppressed retrieval of the irregular version. Presenting an adult subject with a subset of a category of remembered words can impede retrieval of the rest (Slamecka, 1969). We thank Endel Tulving for pointing this out to us.

stem form. The effect might underlie exchanges like this one in Abe's 150th transcript:

> *Father.* What did you hear?
> *Abe.* I heared something like the TV.

There is suggestive evidence that higher levels of past tense elicitation in general may indeed increase overregularization rates. The number of times Abe heard *what did, what'd,* and *happened* per month correlated positively with his overregularization rate for that month, $r(31) = .35, p < .05$. (Across children, the overregularization rate correlates positively, although nonsignificantly, with the number of these forms per parental utterance, $r[23] = .18, p = .20$.) To see if these correlations might reflect a causal relation, we extracted all of Abe's stem overregularizations and correct past tense forms (excluding *get, read,* and the no-change verbs).[18] The preceding parental utterance was then scored manually either as a clear past tense elicitation (e.g., *Tell me what you did, What did you* [verb]*?*, and so on) or as some other sentence type. Overregularizations were significantly more likely after past tense elicitations than other kinds of sentences (27% vs. 19%, $\chi^2[1] = 9.64, p < .005$).

We also tested for one of the specific mechanisms by which certain kinds of past tense elicitations might increase overregularization: the priming of the child's representation of the stem form by its immediately preceding use in a parental question. Abe was significantly more likely to produce a stem overregularization of a particular verb (compared to the correct irregular form) when his parents used the stem form of that verb in the conversational turn immediately preceding the overregularization than when they did not use the stem form in that turn (32% vs. 21%, $\chi^2[1] = 5.60, p < .05$).

To see if these discourse influences operate generally in children, we ran similar tests on the much smaller set of overregularizations from Adam, Eve, and Sarah. We collected all the stem overregularizations in their transcripts and paired each one with the nearest correct irregular past tense form in the transcript. All three children showed a greater overregularization rate following past tense elicitations (9% vs. 2% for Adam, 44% vs. 15% for Eve, and 25% vs. 18% for Sarah); the difference was significant by a chi-square test for Eve individually and in a meta-analysis combining the probabilities of the chi-square tests for the four children ($p < .01$). However, we were unable to confirm the operation of a specific mechanism contributing to this effect that we tested for, namely, the priming of the stem by an

[18] Only stem overregularizations, not past overregularizations, were extracted, because this analysis was conducted simultaneously with the one described in the following paragraph, which requires stem overregularizations.

immediate prior occurrence in the parent's prompt. Tests of this effect were inconclusive: Adam's and Eve's samples contain more overregularizations of a verb after the parent had just used its stem; Sarah's contained fewer.

In sum, there are reasons to believe that the higher overregularization rates among the children Kuczaj studied, including Abe, are partly artifactual. The data are, as Kuczaj noted, not "representative samples of normal conversation"; rather, they appear to be part way between naturalistic speech and experimentally elicited speech. Our analyses of discourse effects on overregularization, together with our review of data from actual elicitation experiments in the next section, suggest that Kuczaj's methodology might have led to systematic overestimates of children's spontaneous rate of overregularization.

Note that we are not suggesting that the entire difference between Kuczaj's subjects and those in the rest of the literature is artifactual; in Chapter VI, we will examine the possible effects of high levels of marking tense on overregularization, a difference between Kuczaj's subjects and the other children that is of some theoretical interest. Note as well that these analyses are an attempt to resolve the discrepancy between Kuczaj's data and the others in the literature and should not be interpreted as a criticism of Kuczaj's methodology in general. Three of the four hypotheses he was testing in Kuczaj (1977a) had nothing to do with overall overregularization rates; rather, they compared the two different kinds of overregularization errors (*eated* and *ated*) and the relative overregularization rates of verbs with different properties. For these purposes there were good reasons to have sought samples with large numbers of past tense forms, just as we focus on Abe in our investigation of the time course of individual verbs in Section IV above.[19] It is only when treating Kuczaj's data as estimates of children's overall overregularization rates in spontaneous speech that the nonrepresentativeness of the samples must be taken into account.

[19] Kuczaj's tests of his fourth hypothesis, however, may have been affected by his methodology, although of course he was not aware of the effects we now point out. Kuczaj disagreed with Brown's (1973) claim that irregular past tense marking was acquired before regular past tense marking, which Brown had based on differences in the relative ages at which the two kinds of marking were supplied in obligatory past tense contexts more than 90% of the time. Kuczaj noted that the finding might depend on whether overregularizations had been counted as incorrect forms or ignored when the percentages were tallied, which had not been made clear in Brown (1973). (In fact, they were ignored; Brown et al., 1971.) Kuczaj counted the overregularizations twice: as incorrect irregular past tense forms and as correct regular past tense forms. The resulting percentages of correct use in obligatory contexts showed an advantage to regular marking, contrary to Brown's claim. Thus, Kuczaj's "nonreplication" was partly just due to differences in definitions, but it was also due to how these differences interact with his special recording circumstances. Because these circumstances may have led to unusually high overregularization rates, Kuczaj's estimates of irregular marking were thereby depressed and his estimates of regular marking inflated.

VIII. PREVIOUS ESTIMATES OF OVERREGULARIZATION FROM ELICITED PRODUCTION EXPERIMENTS

Several experimental studies have elicited past tense forms in sentence completion tasks using existing irregular English verbs. For example, in the experiment by Kuczaj (1978), the overregularization rates for the groups of 3–4-year-olds, 5–6-year-olds, and 7–8-year-olds were, respectively, 29%, 49% (42% stem overregularizations, 7% past + *ed* overregularizations), and 1%. Bybee and Slobin (1982a) found that their third graders (8-6–10-1) overregularized between 2% and 55% of the time, depending on the verb subclass. Marchman (1988) found the following overregularization rates for her different age groups: 4-year-olds, 32%; 5-year-olds, 33%; 6-year-olds, 22%; 7-year-olds, 10%; and 9-year-olds, 5% (calculated from her table 1, based on 76% of the test items being irregular, as mentioned in her text). Note that in all such studies the overregularization rates are generally less than 50%; once again, there is virtually no evidence that young children overregularize exclusively or in free variation with correct irregular forms.

Of course the overregularization rates in elicited production tasks are still far higher than those obtained from spontaneous speech, but the two kinds of estimates are not comparable. Bybee and Slobin (1982a), Prasada, Pinker, and Snyder (1990), and Stemberger and MacWhinney (1986) found that adults, when put under time pressure, are prone to making overregularization errors at even higher rates than children (from 6% to 31% of the time in the Bybee-Slobin study, depending on the subclass), presumably because of a greater likelihood of retrieval failure. It is plausible that many children feel that they are under pressure in experiments even if it is not explicitly stated. Furthermore, if children ever fall into a strategy of treating each experimental item as a pure sound, rather than as a word they know, it essentially becomes a novel form, and regularization is the most accessible option.

But most important, in all such tasks children are being supplied with the stem itself seconds before they are asked to supply the past form (e.g., *This is a girl who knows how to swing. She did the same thing yesterday. She* ———). This contrasts with naturalistic settings in which children produce a past form for an irregular in response to a mental representation of the verb's meaning plus the feature for past tense; the phonetic form of the stem need never be activated. Thus, experimental elicitations of irregular past tense forms using the stem as a prompt, like parents' leading questions containing the stem, are likely to prime the child's representations of the stem form and possibly suppress the irregular past, leading to an increased likelihood of overregularization, an effect we were able to document for Abe in the preceding section.

IX. PREVIOUS ESTIMATES OF OVERREGULARIZATION FROM JUDGMENT AND CORRECTION EXPERIMENTS

Another source of data that might be thought to show that children are indifferent to the past tense forms of their irregular verbs comes from Kuczaj's (1978) judgment task. In one experiment, children aged 3–9 years had to judge whether any member of a group of puppets "said something silly." One puppet produced a sentence with a correct irregular past tense, a second produced an overregularization, and, for verbs other than no-change verbs, a third produced a past + *ed* form. In a second experiment, children of the same ages produced past tenses for irregular verbs supplied in the future tense (discussed in the preceding section), then judged a puppet's version of the verb (always different from the child's version), and then judged a second puppet's version (the third possible kind of past tense form). Finally, children were offered a forced choice among the three versions and asked which of the three they thought their mother would use. In many conditions, overregularizations were judged as acceptable a large proportion of the time, as high as 89% for stem overregularizations for the youngest children in the first experiment.

However, here too the data are not comparable to overregularization rates from spontaneous speech. Grammaticality judgment is a signal detection task, and it is fallacious to assume that every time a child accepts or fails to correct a given form, the child's grammar deems it well formed. Rather, just as with all yes-no data, the perceived payoffs for hits, misses, false alarms, and correct rejections affect rates of saying yes. For children in an experimental setting this could involve a variety of demand characteristics such as the perceived politeness of rejecting or correcting another creature's language more than a given proportion of the time. In the language of signal detection theory, this defines a "criterion" or bias for saying yes that is superimposed on their "sensitivity" in internally representing grammatical and ungrammatical utterances as different, which we can assume is a probabilistic process. Lacking direct manipulations of bias, the best one can do in determining whether children have knowledge of irregular pasts is to compare their yes rate for correct irregulars to that for incorrect overregularizations; if the former are higher, children must be discriminating between them (see Grimshaw & Rosen, 1990). Kuczaj's data provide 15 opportunities to make such comparisons: three age groups in experiment 1, each of which was asked to judge overregularizations of no-change irregulars and to judge overregularizations of other irregulars; and three age groups in experiment 2, each of which was asked to judge stem overregularizations, to judge past overregularizations, and to choose their favorite from among the three. (The children's choice of their mother's favorite form was almost always identical to their own choice and thus is not an independent data set.) Of these 15 comparisons, only one involved a failure to discriminate irregulars from overregularizations: the middle age group (5–7) in experiment 2 preferred past overregularizations over irregulars or stem overregularizations in the forced choice task (although they did not even produce many such forms in the elicited production task, as noted above). In other words, the judgment data confirm that children systematically favor irregular forms as the preferred past tense version of irregular verbs (see also Lachter & Bever, 1988).

More recently, Cox (1989, p. 204) told children that a puppet "was learning to talk but was having trouble with some of his words," and the child was asked to help him say the correct words. Twelve sentences, each with an overregularized noun or verb, were provided. Children were not asked to judge the sentences, and there were no correct irregulars among the experimental stimuli, so we cannot assess children's discrimination abilities from the data. Correction performance was surprisingly poor: none of the six sentences with verbs was corrected by more than 16% of the children around the age of 5, and none of the six sentences with nouns was corrected by more than 28%, except, inexplicably, *tooths*. Since, as Cox herself notes, the children who failed to correct an overregularization did not necessarily use it themselves, a response bias against correcting the puppet too often is a likelier explanation than an absence of knowledge, especially since she told the children that the puppet was having trouble with only "some" of his words but presented no sentences that were actually correct.

Finally, the consistent findings that overregularization rates are low and that irregulars are preferred to them help explain the otherwise paradoxical phenomenon that children who have been observed to overregularize will vehemently correct their parents when they mimic the children's errors (Bever, 1975; Slobin, 1978; see also Lachter & Bever, 1988). Similarly, Ervin and Miller (1963) noted that their subjects often corrected their own overregularizations; we do not know of any reports of children correcting one of their irregular past tense utterances to an overregularization.

X. SUMMARY

Overregularization percentages in the single digits are characteristic of most children, ages, and commonly used verbs. This suggests that, during the ages at which they are overregularizing, children are neither failing to discriminate irregular verbs from regulars nor freely alternating between overregularizations of irregulars and the corresponding correct past tense forms but instead show a pervasive strong bias for the correct form. Such a bias is predicted by the hypothesis that children block regularization whenever they retrieve an irregular form from memory (MacWhinney, 1978; Pinker, 1984) but is not predicted by any other hypothesis in the literature. Finally, what has been called "U-shaped development" corresponds to the following two events: before the first overregularization, there is a measurable extended period during which all irregular past tense forms are correct, and overregularization tails off gradually during the school-age years.

V. THE RELATION OF OVERREGULARIZATION TO CHANGES IN THE NUMBER AND PROPORTION OF REGULAR VERBS IN PARENTS' SPEECH AND CHILDREN'S VOCABULARY

In this chapter, we review the operation of the Rumelhart-McClelland model and how it models children's U-shaped developmental sequence. Then we examine the empirical assumptions justifying the sequence of inputs that Rumelhart and McClelland trained the model on. We test whether these assumptions are reasonable using the available data from the spontaneous speech of Adam, Eve, and Sarah, the three children we have been focusing on who displayed a U-shaped sequence in their longitudinal development.

I. WHY THE RUMELHART-McCLELLAND MODEL OVERREGULARIZES

The core of the Rumelhart-McClelland model is a pattern associator network that takes a phonological representation of the stem as input and computes a phonological representation of the past tense form as output. The pattern associator consists of two layers of nodes—a set of input units that are turned on in patterns that represent the sound of the verb stem and a set of output units that are turned on in patterns that represent the sound of the verb's past tense form—and weighted connections between every input unit and every output unit. Each unit corresponds to a sequence of phonological features, such as a high vowel between two stop consonants or a back vowel followed by a nasal consonant at the end of a word. The word itself is represented solely by the set of feature sequences it contains. When a set of input nodes is activated, each node sends its activation level, multiplied by the link weight, to the output nodes it is connected to. Each output node sums its weighted inputs, compares the result to a threshold, and probabilistically turns on if the threshold is exceeded. The output form is the word most compatible with the set of activated output nodes.

During a learning phase, the network compares its own version of the past tense form with the correct version provided by a "teacher," and it adjusts the strengths of the connections and the thresholds so as to reduce the difference between the actual state of each output node and the correct state. By this process of recording and superimposing contingencies between bits of sounds of stems (e.g., the distinctive features of endings such as *-op* or *-ing*) and bits of sounds of past tense forms (e.g., the features of *-opped* and *-ang*), the model improves its performance over time, and it can generalize to new forms on the basis of their featural overlap with old ones. The model contains nothing corresponding to a word or rule and thus makes no qualitative distinction between regular and irregular mappings; both are effected by connections between stem sounds and past sounds.

Rumelhart and McClelland's explanation of the sequence of overregularization flowed from the ways in which parallel distributed processing (PDP) models generalize. In building such a model, there are numerous ways to bias it toward conservative recording of individual input items, toward liberal overgeneralization according to frequent patterns, or some combination. The challenge was to duplicate the child's transition from conservatism to overgeneralization in a single model. Rumelhart and McClelland proposed a simple and ingenious hypothesis. Not only are irregular verbs high in frequency, but the reverse is true as well: the verbs highest in frequency are irregular. For example, the top 10 verbs in Kucera and Francis's (1967) frequency list are all irregular. If children acquire verbs in order of decreasing frequency, they will develop a vocabulary with an increasing proportion of regular verbs as they begin to run out of the high-frequency irregulars and encounter more and more regular verbs. In particular, Rumelhart and McClelland assumed that, at some point in development, the child shows "explosive" vocabulary growth, which would result in a sudden influx of a large number of regular verbs. Because the regular pattern will be exemplified by many different verbs, the learning procedure will strengthen many links between stem features and the features defining the *-ed* ending. The effects of these newly modified link weights could overwhelm the existing weights on the links between idiosyncratic features of irregular stems and the idiosyncratic features of their pasts, resulting in overregularization. As the irregulars continue to be processed, the discrepancies between the overregularized and teacher-supplied correct forms will be registered, and the crucial idiosyncratic links will be strengthened over time, eventually allowing the irregular forms to reappear.

Given these assumptions, Rumelhart and McClelland were able to model the developmental sequence with one additional assumption: the vocabulary explosion occurs after the child has just acquired his 10th verb. Their 10-verb decision results in two training phases. First, the model is presented with the 10 highest-frequency verbs (excluding *do* and *be,* which can also be auxiliaries), of which only two (20%) happen to be regular,

10 times apiece. Then the model is presented with that list plus the 410 next-most-frequent verbs, constituting a set in which 80% of the verbs are now regular, 190 times apiece. In phase 1, the model learned the 10 verbs successfully; when phase 2 begins on the eleventh cycle and it is suddenly swamped with regulars, the model overregularizes the irregulars. The recovery process begins immediately, reaching asymptote shortly before the 200th epoch (see Figs. 16 and 17, taken from Rumelhart & McClelland, 1986).

The Rumelhart-McClelland model challenges the traditional account of overregularization, which depended on separate rote and rule mechanisms, in favor of a single mechanism that begins to overregularize because of an influx of newly acquired regular verbs, a presumed consequence of a vocabulary growth spurt. Let us call this explanation of the cause of overregularization the vocabulary balance hypothesis; it is also a feature of the more recent network simulations by Plunkett and Marchman (1990).

II. PINKER AND PRINCE'S CRITIQUE

Pinker and Prince (1988; see also Prince & Pinker, 1988) examined Rumelhart and McClelland's assumptions about development. Rumelhart and McClelland cited Brown (1973) in support of their assumption of a vocabulary spurt near the onset of overregularization, but Brown did not discuss vocabulary acquisition at all. According to standard sources (see, e.g., Ingram, 1989) children's "word spurt" usually occurs at 1-6, about a year too early to account for the onset of overregularization for most children, which occurred at a mean age of 2-5 for the seven children examined in Chapter IV. Pinker and Prince examined Brown's (n.d.) vocabulary lists for Adam, Eve, and Sarah, which were drawn from five evenly spaced samples spanning the overregularization sequence, plus a fourth child in the one-word stage. They found neither an explosive growth in vocabulary near the onset of overregularization nor, more significant, an increase in the percentage of the child's vocabulary samples that was regular: the proportion regular stayed around 50% before, during, and after the onset. Pinker and Prince also cited data (partly from Slobin, 1971) suggesting that the proportion of regular verb tokens among all verb tokens in parental speech to children is about 20%–30% during overregularization, nowhere near the 80% proportion that Rumelhart and McClelland used to override the irregular patterns. They argued that an endogenous transition from rote to rule is still required to account for the data, as in the traditional account.

Pinker and Prince's (1988) data showing that the proportion of regular verb types in children's longitudinal samples' stays at around 50% seem paradoxical at first: if there are only 180 irregular verbs and thousands of

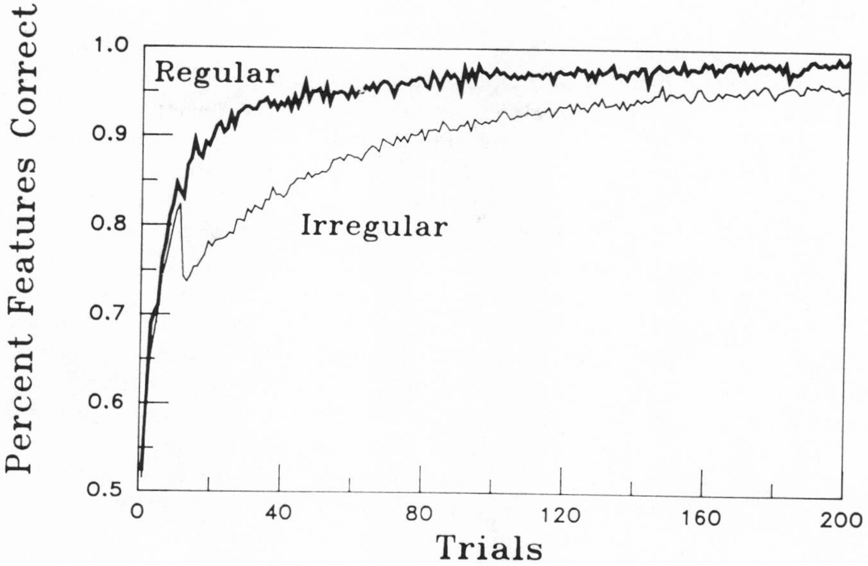

FIG. 16.—Performance of the Rumelhart-McClelland model on regular and irregular verbs as a function of training epochs. The dip in the curve for irregular verbs following the 10th epoch corresponds to the onset of overregularization. From Rumelhart and McClelland (1986).

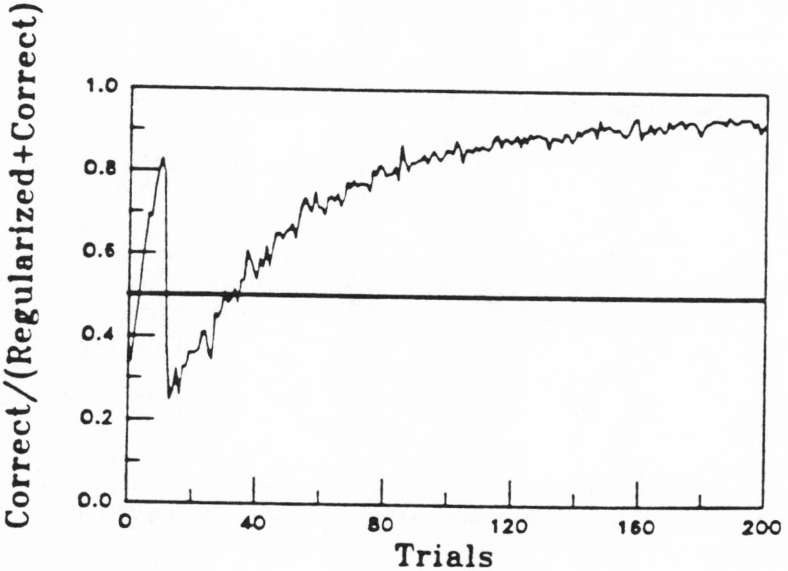

FIG. 17.—Tendency of the Rumelhart-McClelland model to overregularize irregular verbs as a function of training epochs. Overregularization tendency is measured as the ratio of the strength of the correct irregular response to the sum of the strengths of the correct and the overregularized responses. Points below the line correspond to a tendency to overregularize. From Rumelhart and McClelland (1986).

regulars, isn't an increase in the percentage of regular verbs a mathematical certainty after the 180th irregular is acquired, and a statistical near certainty well before that? The answer is that Pinker and Prince's type estimates were from fairly small samples (about 700 utterances per child per stage) and hence were not pure estimates of type frequency but something combining type and token frequency: types with higher token frequency were more likely to have been sampled. Because the token frequency of irregulars is much higher than that of most of the regulars, it is possible that when children learn lower-frequency regular verbs, they may not displace the earlier acquired irregulars. *Permit, understand, remember, misbehave,* and so on may compete among themselves for air time in children's speech, leaving general-duty verbs like *come, go, take, put, eat,* and so on to occupy a constant proportion of verb slots in conversation throughout development.

Because Pinker and Prince's data reflected both type and token frequencies, the force of their critique is uncertain. To evaluate the vocabulary balance hypothesis, then, one must first establish whether it is the proportion of regular types, tokens, or some other index that is relevant. Two issues must be addressed. What is the psychological event that corresponds to an episode of network learning, according to Rumelhart and McClelland's theory? And what kinds of changes in the schedule of learning episodes cause overregularization in pattern associator networks?

III. WHAT IS A LEARNING EPISODE?

Rumelhart and McClelland make the following assumptions about the real-world events that correspond to a learning episode:

> The [simulation] run was intended to capture approximately the experience with past tenses of a young child picking up English from everyday conversation. Our conception of the nature of this experience is simply that the child learns first about the present and past tenses of the highest frequency verbs; later on, learning occurs for a much larger ensemble of verbs, including a much larger proportion of regular forms.
>
> Although the child would be hearing present and past tenses of all kinds of verbs throughout development, we assume that he or she is only able to learn past tenses for verbs already mastered fairly well in the present tense. This is because the real learning environment does not, in fact, present the child with present-tense/past-tense pairs. Rather, it presents the child with past-tense words in sentences occurring in real-world context. The child would therefore have to generate the appropriate present tense form internally with the aid of the entire sentence and context, and this, we suppose, requires that the

child already know the present tense of the word. [Rumelhart & McClelland, 1987, p. 222]

The assumption here is that an episode of learning consists of hearing a past tense form, using the context to recover its corresponding stem from the mental lexicon,[20] feeding the stem into the internal pattern associator, comparing the output with the past tense form actually heard, and adjusting the weights in response to discrepancies. A stem-past pair would be fed into the model only when an adult used the past *and* the child possessed the stem in his or her vocabulary (and knew it was related to the past form).

This means that the proportion of regulars fed into the past tense learning system would be determined by the proportion of occasions that the parent used a regular past tense that the child already possessed in stem form. However, it is impossible to tell from transcripts exactly when this conjunction of parent's use and child's knowledge occurs. Instead, there are three ways to estimate the relevant proportions indirectly, each with different assumptions.

For all three, it is useful to assume that all verbs have an approximately constant distribution of uses in different tenses, so we can collapse across tenses and increase sample sizes, reducing the danger of underestimating the number of regular verbs. Counting all verbs, not just past tense forms, also reduces the size of a possible confound: if one were to find a positive correlation between the increase in the number of regular past tense forms and the tendency to overregularize, it could reflect the effects of a newly acquired regularization process on the ease of generating past tense forms of regular verbs rather than the effects of having many regular verbs on the development of an ability to regularize.[21] In fact, we have found that irregular verbs take up a somewhat larger proportion of past tense tokens than of total verb tokens (about 85% vs. 65%–75%), but this difference only strengthens the conclusions that we will be making on the basis of all verb tokens.

[20] Rumelhart and McClelland refer to the input form as the "present," but the present tense form would include an irrelevant *-s* affix for the third person singular; "stem" is actually what they had in mind.

[21] Lachter and Bever (1988) point out that the direction of a cause and effect relation between possessing regular verbs and overregularization cannot completely be resolved, even if one were to examine possession of regular verbs per se rather than mastery of the past tense form of such verbs. The problem, they note, is that once a child has developed the ability to generate and analyze regular past tense forms productively, he or she no longer has to memorize such forms from parental speech. As a result, the learning events and memory space that beforehand would have been dedicated to acquiring regular past tense forms can now be applied to the learning of brand new verbs, and such verbs should be acquired at a more rapid rate. We will not pursue this possibility further, although it would be an important consideration if one were to find the relevant correlation.

The first method assumes that children produce regular and irregular verbs in approximately the same proportions that they process regular and irregular past tense forms in their parents' speech (i.e., it assumes that if a child uses a verb, he or she knows it, and that children in conversation with parents will use different verbs in roughly the same proportion as their parents). Under this assumption, *the proportion of verb tokens that are regular in the child's speech* indirectly estimates the proportion of regular learning episodes.

Second, since the occurrence of a parental token is necessary for a learning episode to take place, if we assume that children know a constant proportion of the verb tokens their parents address to them, we can measure *the proportion of verb tokens that are regular in the parent's speech.*

In practice, Rumelhart and McClelland ignored token frequency entirely in assembling the training set for their model: every verb was fed in the same number of times, once per epoch. This assumes that a third measure, the proportion of regular verb types among all verb types, is the relevant factor—although it is inconsistent with their psychological interpretation of a learning episode, which would be driven by parental tokens. Rather, the teaching schedule they actually modeled is more consistent with some kind of off-line learning, fed by a preprocessor: the child takes a pass through his entire verb lexicon, feeding each stem-past pair into the pattern associator once per scan. If we entertain this interpretation of a learning episode, which corresponds literally to Rumelhart and McClelland's learning schedule, rather than the token-driven interpretation they discuss, we can test the vocabulary balance hypothesis by trying to estimate *the proportion of verb types in the child's vocabulary that are regular.* Note that it is not valid to use the percentage of a child's vocabulary that is regular as a surrogate for the number of on-line learning episodes even if it turns out that the proportion of regular verbs among parental tokens is constant. That is, one cannot assume that the proportion of regular learning episodes is determined by the proportion of the child's vocabulary that is regular, because this larger regular vocabulary could correspond to a larger number of regular types that the parent is cycling through a constant number of regular tokens in his or her speech, leaving the proportion of regular learning episodes constant.

IV. HOW DO CHANGES IN LEARNING EPISODES LEAD TO OVERREGULARIZATION?

Assuming that we know what a learning episode is, what kind of changes in the distribution of learning episodes lead to overregularization, according to the vocabulary balance hypothesis?

A. Type versus Token Frequency

First, it is clear that both type and token frequency have important consequences. The Rumelhart-McClelland model overregularized because it changed its connection strengths with each input pair in a direction that reduced the discrepancy between computed and input past forms. After the first epoch, in which the model was suddenly bombarded with regulars, about 80% of the changes that the model made were designed to make it more likely to generate regular forms, because 80% of the inputs were new regulars. Many of the changed connections involved links from phonological features that were also shared with irregulars (since most irregulars are phonologically similar in some way to at least some regulars). Because the network did not have enough specific feature units to register each verb on its own set of units, the overlap was high enough that each irregular was represented by many units whose links had just been adjusted to help produce the regular ending, and overregularization resulted. This effect would obviously depend strongly on the number of regular types, because the wider the range of regular forms that are fed in, the greater the probability that a given phonological feature of an irregular verb will be shared by some regular verb and hence develop stronger links to the incorrect regular pattern. But this effect can also be mitigated by token frequency: if, say, each irregular had been repeated four times for each regular (reflecting the real-world higher token frequency of irregulars), the links that joined features unique to the irregulars to their corresponding irregular past forms would have been strengthened several times during the epoch to reduce the errors with such forms, and overregularization would be less likely. Indeed, one of the noteworthy properties of the Rumelhart-McClelland model is its distributed phonological representation of words, with no units dedicated to words per se (see Pinker & Prince, 1988), so there is no physical basis for a distinction between types and tokens in the model at all. Only feature-to-feature mappings, whether they be from a single word or a set of similar words, are represented. The actual behavior of the model will depend on the number of regular types, the phonological range of the regular types, their degree of overlap with irregulars, the token frequencies of both irregulars and regulars, and other factors. In any case, it is clear that overregularization of an irregular does depend on the ratio of regular to irregular tokens and hence is relevant to testing the vocabulary balance hypothesis.

B. Proportion versus Changes in Proportion

Second, the percentage of regular learning episodes at a given time is not the relevant factor in predicting overregularization. In the Rumelhart-

McClelland model, unlike in children, the process of recovery from overregularization begins immediately after its onset (see Fig. 17), correct irregular forms predominate within a few epochs, and at asymptote they are produced most of the time, all with a constant level of 80% regular learning episodes. This is an obvious property of any model that is designed to perform correctly at asymptote: even with the most unfavorable proportion of regular episodes, the irregulars must eventually reassert themselves. Overregularization is a short-term consequence of the *increase* in the percentage of regular episodes with development. Although a properly designed model could learn to overcome any particular level of dominance of regulars, this adjustment cannot take place instantaneously, and influxes of regulars will cause temporary overregularization, before the crucial links between nodes unique to an irregular and its idiosyncratic past have been sufficiently strengthened. For this reason, the difference between the rapid recovery of the Rumelhart-McClelland model and the protracted period of overregularization of children does not speak against the model. It is possible that as children learn more and more words, new regulars are constantly washing over them; no sooner do they adjust their irregulars to the leveling effect of one wave of regulars than a new wave comes in. Thus, the proper test of the vocabulary balance hypothesis involves a correlation between the most recent *increase* in regular learning episodes and the current rate of overregularization; this is why Rumelhart and McClelland appeal to a period of explosive *growth* in vocabulary to trigger overregularization.[22]

C. *Proportion of Regular Verbs versus Number of Regular Verbs*

Third, for the analyses in which types are being examined, it may not be the proportion of verb types that are regular that is the relevant predictor. The problem is that the competition in pattern associators is not between the regular pattern and a single irregular pattern shared among all the irregulars. Rather, irregulars are different from each other, not just from the regulars. Imagine that at one stage there are six different irregulars, each with a different change (e.g., *go-went, come-came, hit-hit,* etc.), and six regulars. At the next stage, there are 12 different irregulars, each with a different change, and 12 regulars. The proportion of regulars in the sample remains the same, but the ratio of regulars to *any particular irregular*

[22] In recent experiments on the behavior of connectionist networks at learning inflectional mappings in sets of artificial verbs with different training schedules and vocabulary mixtures, Plunkett and Marchman (1990, 1991) have confirmed that both token frequencies and rate of vocabulary increase have direct effects on the tendency of standard connectionist models to produce outputs analogous to overregularizations.

pattern has doubled. Therefore, in this scenario it is the number of regulars, not the proportion of regulars, that would predict overregularization.

The preceding scenario is not fully accurate, however: the ratio of learning episodes for the regular pattern to a given irregular pattern would be identical to the number of regulars only if every irregular were *totally* idiosyncratic. But virtually all the irregulars share their patterns of change with other irregulars, so the calculation is too extreme. Consider a scenario that is extreme in the other direction: the six irregulars in phase 1 fall into three classes (e.g., *sing-sang, ring-rang, feed-fed, breed-bred, wear-wore, tear-tore*), and the new irregulars in phase 2 fall into the same classes (e.g., *spring-sprang, lead-led, swear-swore*). Here, the ratio of regulars to any irregular vowel change pattern is 3 : 1 in both phases, and we would expect overregularization to be less likely; only a change in the proportion of regulars would clearly induce it.

In reality, the situation is likely to be somewhere between these extremes because while English irregulars do fall into a restricted number of kinds of change, we would expect the number of patterns in a child's vocabulary, not just the number of irregulars per pattern, to increase somewhat with development. Therefore, it is not clear whether overregularization rates should be correlated with the proportion of total types that are regular (appropriate if all new irregulars fall into old patterns and hence protect old irregulars) or with the number of types that are regular (appropriate if each new irregular is unique), and we will examine both correlations.

D. Summary of Tests

We will examine whether there are increases over time in the proportion of verbs that are regular verbs among the child's tokens, the parents' tokens, and the child's types and, if there are, whether such increases are related to the child's tendency to overregularize. The relations will be tested at two levels of temporal detail.

First, we will compare the monthly rate of increase in each vocabulary factor for the months before the first overregularization with the monthly rate of increase for the months during which overregularization is taking place (i.e., the first month containing an overregularization and all the months after it). This is an objectively specifiable dividing line but requires some further comments. For Eve, there are a small number of tokens before the first overregularization, and recall that there is no statistical evidence that she in fact underwent a transition between stages (see Chap. IV, Sec. IV*A*). For Sarah, the dividing line could be questioned. Brown (n.d.; see Pinker & Prince, 1988) noted that Sarah produced a past tense of *hear* at 2-10 that was literally pronounced as an overregularization (*heared,* with a schwa instead of the *r*), but he worried whether it could have been an odd pronunciation of *heard*. The first completely unambiguous overregularization does not occur in her transcripts for another 5 months. However, the hypothetical pattern of distortion that Brown considered is not independently motivated by Sarah's other mispronunciations: for example, at 3-2 she pronounced *hurted* as *hahted,* suggesting that if *heard* was intended but mispronounced, it would have surfaced as *hahd,* not *hea-əd* (Alan Prince, personal communication, January 10, 1989). Furthermore, excluding this datum has the effect of weakening the evidence for the vocabulary balance hypothesis. Therefore, we will not second-guess the transcription, and we will count *heared* as Sarah's first overregularization. In any case, the first recorded overregularizations of all three children should be taken, not as the literal moment of arrival of the ability to overregularize, but as a partly arbitrary dichotomization of the developmental span into a period when overregularizations are likely to occur and a preceding span when overregularizations are unlikely to occur.

A more precise test comes from correlating the monthly rate of increase in a vocabulary measure between month t and month $t + 1$ with the overregularization rate at time $t + 1$. This analysis combines the factors that differentiate the pre-overregularization stage from the overregularization stage and the factors that cause overregularization to be more frequent in one month than another during the overregularization stage. According to the Rumelhart-McClelland model, there is no qualitative difference between the two. Because longitudinal transcripts from a given child are not independent sampling units, the correlation coefficients are best treated as descriptive statistics; the meaning of tests of significance is not clear. Fortunately, the issue will seldom arise, as the sign of the correlation coefficients we find will usually obviate the need for significance testing.

V. PARENTAL TOKENS

The proportion of regular verb tokens among all adult verb tokens is plotted for Adam, Eve, and Sarah in Figures 18, 19, and 20. As mentioned in Chapter III, the data come not only from the child's parents but also from the other adults speaking to the child in the transcripts. For all three children, a bit more than one-quarter of the parental verb tokens were regular, and this did not change over the course of development. As mentioned, the reason the proportion is constant is that most of the high-frequency verbs that are indispensable for casual conversation are irregular, and they do not move aside to make way for the more numerous but lower-frequency regulars.

The proportions are similar before and after overregularization begins:

for Adam, 30% before, 29% during; for Eve, 29% before, 25% during; for Sarah, 25% before, 26% during. More important, the rate of change in the proportions was not systematically larger during the overregularization period: for Adam, 1.2 percentage points per month before, −0.1 during; for Eve, 0.9 before, −0.7 during; for Sarah, 0.2 before and during. The correlations between the rate of monthly change in proportion regular and the child's overregularization rate are in the wrong direction for Adam (−.40) and Eve (−.29) and close to zero (.03) for Sarah.

VI. CHILD'S TOKENS

The proportion of the child's tokens that consists of regular verbs is plotted on the same axes as their adults' proportions, also in Figures 18–20. The proportion oscillates between 26% and 45% for Adam, actually declines for Eve from around as high as 54% (possibly sampling error) to a steady state between 23% and 30%, and shows some early dips to the teens for Sarah before mainly oscillating within the 20%–40% range. The reasons for regular verbs being used a steady minority of the time are no doubt the same as for the adults.

The proportion of tokens that are regular does not systematically increase after overregularization begins: 37% versus 34% for Adam; 50% versus 27% for Eve; and 25% versus 30% for Sarah. The monthly rates of change for these figures are actually higher before overregularization than during: respectively, 2.4 and −0.3 percentage points for Adam; 7.9 and −3.8 for Eve; and 4.2 and −0.6 for Sarah. The correlations between monthly change in percent tokens regular and the child's overregularization rate are −.03 for Adam, −.22 for Eve, −.10 for Sarah.

VII. CHILD'S TYPES

As mentioned, measures based on the child's types are the least psychologically realistic measures to focus on, because they are meaningful only if rule learning is an off-line pass through the child's vocabulary, which does not correspond to Rumelhart and McClelland's psychological assumptions. But the measures are worth examining both because they represent the form of the vocabulary balance hypothesis that is most likely to be consistent with some developmental trend (since the proportion of regular types *must* increase with development) and because it was in fact a change in regular types that defined the training sequence given to the Rumelhart-McClelland model.

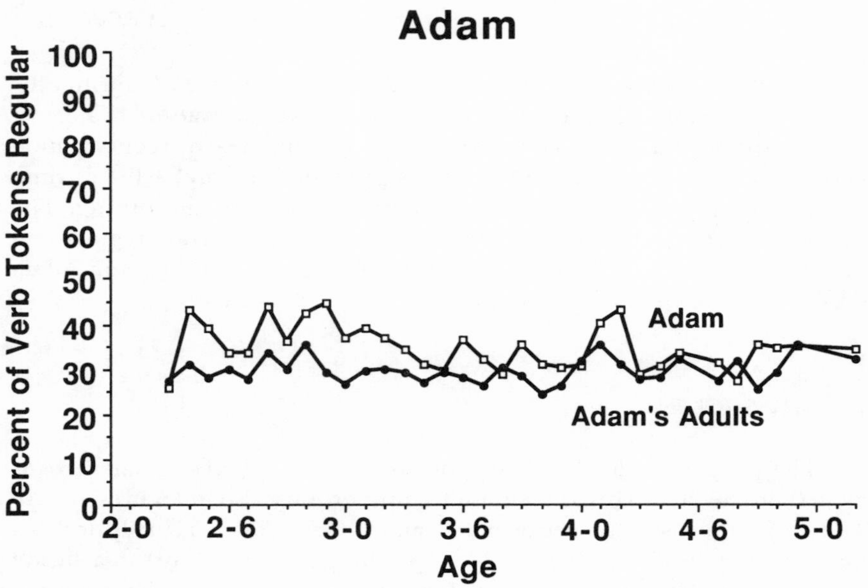

FIG. 18.—Percentage of verb tokens that are regular for Adam and the adults conversing with Adam.

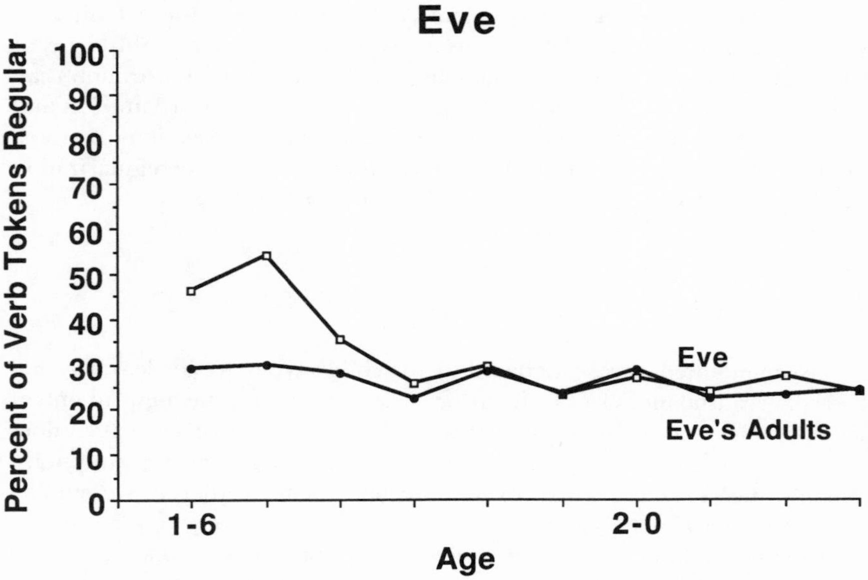

FIG. 19.—Percentage of verb tokens that are regular for Eve and the adults conversing with Eve.

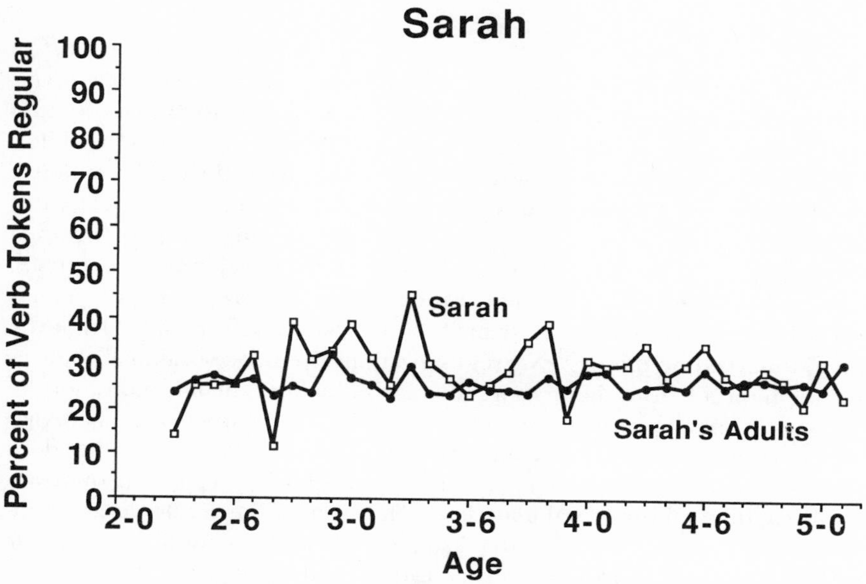

FIG. 20.—Percentage of verb tokens that are regular for Sarah and the adults conversing with Sarah.

Measuring the proportion of children's vocabulary that consists of regular verbs is an extremely difficult problem, for it faces the notorious pitfalls involved in estimating children's vocabulary size in general (for extensive discussion, see, e.g., Lorge & Chall, 1963; Miller, 1977; Moe et al., 1982; Seashore & Eckerson, 1940; Templin, 1957). The source of the problem here is that we are confined to the actual words that children used in samples. Obviously, the child will use only a small fraction of his or her total vocabulary in any given sample. Since high-frequency verbs are more likely to appear than low-frequency verbs, the number of low-frequency verbs will be systematically underestimated. And since there are more low-frequency regulars than low-frequency irregulars, counting types per sample will systematically underestimate the proportion of regulars (this was a problem with Pinker and Prince's 1988 estimates). There is no completely adequate solution to the problem of measuring children's vocabulary, but there are various estimates that can be examined, and at the very least the direction of changes in the proportion that is regular can be compared for months associated with different levels of overregularization, and the resulting conclusions can be compared across different methods in an attempt to arrive at converging conclusions.

A. Method 1: Cumulative Vocabulary

One measure that is designed to be generous to low-frequency forms is the child's *cumulative* vocabulary totals. That is, one assumes that the child never forgets. If a word is used in a given month, it is credited to the child's vocabulary from then on. Figures 21–26 show the children's cumulative vocabulary growth for regular and irregular verbs, and the proportion of cumulative vocabulary that is regular; overregularization rates are included in these graphs for ease of comparison of their developmental courses. Table 5 shows the rate of change of the number and proportion of regular verbs in the vocabularies of Adam, Eve, and Sarah before and during the period marked by the first overregularization; the static vocabulary figures for the month before the first overregularization and the last month of the transcripts are also provided as reference points. By mathematical necessity each child possesses a larger cumulative regular vocabulary later in development than earlier, and, as expected, the regulars take up a larger proportion of the child's total verb vocabulary later. However, as the decelerating vocabulary curves (most visible for Adam) suggest, for both the number of regular verbs and the proportion of verb vocabulary that is regular, the rates of increase are much larger for the stages before than during overregularization, contrary to the vocabulary balance hypothesis. Similarly, the monthly changes in the number of regular verbs and in the proportion of regular verbs among all verbs correlate negatively with overregularization rate for all three children.

Unfortunately, the decelerating vocabulary curve and concomitant negative correlation with overregularization may be a direct consequence, even an artifact, of the cumulative measure for vocabulary. Cumulative vocabulary is equivalent to sampling without replacement. Imagine that parents use 500 regular verbs, with equal token frequencies, when speaking to their children, at all ages. Imagine that every month children attend to and acquire 10% of the verbs they hear and produce every word they have acquired at least once. At the end of month 1 their cumulative vocabulary is 50 words. At the end of month 2 it is not 100 words but only 95—the 50 they learned in month 1, plus 10% of the 450 words that they had not previously acquired in month 1 (i.e., 45 words; the other five they attended to do not count because they had already been acquired). In month 3 their cumulative vocabulary will be 136 words, reflecting the addition of only 40 new words (10% of the 405 remaining), and in month 4 it will be 172 words (36 new ones). In other words, new words will be acquired at a faster clip early in development than later, even with a constant learning rate and a constant number of words in the environment. If there is indeed a relatively limited set of regular verbs for the child to acquire during the preschool years, this is one reason why the vocabulary balance hypothesis could be false.

However, these sampling considerations could also mean that the decelerating growth curve is an artifact. Imagine that the child possesses a constant 500 words throughout development, but manages to produce only 50 during a month's worth of samples. Following the same arithmetic as described above, the fact that cumulative vocabulary is a form of sampling without replacement means that we as investigators will spuriously credit the child with having "acquired" fewer and fewer new words with each succeeding month. It is very difficult to tell to what extent the curves in Figures 21–25 represent a genuine sampling effect in vocabulary learning, a sampling artifact in measuring vocabulary from production data, or both. Thus, it is important to supplement these direct estimates with some indirect measure that is free of this possible bias.

B. Method 2: Jackknife Estimates Using ''Mark-Recapture'' Patterns

There is a family of techniques commonly used in biology and demography for estimating population sizes from multiple samples. The simplest version is commonly known as "mark-recapture" (see Seber, 1986). Here is an idealized example of how one might estimate the number of squirrels in a forest. Trap 50 squirrels, paint their tails orange, release them, allow enough time for them to diffuse through the forest, trap 50 squirrels again, and see how many have orange tails. If there are 10 such recaptures, then the first trapping session must have represented 10/50 or one-fifth of the total population. Since 50 were trapped initially, the forest population must be 250.

This logic can be applied to vocabulary estimation as follows. A verb is a squirrel, a transcript is a trapping session, and a verb that appears in two successive transcripts has been recaptured. The proportion of verbs at t_2 that also appeared at t_1, multiplied by the number of verb types recorded at t_1, is an estimate of the vocabulary size. Note that this procedure avoids the possibly artifactual deceleration in vocabulary acquisition inherent in cumulative measures. If a child had a static vocabulary of 500 words, 50 of which were recorded in each sample, then the second sample would consist of five of the words that appeared in the first sample (1/10 × 50) and 45 new words (1/10 × 450), and the recapture rate of 1/10 (5/50), multiplied by the first sample size (50), would yield the correct figure of 500. This would be true of every pair of successive samples. Note as well that, if new verbs are acquired between t_1 and t_2, the estimate will be an unbiased estimate of the vocabulary at t_2. Imagine an idealized case in which 100 baby squirrels were born between capture and recapture. Orange-tailed squirrels

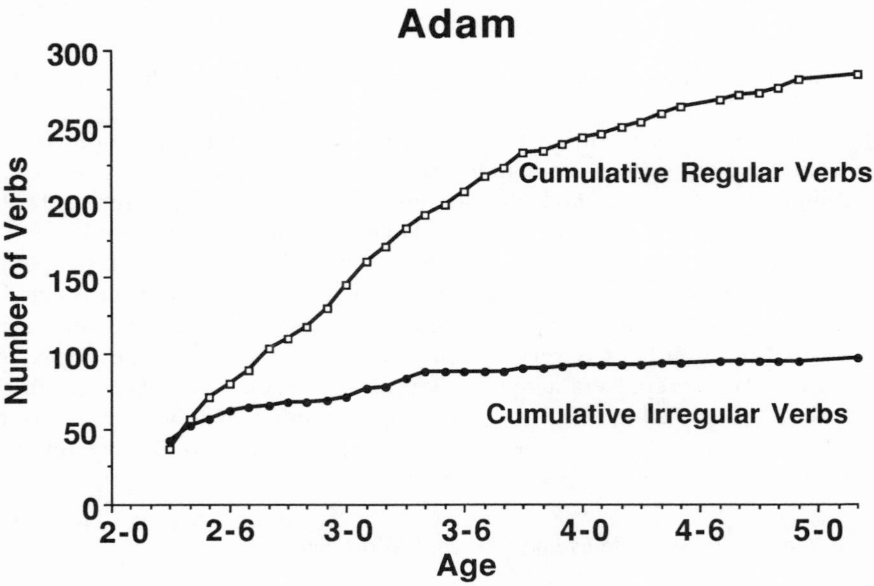

FIG. 21.—Adam's cumulative regular and irregular verb vocabulary

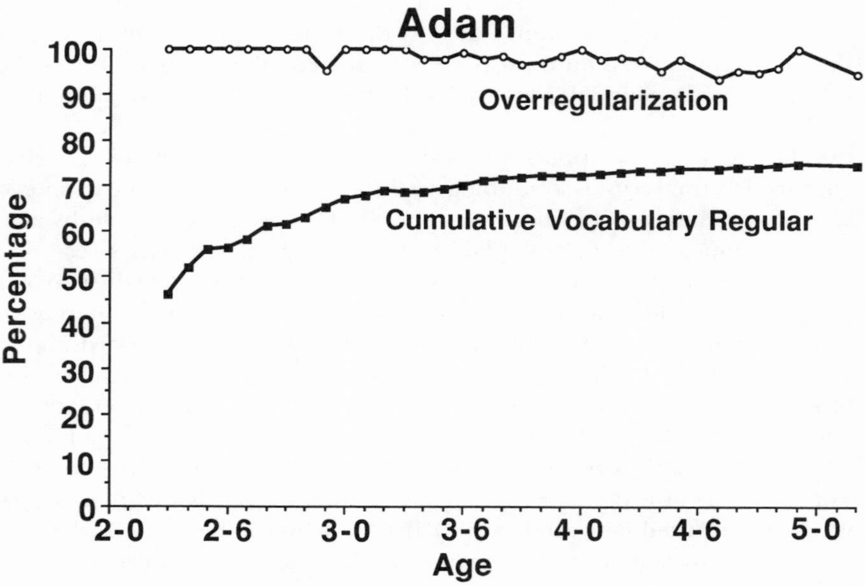

FIG. 22.—Proportion of Adam's cumulative verb vocabulary that is regular and his overregularization rate (subtracted from 100%).

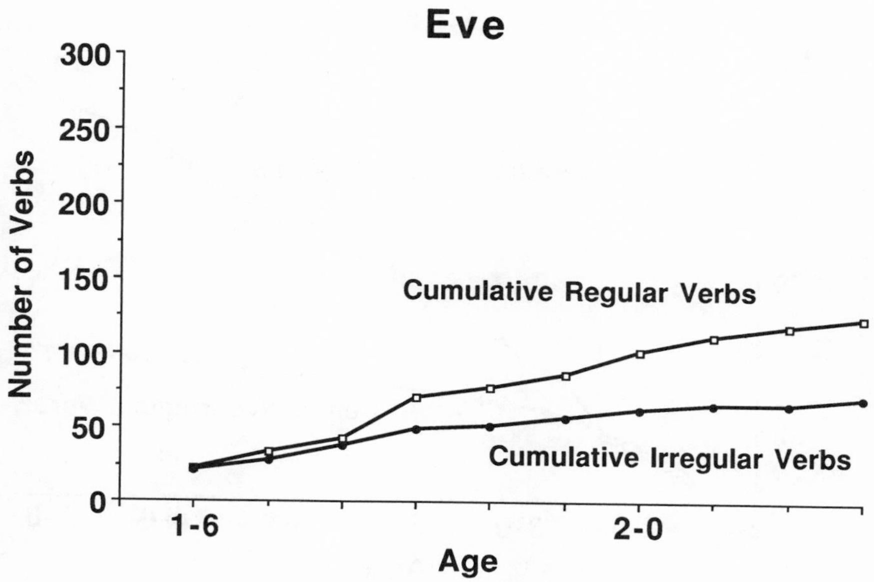

FIG. 23.—Eve's cumulative regular and irregular verb vocabulary

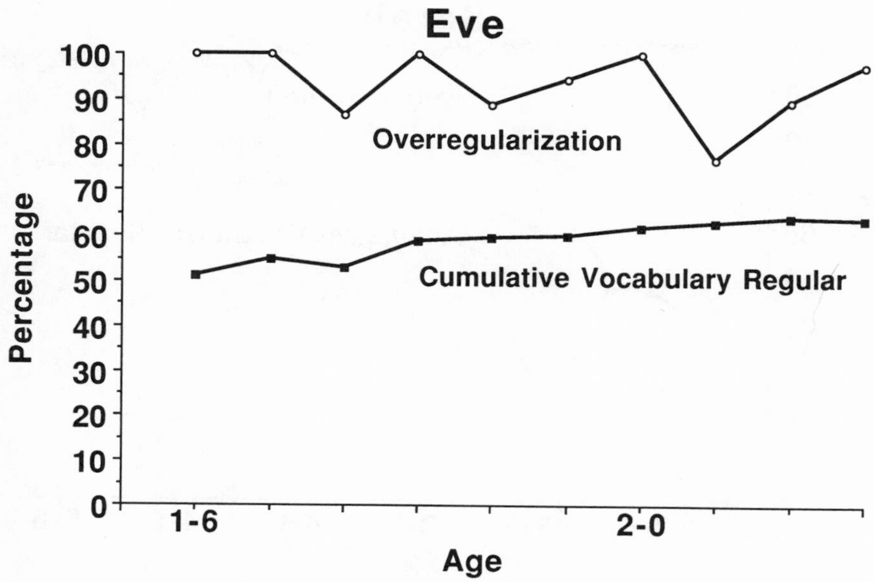

FIG. 24.—Proportion of Eve's cumulative verb vocabulary that is regular and her overregularization rate (subtracted from 100%).

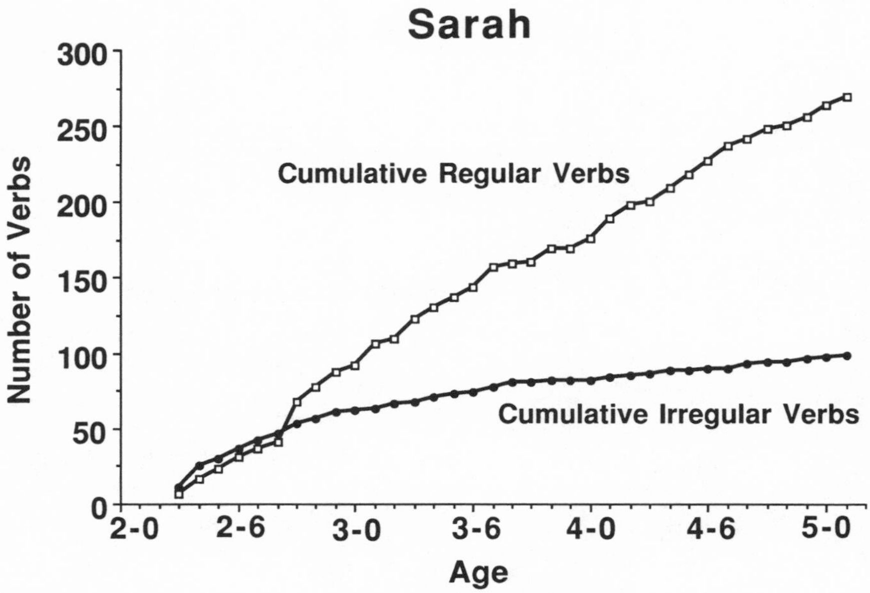

FIG. 25.—Sarah's cumulative regular and irregular verb vocabulary

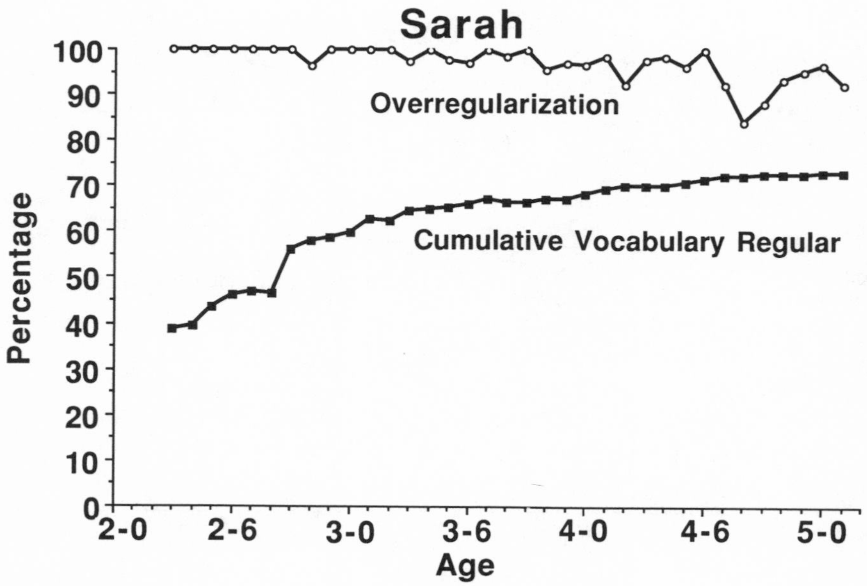

FIG. 26.—Proportion of Sarah's cumulative verb vocabulary that is regular and her overregularization rate (subtracted from 100%).

TABLE 5

Growth of Cumulative Regular and Irregular Vocabulary

	Adam	Eve	Sarah
Average monthly rate of increase before first overregularization:			
Number of regular verbs	11.6	12.0	10.2
Proportion of verbs regular	2.4	3.6	2.9
Level at month before first overregularization:			
Number of regular verbs	117	34	68
Number of irregular verbs	68	28	53
Total	185	62	121
Percentage regular	63	55	56
Average monthly rate of increase during overregularization:			
Number of regular verbs	6.6	11.3	7.2
Proportion of verbs regular	.5	1.1	.6
Level at end of transcripts:			
Number of regular verbs	283	124	269
Number of irregular verbs	99	70	99
Total	382	194	368
Percentage regular	74	64	73

are now recaptured with probability 50/350, so the recapture proportion is 1/7. Seven times the capture sample size of 50 is 350, the true population size at recapture.

Unfortunately, unequal token frequencies for different verbs lead to systematic underestimates if one were to use this procedure unmodified. Imagine that some squirrels are more trap shy than others—in a simple case, 40% of the squirrels might be "shy," where "shyness" means that the probability of blundering into a trap (1/5, in our example) is cut in half. One expects the first sample to capture 30 of the 150 bold squirrels but only 10 of the 100 shy squirrels. Sixteen percent (40/250) of the squirrels in the forest now have orange tails, but the second trapping session will recapture only seven of them: six bold ones (1/5 × 30) and one shy one (1/10 × 10). Since the second sample consists of 40 squirrels in all ([1/5 × 150] + [1/10 × 100]), the 7/40 recapture rate, multiplied by the 40 squirrels in the first sample, yields an estimate of 229, 21 less than the true figure. For children's vocabulary, verbs with lower token frequencies are "trap shy," and because many of them are regular, one would obtain systematic underestimates of total verb vocabulary, regular verb vocabulary, the percentage of vocabulary that is regular, and the rate of increase in regular vocabulary (although comparisons of higher- versus lower-growth months might still be roughly accurate).

Biostatisticians have dealt with the trap-shyness problem by applying the "generalized Jackknife" estimator to the mark-recapture methodology, first developed by Burnham and Overton (1978, 1979) and extensively investigated by Otis, Burnham, White, and Anderson (1978). Instead of two trapping sessions, there are *k* of them. The numbers of squirrels that have been captured only once, twice, three times, and so on are tallied. The effects of unequal capturability can thus be estimated by taking into account the distribution of multiple recaptures. While the simple capture-recapture estimate assumes a uniform distribution of capturability, with the extra information of number of recaptures one can assume that individual capture probability is a random variable from an arbitrary distribution. Otis et al. (1978) found empirically that the Jackknife estimator produces accurate estimates if many individuals are caught a relatively large number of times—that is, if the multiple recapture rate across samples is high.

In our case, this procedure consists of comparing sets of five consecutive transcripts and counting how many verbs were used in each of the five transcripts, how many in only four, and so on. (To make the estimates for the three children comparable, for Sarah we use five consecutive *pairs* of transcripts because her speech was sampled for 1 hour once a week, whereas Adam's and Eve's was sampled for 2 hours once every 2 weeks.) As required, many verbs did appear in multiple transcripts from such sets. This set of numbers is fed into the Jackknife algorithm, providing an estimate of vocabulary size for that period. With nonoverlapping sets of five consecutive transcripts, we obtain independent estimates for different ages. The deceleration in cumulative estimates is eliminated, as is the underestimation inherent in simple mark-recapture estimates.

The estimates span periods of 2½ months rather than a single month, which has both disadvantages and advantages. The growth estimates are temporally coarser, and there is no vocabulary estimate at all for Eve that corresponds exclusively to the period before her first overregularization. However, a larger temporal window may catch effects of vocabulary growth that act over longer time spans than the 1-month window used so far.

The estimator is not free of complications. Because the kind of context in which the recording takes place is similar in all recording sessions, those verbs most appropriate to those contexts will be recorded more often. (In the ecology literature, it has also been noted that achieving equal capturability is impossible, even with randomized capture locations on each sampling occasion; see Chao, 1987.) Furthermore there is a free parameter that must be decided on in calculating the estimates: the "order" of the estimate, corresponding to the maximum number of recaptures (out of five, in our case) that are counted in the calculations. Higher-order estimates have lower bias but higher variance; there is a complex procedure for selecting the optimal order for a given estimate. For simplicity's sake, we will uniformly report estimates of order 4. We have found these generally to be the highest of the estimates of different order, especially for regular verbs; hence, they are fairest to the vocabulary balance hypothesis. But in any case we also found that the growth curves for different order estimates are almost perfectly parallel, so the correlations we calculate are not notably affected by this choice. With these considerations in mind we can cautiously compare periods of high regular vocabulary growth with periods of low regular vocabulary growth, even if the magnitudes of particular increases and totals are not to be taken as perfectly accurate estimates.

Figures 27–32 show that the vocabulary estimates obtained from this method are higher for young children and somewhat lower for older children than the cumulative estimates, eliminating the severe deceleration that was inherently unfavorable to the regular vocabulary balance hypothesis. They also do not display the unlikely constant 50/50 regular-irregular ratio that would correspond to interpreting Pinker and Prince's figures as estimates of types.

Overregularization rates are included in the graphs for ease of comparison of their developmental courses. Table 6 shows the rate of growth of estimated vocabulary per interval during the period preceding the first overregularization and the period beginning with it; numbers and proportions of regular verbs at the end of these two intervals are shown as well. The number of irregular types shows a very small increase with time; the number of regulars shows a larger one. As Table 6 shows, for Adam, the rate of increase in the proportion of verbs that are regular is larger during the overregularization stage than before it (1.1 and −0.2 percentage points, respectively, per five-sample interval). This, however, is the only comparison from among all those we have performed that is in a direction consistent with the vocabulary balance hypothesis. For Adam, the rate of increase in the proportion of verbs that are regular from one interval to the next shows no correlation with the overregularization rate at the end of the interval (r = .004); there was virtually no difference in the number of regular verbs acquired per interval during the overregularization stage versus before it (9.7 and 9.1 new regular verbs per interval, respectively); and the sample correlation coefficient for the relation between the size of the increase between intervals and the overregularization rate for the second interval is negative (r = −.08). Sarah acquired regular verbs at a faster rate before her overregularization period than during it (42.2 and 10.2 additional verbs per interval, respectively), and these increases correlated negatively with their ensuing overregularization rates (r = −.26). Similarly, the proportion of her vocabulary that was regular increased much more rapidly before than during her overregularization stage (8.3 and 0.4 percentage points per

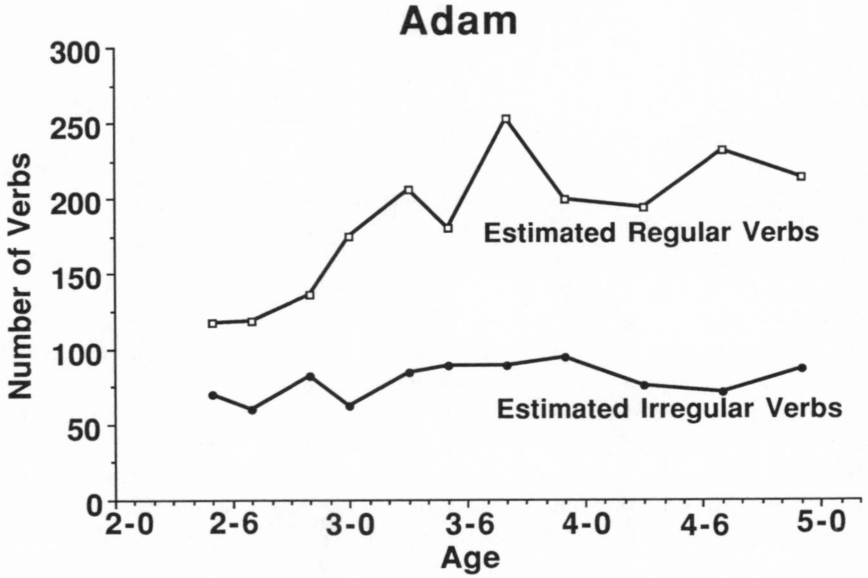

FIG. 27.—Adam's Jackknife-estimated regular and irregular verb vocabulary

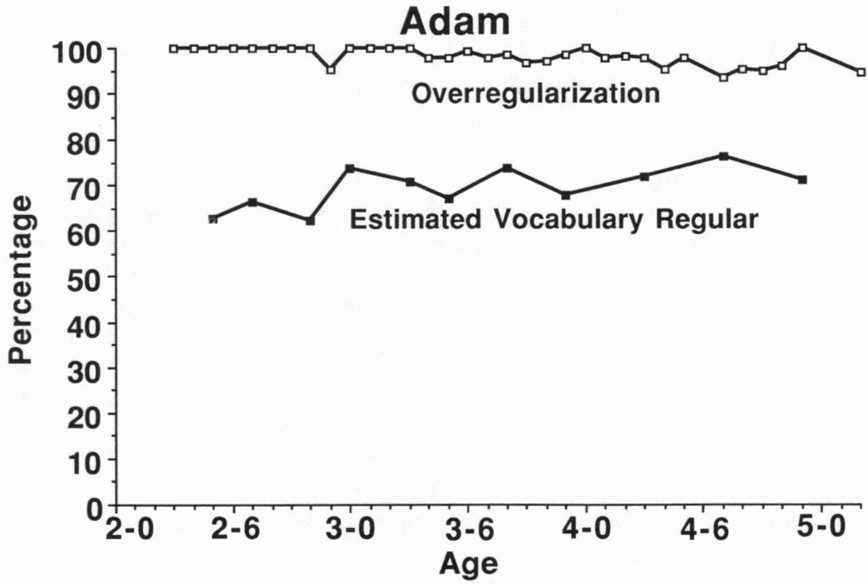

FIG. 28.—Proportion of Adam's Jackknife-estimated verb vocabulary that is regular and his overregularization rate (subtracted from 100%).

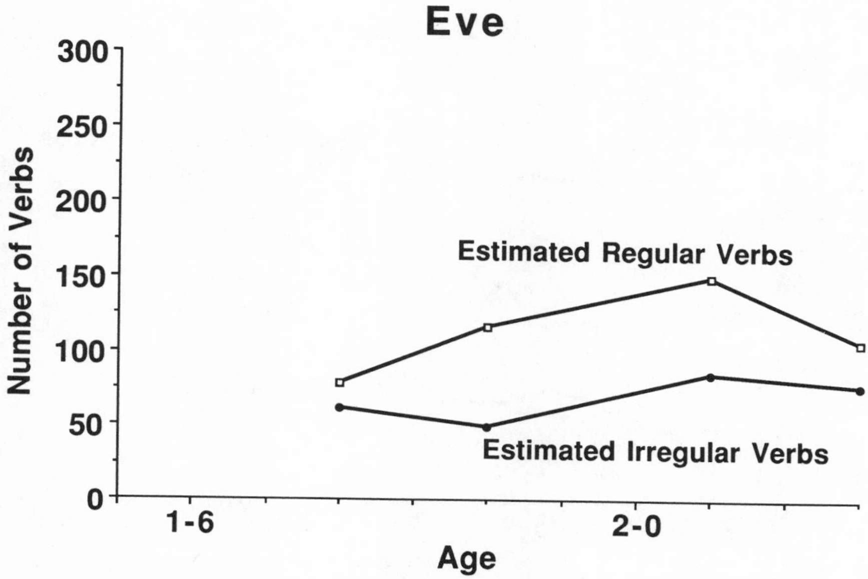

FIG. 29.—Eve's Jackknife-estimated regular and irregular verb vocabulary

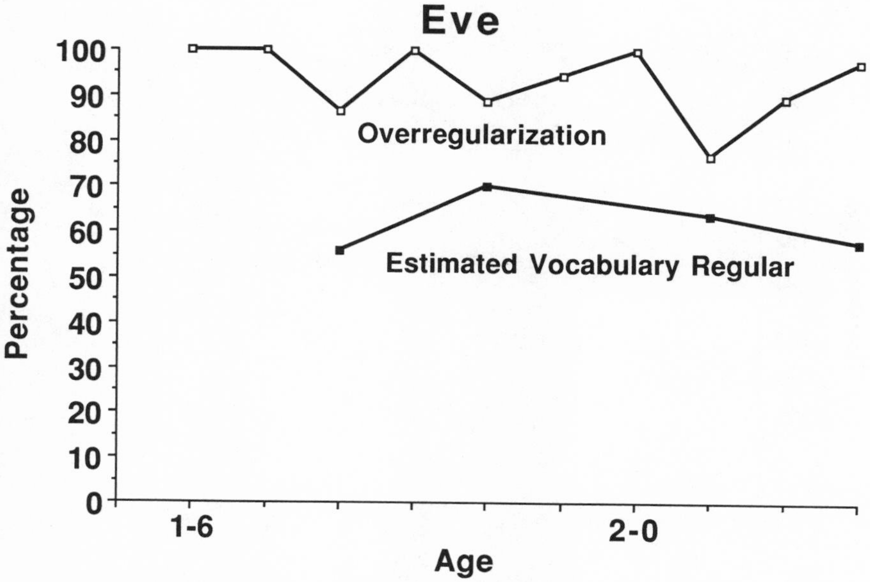

FIG. 30.—Proportion of Eve's Jackknife-estimated verb vocabulary that is regular and her overregularization rate (subtracted from 100%).

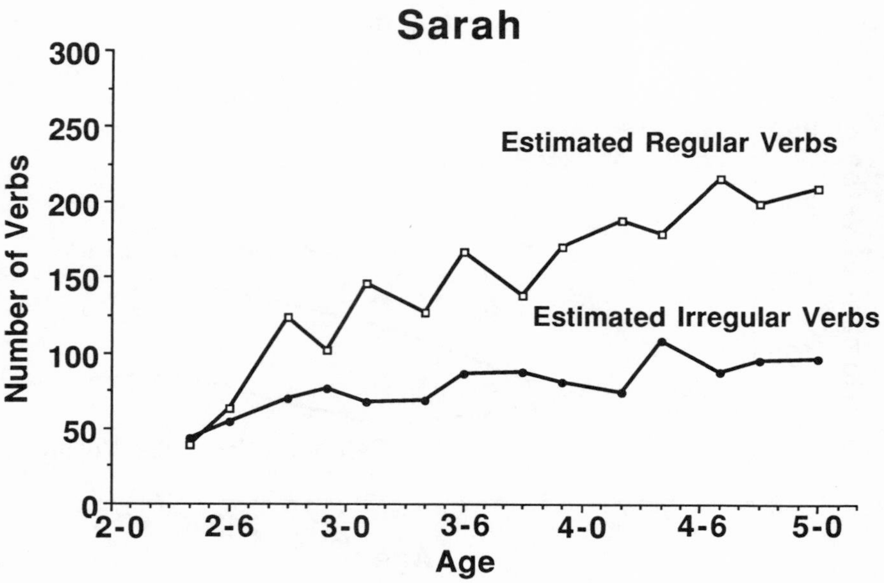

FIG. 31.—Sarah's Jackknife-estimated regular and irregular verb vocabulary

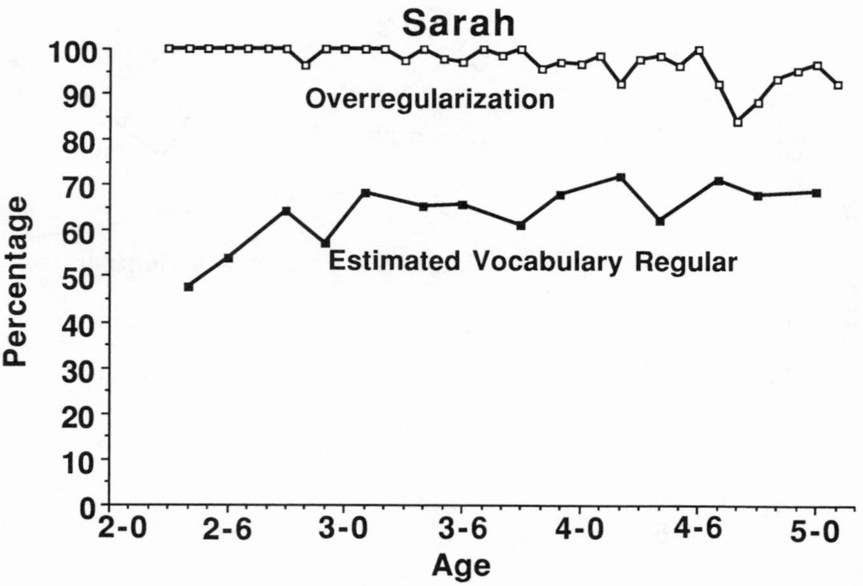

FIG. 32.—Proportion of Sarah's Jackknife-estimated verb vocabulary that is regular and her overregularization rate (subtracted from 100%).

TABLE 6

Growth of Regular and Irregular Vocabulary, Jackknife Estimates

	Adam	Eve	Sarah
Average rate of increase before first overregularization:			
Number of regular verbs	9.1	[a]	42.2
Proportion of verbs regular	−.2	[a]	8.3
Level at month before first overregularization:			
Number of regular verbs	136	[a]	124
Number of irregular verbs	82	[a]	69
Total	218	[a]	193
Percentage regular	62	[a]	64
Average rate of increase during overregularization:			
Number of regular verbs	9.7	9.5	7.8
Proportion regular	1.1	.6	.4
Level at end of transcripts:			
Number of regular verbs	213	106	209
Number of irregular verbs	87	78	96
Total	300	184	305
Percentage regular	71	58	69

[a] Eve had too few samples before her first overregularization to yield Jackknife estimates.

interval, respectively) and correlated negatively (−.17) with overregularization rate. For Eve, the temporal coarseness of the Jackknife estimates prevents a before-and-after comparison, but both the increase in number of regular verbs and the increase in proportion of verb vocabulary that is regular correlate negatively with overregularization rate at the end of the relevant interval.

C. *Comparison to Previous Estimates of Vocabulary Size and Composition*

With all the hazards of vocabulary estimates it would be reassuring to compare ours with previous estimates in the literature that report type and token counts from much larger samples of children's speech.

E. Horn (1925) examined the vocabularies of 80 children from 1 to 6, plus 270,000 tokens from kindergartners and first graders. The combined lists yielded 5,000 words, from which he selected 1,084 that recurred a certain minimum number of times across samples. Of these, 233 are unambiguously verbs, 81 irregular and 152 regular, or 65% of types regular. M. D. Horn (1927) amassed 489,555 tokens of the speech of kindergarten children, a set composed of 7,097 types. She reports the 1,003 most frequently used words. The list contains 97 regular verbs and 74 irregular verbs, or 57% of types regular. These figures are somewhat smaller than the cumulative and Jackknife proportions that we find for Adam and Sarah at the end of their transcripts (which range from 69% to 74% regular), but that is to be expected because both Horns excluded lower-frequency words, which in turn systematically underestimates the number of regular verbs. (When we look at single samples of Adam's and Sarah's speech near the end of their transcripts, which introduces a similar bias, we ourselves get lower figures, near 58%.) However, M. D. Horn provided data for the proportion of verb *tokens* that are regular, which should be unaffected by this sampling bias. The token figures are similar to our estimates: 24,581 regular tokens and 80,370 irregular tokens, or 23% regular.

Even better estimates come from Moe et al.'s (1982) figures for first-grade children (mean age 6-9) because they report all verb tokens, not just the most frequent ones. Their lists include 418 regular verb types and 108 irregular types, corresponding to 79% of verb types being regular and 33% of verb tokens. These figures can be compared with the estimates shown in Tables 5 and 6 for Adam and Sarah at the end of their transcripts: Adam (5-2), 74% cumulative types regular, 71% Jackknife-estimated types regular, 33% tokens regular; Sarah (5-1), 73% cumulative types regular, 69% Jackknife-estimated types regular, 20% tokens regular.

D. Comparison to the Analyses of Marchman and Bates

Before we summarize the conclusions of this chapter, we briefly examine contrary claims made in a recent paper by Marchman and Bates (1991). They analyze data on children's vocabulary size and overregularizations, concluding, "Verb vocabulary size is highly predictive of . . . the onset of overregularization errors" (p. 7). In particular, they interpret their data as support for a "critical mass hypothesis" according to which the "vocabulary size is related to . . . the subsequent onset of overregularization errors when verb vocabularies become sufficiently large" (p. 6). They take this as evidence supporting the connectionist models of Plunkett and Marchman (1990, 1991), which also, they suggest, show critical mass effects. In this section, we attempt to resolve the discrepancy between these conclusions and ours.

Marchman and Bates used different methods of vocabulary estimates from ours, different measures of overregularization, and different predictions about the relevant correlations. We examine each in turn before discussing their actual findings.

Method of estimation of vocabulary size and overregularizations.—The vocabulary estimation technique employed a checklist given to 1,130 mothers of children between the ages of 1-4 and 2-6. Each mother filled out the checklist once, so there are no longitudinal data. One section of the checklist contained 680 word stems, including 46 irregular verb stems and 57 regular verb stems. The other consisted of 21 irregular past tense forms and 30 overregularized versions of these verbs (stem overregularizations of all verbs, plus past overregularizations of some of them).[23]

As Marchman and Bates point out, it is desirable to use a variety of methods of vocabulary acquisition, given the limitations inherent to any single technique such as the ones we have noted and dealt with in this chapter. The main advantage they see for parental checklists is that they provide "more accurate estimates of vocabulary size" (1991, p. 3), presumably owing to the potentially larger corpus of speech drawn from (namely, however much of a child's speech a parent can remember). Unfortunately, this putative advantage is vitiated by the fact that Marchman and Bates provided only a small subset of English irregular verbs on their list. For example, Adam at 2-6 and Eve at 2-3 had already produced within their transcripts (a small subset of their total speech) more regular verbs, and more irregular verbs, than Marchman and Bates included on their checklists (see Figs. 21 and 23), and this was true for Sarah by the time of her first overregularization (see Fig. 25). Thus, the verbs that Marchman and Bates's parents had the opportunity to check off constitute a subset of the verbs that we know (from our transcript data) that children of the relevant ages use. Therefore, Marchman and Bates's vocabulary figures, contrary to their claims, are not more accurate than our transcript counts; we know that they must suffer from a greater degree of underestimation.

A more fundamental objection, however, is that the checklist data pertain exclusively to types—Marchman and Bates estimate how many verb types were overregularized at least once but have no data on the overregularization rate either within or across verbs. As we shall see when we return to their empirical claims, this is a crucial limitation, confounding their main conclusion.

The logic of the prediction.—Marchman and Bates, citing the simulations of Plunkett and Marchman (1990, 1991), predict that overregularization should be triggered by the attainment of some absolute size of verb vocabulary. As a result, they tested the correlation between vocabulary size and the number of verbs overregularized. This contrasts with our tests, which test for correlations between the recent *change* in vocabulary size (i.e., the rate of acquisition of new vocabulary) and overregularization.

Examination of the Plunkett and Marchman papers, however, raises

[23] These figures correspond to the number of verbs actually listed in their appendix; their text mentions 20 irregular past tense forms and 31 overregularized forms.

questions about the basis for Marchman and Bates's prediction. First, Plunkett and Marchman repeatedly conclude that the *rate* of vocabulary expansion (the factor that we, but not Marchman and Bates, correlated with overregularizations) is a critical variable in their models' tendency to overregularize (e.g., Plunkett & Marchman, 1990, pp. 12–13, 18). Indeed, they note that their model can attain 100% correct performance on any *absolute* level of vocabulary size (p. 11). Second, when Plunkett and Marchman do discuss a putative effect of a critical mass in vocabulary, the effect in question is "recovery from erroneous performance" (p. 11), exactly the opposite of the *decrement* for irregular verbs that Marchman and Bates are trying to explain. (Later, they discuss generalization to new stems, but this is still different from overregularization of previously learned ones.) Third, Plunkett and Marchman's claim for a critical mass effect in their model (i.e., recovery after vocabulary size reaches 50, constant across different rates of vocabulary increase) bears no obvious relation to the simulation data they present. They cite no numbers, instead inviting the reader to inspect their figures 1 and 2, but neither figure shows any discontinuity in performance for irregular verbs at the point corresponding to the 50th verb acquired. Moreover, their figure 1 shows clear differences in the recovery profile depending on the rate of vocabulary increase.

The empirical claims.—Marchman and Bates report two relevant empirical findings. The first is that overregularizations are rarely reported for children with reported verb vocabularies less than 15–30 words. They take this as evidence for a critical mass effect, but the reasoning is unsound. If children's vocabulary increases with age and they begin to overregularize at a certain point after vocabulary acquisition begins, by logical necessity any finite data set will yield numbers corresponding to the average and minimum sizes of their vocabulary at the time they begin overregularizing. In particular, the minimum will simply correspond to the vocabulary size of the most precocious overregularizer in the sample. This does not constitute evidence for a critical mass effect, that is, that across variation in other factors such as rate and composition of vocabulary, a given child will begin to overregularize when he or she attains a specific vocabulary size.

The second finding is that vocabulary size correlates well with overregularizations, holding linear effects of chronological age constant in a multiple regression. But this finding, too, is close to being a statistical necessity, not an empirical discovery. Recall that Marchman and Bates's data on overregularization consist of the number of irregular types that are overregularized at least once; they have no data on the overregularization *rate* (the probability that the child will use an overregularization as compared to the correct irregular past). Clearly, a child cannot overregularize a verb that is not in his or her vocabulary. If the child has a vocabulary of five irregular verbs, he or she cannot be recorded as having overregularized six verbs. If the child has a vocabulary of 50 irregular verbs, he or she can, in principle, overregularize 50 verbs but no more, and so on. Thus, even if children overregularize at the same rate regardless of vocabulary size, the number of overregularized types recorded will almost certainly be larger for children with larger vocabulary sizes simply because larger vocabularies yield more logical opportunities to overregularize types. Thus, Marchman and Bates's correlation is an artifact that provides no support for the claim that larger vocabularies predict a greater *likelihood* of overregularizing.

In sum, while there may be promise in the use of parental checklists as a corroborating method of estimating vocabulary size, they have no a priori advantages over direct counts from spontaneous speech transcripts, and as Marchman and Bates have deployed them, they have a number of disadvantages. Moreover, Marchman and Bates's conclusion—that children, like connectionist models, overregularize because they attain a critical vocabulary size—must be rejected. First, connectionist models have not been shown to overregularize because they attain a critical vocabulary size; rather, their overregularization is mainly caused by high rates of input of regular verbs, which is the motivation for our own analyses discussed in this chapter. Second, children have not been shown to overregularize because they attain a critical vocabulary size; the correlations that Marchman and Bates report are artifacts.

VIII. SUMMARY

Our estimates of children's types, adults' types, and children's tokens provide virtually no support for the hypothesis that overregularization is triggered by increases in the number or proportion of regular verbs available to the child. Regular verbs remain a roughly constant proportion of adults' and children's conversational tokens, and never dominate. Regular types—which in any case do not correspond to on-line learning episodes—necessarily increase with development, both absolutely and as a proportion of total verb vocabulary, but the sizes of these increases do not correlate positively with children's tendency to overregularize, which is what the vocabulary balance hypothesis requires. It appears that something endogenous to children's grammatical systems, and not a change in either their environments or their vocabularies, causes overregularization errors to begin.

VI. THE RELATION OF OVERREGULARIZATION TO THE DEVELOPMENT OF TENSE MARKING OF REGULAR AND IRREGULAR VERBS

If vocabulary development does not predict the onset of overregularization, does anything? Pinker and Prince (1988) suggested that children's lag in overregularizing might be due to the development of the regular tense-marking process itself. If, consistent with traditional assumptions and contrary to the assumptions behind the Rumelhart-McClelland model, children have an ability to memorize stems and pasts independently of the ability to generate the past from the stem, and if the specifics of English tense marking take time to learn, then before they are learned correct irregular pasts could be produced. Overregularizations would be absent because the child's regular past tense–marking machine is "off," not because it is "on" but starved of regular inputs.

There is nothing in this hypothesis that is incompatible with the Rumelhart-McClelland model being an accurate model of the child's past tense–marking machine. One would, of course, have to give up the idea that there is no rote storage outside the past tense–marking machine and that U-shaped development can be explained entirely by the internal workings of the machine as it processes a changing input mixture. The sequence would be explained by a transition from a stage where only the rote lexicon was working to a stage at which a connectionist model began to process stems and pasts as inputs. MacWhinney and Leinbach (1991) endorse (but do not implement) such a two-module system in their connectionist model of past tense inflection. Indeed, Rumelhart and McClelland themselves briefly entertained such a possibility, and there are numerous suggestions in the connectionist literature for how to implement the equivalent of gates or on-off switches for multimodule network models (see, e.g., Jacobs, Jordan, & Barto, 1991). Thus, the analyses we discuss in this chapter do not speak to how past tense marking is computed (i.e., whether it is computed by traditional symbol processing or by parallel distributed processing), as long as it can be computed independently of rote storage of lexical items.

To see if overregularization begins only when the productive regular process is first activated, we need the results of *wug* tests administered to children at various points before and after they overregularize. Obviously, these data do not exist, and it is not practical to hope for them. One- and 2-year-old children make poor experimental subjects in elicited language production tasks, especially with made-up words introduced on the spot. Fortunately, there are data from spontaneous speech that indirectly bear on the hypothesis.

In principle, a ruleless child with excellent rote memory could produce regular and irregular pasts with equal facility, as long as they were available in the input to be memorized. In practice, however, the young child produces correct irregular past tense forms more reliably in obligatory past tense contexts than regular past tense forms (Brown, 1973; de Villiers & de Villiers, 1973; see also n. 19 above). Presumably, irregulars are easier to memorize and produce because of their higher token frequency, their phonological simplicity (all irregulars have monosyllabic roots, but many regulars do not; Pinker & Prince, 1988), their greater phonological salience (vowel changes might be more perceptible than a word-final *t* or *d*, especially as part of a consonant cluster), or some combination of these factors. However, once the regular process is acquired, the irregular advantage should be nullified: any verb, whether its past tense form is remembered or not, can be supplied with a regular past tense form at that very moment. Therefore, the initiation of the regular process should be visible in spontaneous speech in a reduction or elimination of the difference between the ability to supply the past tense forms of regular and irregular verbs in obligatory past tense contexts. One can then see whether this equalization occurs near the onset of overregularization.

A related signature of the acquisition of a productive regular process can be sought in the absolute rate of marking tense on regular verbs. In English syntax, all main clauses must be marked for tense. Thus, we can think of syntactic processes as issuing a subroutine call to morphology, demanding a tensed form of the particular verb to be used. English, of course, executes this subroutine in different ways: the various irregular forms and the regular process. The beauty of the regular process is that it can always keep the syntax satisfied: any verb, familiar or unfamiliar, can be suffixed to mark tense and hence can be used in a main clause (except possibly in the unusual circumstances discussed in Chap. II, Sec. I*B*). However, for a child who has not yet acquired the regular suffixation process, if the regular past form of a verb had not been previously memorized, the desire to mark tense on it would have to go unsatisfied. Mastery of the regular process, then, should be visible in attainment of high absolute rates of marking the past tense on regular verbs in obligatory past tense contexts. Again, one can see whether attainment of such levels occurs near the time of the first overregularization, and whether degree of successful regular marking correlates with overregularization across time and children. The prediction depends on the assumption that the syntactic requirement of tense marking has itself been acquired (if children do not know that tense is obligatory, they could leave regular verbs in past tense contexts unmarked even if they knew how to mark them), so if children do not reliably mark the tense of either regular verbs or irregular verbs (which do not depend on a productive process) in obligatory contexts, this prediction cannot be tested. But if regular verbs are reliably marked, we have indirect evidence for a productive regular process; if irregular verbs are reliably marked but regular verbs are not, we have indirect evidence that the regular process has not yet developed. (The acquisition of obligatory marking of irregular verbs will be discussed in a separate section.)

Note that these predictions about levels of irregular and regular marking appear to contrast with those of the Rumelhart-McClelland model under the assumption that the model is responsible for early correct performance with irregulars, with no separate lexical storage. During the early period of learning, before the influx of regular verbs triggers overregularization, the model rapidly attained successful performance with both irregular *and* regular verbs (80%–85% of correct features generated), with, if anything, a slight advantage for the regulars (see their fig. 4, reproduced here as Fig. 16). Furthermore, Rumelhart and McClelland point out that their model is not just doing the equivalent of rote memorization before it overregularizes but is showing "substantial generalization." Newly presented regular verbs are inflected with 75% accuracy (chance is 50%) on their very first exposure, based on the training during the period in which irregulars are being produced correctly.

I. THE DEVELOPMENT OF REGULAR TENSE MARKING AND OVERREGULARIZATION

In this section, we examine whether there is an association between overregularization and the development of the productive regular affixation process. We begin with Adam, Eve, and Sarah, who show initial overregularization-free months in their longitudinal samples, allowing tests of whether the onset of overregularization coincides with development of high levels of marking regular verbs in obligatory past tense contexts (high both in absolute terms and in terms of a rate comparable to the rate of marking the tense of irregular verbs).

A. The Brown Children

We present Cazden's data on rates of supplying correct past tense forms of irregular and regular verbs in obligatory past tense contexts in Figures 33–38 and in Appendix Tables A1–A3.[24]

As Brown (1973) pointed out, curves plotting use of a morpheme in obligatory contexts as a function of age are invariably noisy. In particular, early points often represent a tiny number of instances, because the grammatical structures that allow obligatory contexts to be recognized themselves develop with age, and this can result in severe sampling error. For example, the early spikes where Sarah anomalously marks irregular and regular verbs 100% of the time represent two out of two and three out of three tokens, respectively.

Nonetheless, several general qualitative features of the data are noticeable. First, for all three children, the first month with an overregularization displayed a high level of marking of irregular past tense: 84% for Adam, 93% for Eve, and 70% for Sarah (although the neighboring months are higher for Sarah and much lower for Eve). Second, regular marking is low before the first overregularization but displays rapid increases to high levels, overlapping those seen for irregular verbs, shortly afterward. Adam's first overregularization occurred during a 3-month period in which regular marking increased from 0% to 100%; Eve's occurred during a 7-month period in which she went from 0% to 95%; Sarah's occurred during a 4-month interval in which she went from 0% to 78%. (Moreover, for Adam and Sarah there appears to be a brief decline in regular marking coinciding with a reversion to several months of no overregularizations immediately after the first recorded one, followed by a rise to levels close to 100% around the time when overregularization resumes.)

Table 7 confirms that rates of regular marking are low and smaller than those for irregular marking for the period before the first overregularization, and that the difference is narrowed or eliminated for the period beginning with the first overregularization. The increase in both kinds of marking and the relatively larger increase for regular marking can be captured in a 2 × 2 ANOVA whose factors are regular versus irregular verbs and before versus during overregularization and whose dependent variable

[24] The data are grouped into months to be commensurable with our overregularization data. Sarah's recording sessions were half as long but twice as frequent as those of Adam and Eve; to facilitate comparisons among the three children, Cazden pooled successive pairs of Sarah's samples. Sometimes these pairs straddled a boundary between months of chronological age, the units we have been using. When this happened, we divided the tokens in that pair of samples by two, assigning half to the month preceding the boundary, half to the month following it.

TABLE 7

Proportion of Verb Tokens in Obligatory Past Tense Contexts That Were Marked for Tense before the First Month with an Overregularization and in the Period Beginning with the First Month

	Irregular		Regular	
	Proportion Marked	No. of Obligatory Contexts	Proportion Marked	No. of Obligatory Contexts
Adam, before	.74*	369	.08*	123
Adam, during	.91*	559	.73*	173
Eve, before	.18*	11	.11*	19
Eve, during	.62*	259	.66*	118
Sarah, before	.65*	131	.44	26
Sarah, during	.90*	508	.85*	134

* Proportions significantly different from .5.

is the proportion of verb tokens marked for tense in obligatory contexts. Verbs were marked more reliably after overgeneralization began than before, $F(1,2) = 199.80$, $p < .005$, and, marginally, the increase was larger for regular than for irregular verbs (for the interaction between the factors of regular/irregular and before/during, $F[1,2] = 8.77, p < .10$). The correlation between tense marking and overregularization can also be shown in continuous measures: there are positive correlations over months between the proportion of regular verbs marked in obligatory past tense contexts and the overregularization rate: $r(14) = .33$ for Adam; $r(8) = .48$ for Eve; $r(22) = .44$ for Sarah. Correlations with irregular marking rate are positive, although smaller, for all three children: .29, .42, and .21, respectively.[25]

How might one examine the second prediction of the hypothesis that overregularization is associated with the acquisition of a productive regular past tense–marking process, namely, that children mark regular verbs "obligatorily" during the overregularization period? Of course literally "obligatory" means nothing less than 100% marking, which none of the children attained. Brown (1973) employed the criterion that a morpheme was being marked "obligatorily" if it was supplied in 90% of its obligatory contexts in six successive hours of speech. However, he was interested, not in obligatory marking for any particular morpheme, but in the relative order of acquisition of 14 heterogeneous morphemes; the reason he

[25] Sarah's correlation with regular marking would be statistically significant if one were to treat months as independent sampling units; the other correlation coefficients would not be. Such significance tests, however, are meaningless because monthly transcript sets are not independent samples from a population, as noted earlier.

adopted the 90% over 6 hours criterion was because it could be used to derive an objective rank ordering of the age of acquisition of the morphemes. For our purposes, which do not involve ordering heterogeneous morphemes, the criterion is in some ways too strict (because extended use of a morpheme in, say, 75%–85% of obligatory contexts clearly indicates relevant knowledge) and in others too lax (because a span with a lucky streak of correct usages could be counted as mastery, only to return to lower levels because of regression to the mean). Brown notes that the developmental curves show such patterns in several instances.

One convenient benchmark is whether a child marks tense more often than not in obligatory contexts (i.e., if significantly more than 50% of verb tokens are marked). The 50% figure is, of course, partly arbitrary, but it does literally reflect a systematic preference that tense be marked. Moreover, because children initially mark most morphemes at rates far less than 50% (most notably, the regular past tense), it is unlikely to represent the base rate for the proportion of times a past tense is called for on pragmatic communicative grounds, and attainment of a level of marking greater than 50% represents movement toward the adult state where tense marking is truly obligatory.

In Table 7, marking rates that are significantly greater than .5 by a two-tailed binomial test (computed by the approximation to the normal distribution) are indicated with an asterisk. All three children, before they began to overregularize, left regular verbs unmarked more often than they marked them (Adam and Sarah marked irregular verbs more often than they left them unmarked). After overregularization had begun, all three children marked both irregular verbs and regular verbs more often than they left them unmarked. In sum, for Adam and Sarah, and to a lesser extent Eve, there is evidence that the onset of overregularization is temporally associated with attainment of high rates of marking tense on regular verbs, comparable to rates of tensing irregular verbs.

The data from Adam, Eve, and Sarah help resolve a paradox noted long ago in the developmental literature. Ervin (1964) remarked that for some of her subjects there were no regular past tense forms preceding the first overregularizations. Among the nine children with extended longitudinal transcripts in our sample, we found this to be true for Naomi and April as well: the first regular verbs marked for past tense appeared a few days *after* their first overregularization. The puzzle arises because no specific rule of morphology can be innate. Therefore the child must acquire any particular rule on the basis of individual regularly inflected forms memorized from parental speech. All children, then, should be capable of producing at least some regular past tense forms before their first overregularization. The paradox disappears when we see that Adam, Eve, and Sarah used regular past forms at very low rates before their first overregularization, presumably because memorizing them or retrieving them from memory is difficult (although not impossible) owing to their relatively low frequency and salience. For some children, then, the rates can be as low as zero, or at least low enough that no examples turn up in their transcripts. At some point the child extracts a suffixation process capable of generating regulars freely, apparently from a small amount of evidence if the frequency of producing regular forms reflects the number serving as the basis for the rule, and uses it simultaneously to inflect regular verbs and occasionally to overregularize irregular verbs.

B. The Kuczaj Children

Let us turn to Abe. As mentioned, before-and-after comparisons are not possible for him, because he overregularized in his first sample. However, Kuczaj (1977a) noted that in the period ending at 2-6, Abe's overregularization rate and his rate of marking regular and irregular verbs in obligatory contexts were both lower than they were in subsequent months. Figures 39 and 40, taken from the appendices to Kuczaj (1976) (reproduced in our App. Table A4), show the data in full.[26] High rates of regular marking (often higher than the rate of irregular marking) characterize the entire period, starting at 76%, increasing in 4 months to 98%, and staying close to that level thereafter. Because Abe's data, unlike those from Adam, Eve, and Sarah, include the later phase where overregularization begins to diminish (the right-hand arm of the U), the correlation coefficient between regular marking and overregularization calculated over the entire period is low (.09). The reason is that although overregularization is lower in some of the very early months, when regular marking is also low, overregularization becomes low again in the latest months, when regular marking, of course, remains high. When the late reduction of overregularization is held constant by partialing out age, the correlation between overregularization and regular marking is far higher, .44.

As Kuczaj (1977a) points out, his cross-sectional sample shows a similar distribution to Abe's longitudinal sequence. All 14 children overregularize, and the sample includes the late span when overregularizations decrease: the three oldest children in the sample overregularize the least. All the children marked regular verbs in obligatory contexts at high rates (84%–100%) except one, the child who was youngest and had the lowest MLU,

[26] These percentages were taken directly from Kuczaj (1976) rather than being calculated from the transcripts or raw data tables, so in some cases they are based on slightly different token counts for number of correct irregulars than the ones we have been using (i.e., the data listed in the second column of App. Table A4).

and this child also had the lowest overregularization rate except for the three oldest children. Statistically, the children in the cross-sectional sample behave similarly to Abe's months; although the simple correlation coefficient between overregularization and regular marking is low (−.09), the partial correlation with age held constant is high ($r = .47$, $p < .05$).

Summary of developmental patterns.—Several general relations appear to hold consistently among the children we have examined. Before the first overregularization, regular verbs in obligatory past tense contexts are left unmarked more often than they are marked, and they are marked at lower rates than irregular verbs. In the period beginning with the month of the first overregularization, there is no consistent difference between the rates of marking regular and irregular verbs; both are marked more often than they are left unmarked, often at very high rates. During developmental spans before overregularization begins to diminish, rates of regular marking correlate positively with the rate of overregularization.

The pattern is consistent with the hypothesis that the immediate trigger for overregularization is the acquisition of the process responsible for regular tense marking, which is independent of early use of correct irregular forms. Once productive regular marking has been acquired, children can now inflect the stem productively on any occasion that they try to mark the past tense of an irregular verb but fail to retrieve its past form. They do so for the same reason that they can now inflect regular stems at high rates, despite the initial disadvantage in memorizability that the regulars had faced.

Of course with these correlational data we do not have strong evidence that a common underlying acquisition event *causes* the correlation between overregularization and regular marking, as opposed to both phenomena simply increasing with age for independent reasons. At this point the most that can be said is that we have found consistent relations in the predicted direction between overregularization and the level of regular marking in obligatory contexts, both of them showing their major developmental increases in the same general window, before the later diminishment of overregularization decouples them. The consistent correlations in the predicted direction contrast with the results of tests of the vocabulary balance hypothesis in the preceding chapter, where all the predictor measures of vocabulary either remained constant or correlated in the wrong direction with overregularization.

Note, finally, that although children systematically mark tense by the time they begin to overregularize, the rates vary from child to child. It is possible that some of the individual differences among children in overregularization rates are related to these differences. Recall that Abe and Kuczaj's cross-sectional sample showed unusually high overregularization rates

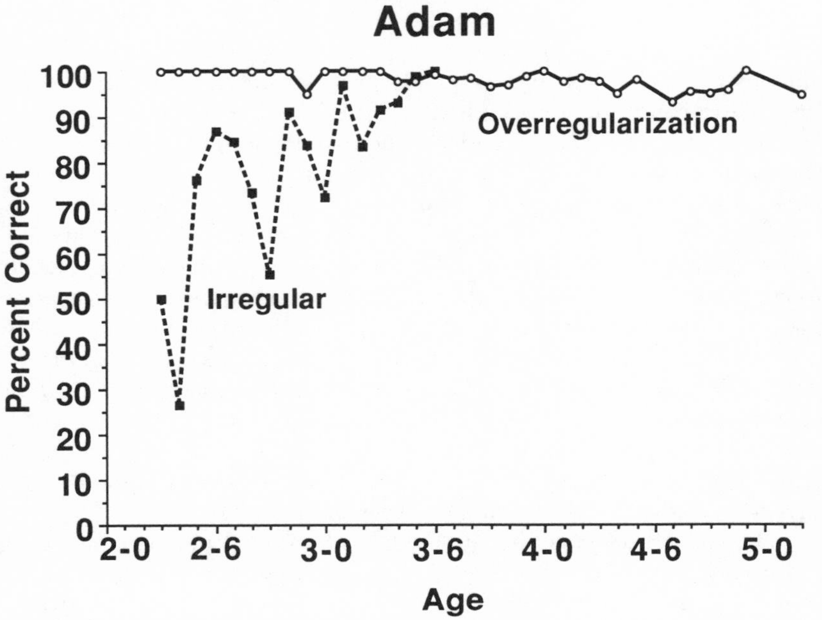

FIG. 33.—Proportion of Adam's irregular verbs in obligatory past tense contexts that were correctly marked for tense. Overregularizations do not enter into these data but are shown in the curve at the top (subtracted from 100%).

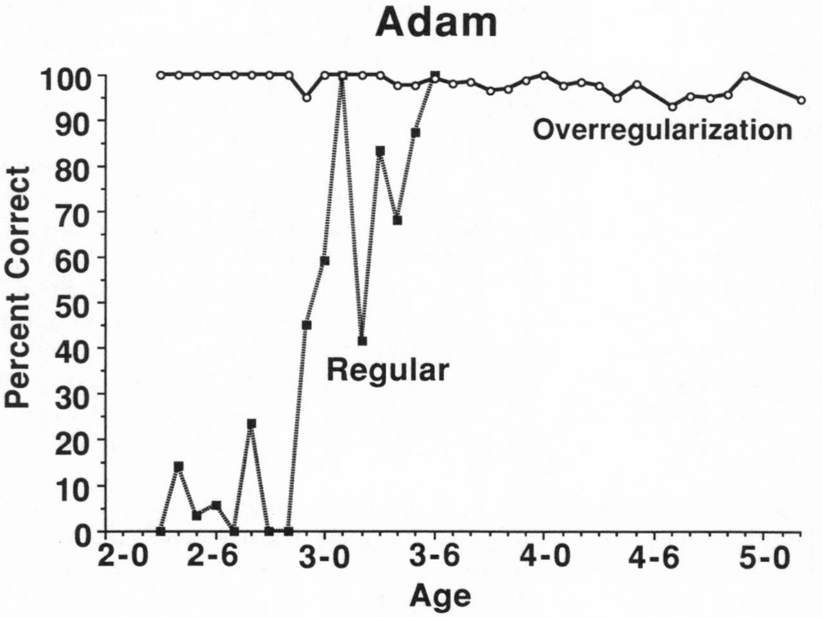

FIG. 34.—Proportion of Adam's regular verbs in obligatory past tense contexts that were correctly marked for tense and his overregularization rate (subtracted from 100%).

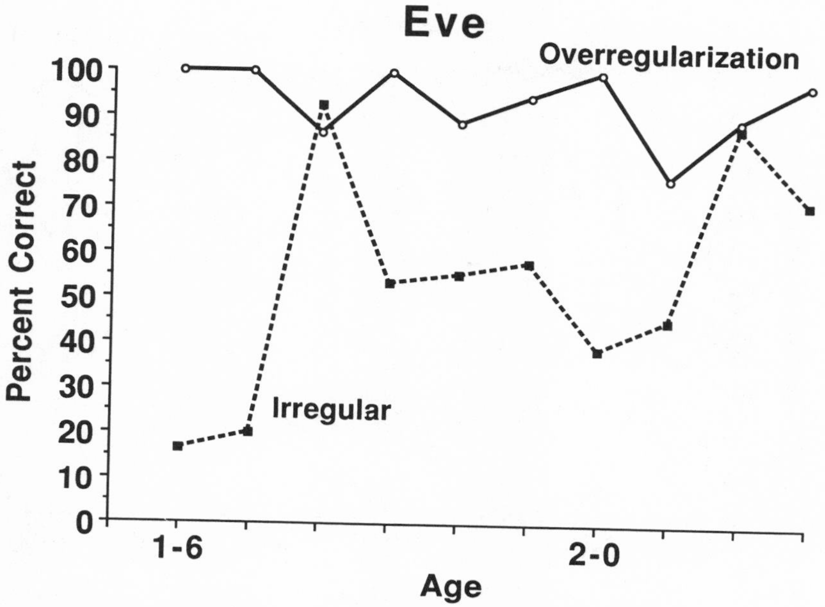

FIG. 35.—Proportion of Eve's irregular verbs in obligatory past tense contexts that were correctly marked for tense. Overregularizations do not enter into these data but are shown in the curve at the top (subtracted from 100%).

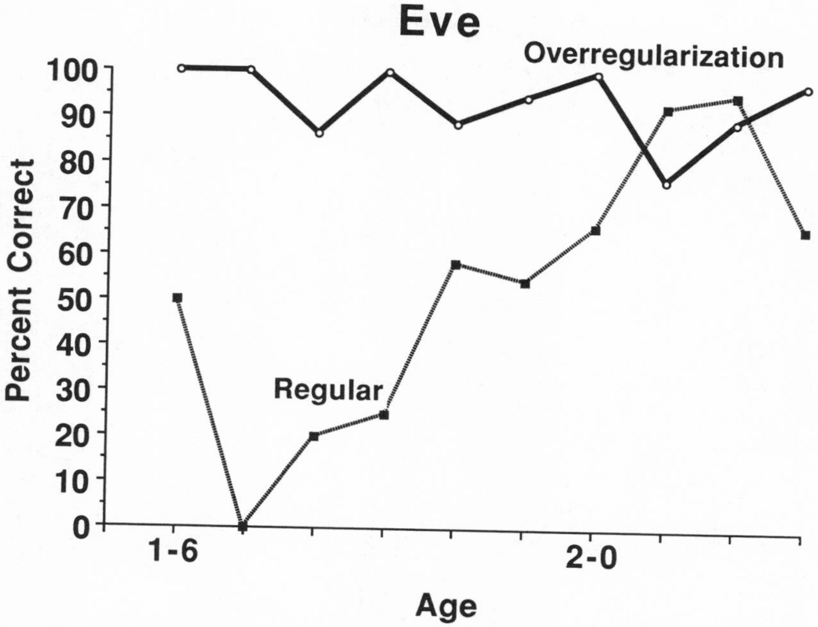

FIG. 36.—Proportion of Eve's regular verbs in obligatory past tense contexts that were correctly marked for tense and her overregularization rate (subtracted from 100%).

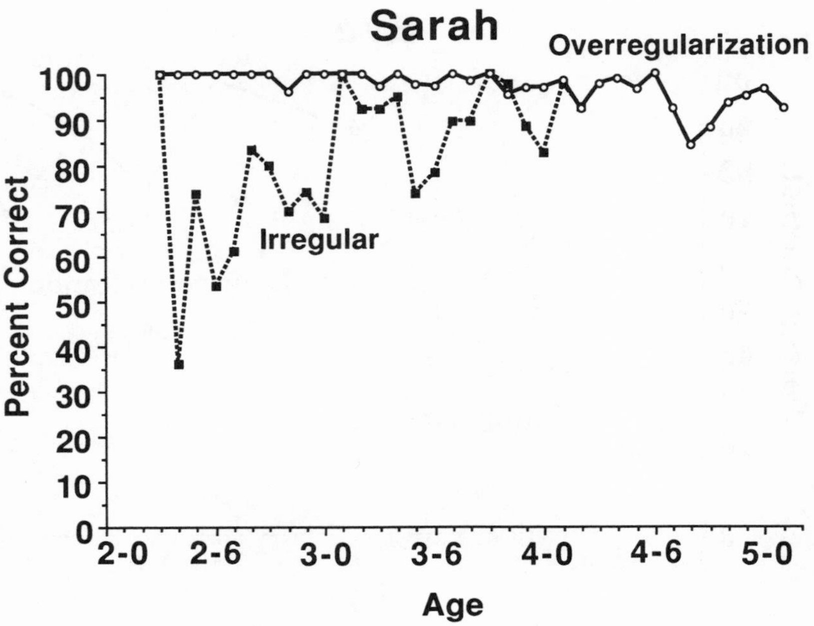

FIG. 37.—Proportion of Sarah's irregular verbs in obligatory past tense contexts that were correctly marked for tense. Overregularizations do not enter into these data but are shown in the curve at the top (subtracted from 100%).

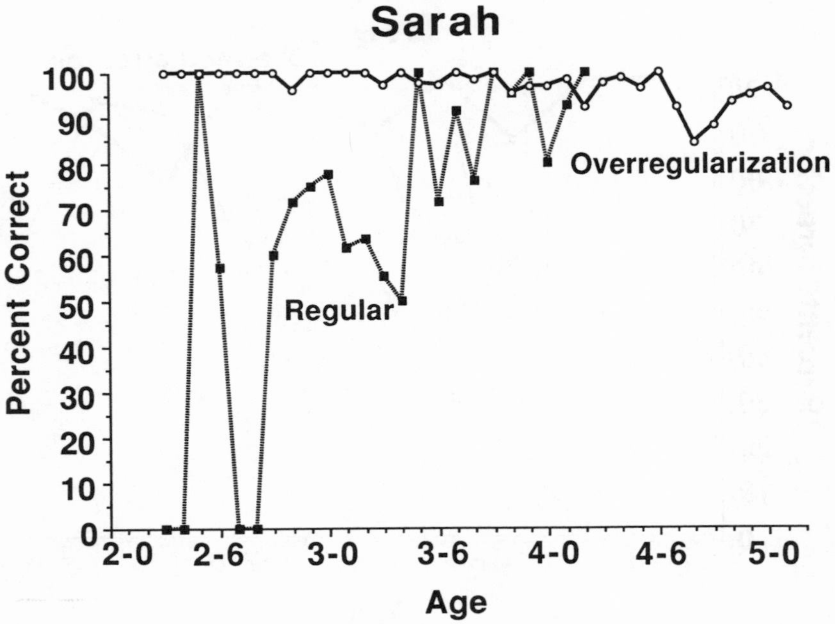

FIG. 38.—Proportion of Sarah's regular verbs in obligatory past tense contexts that were correctly marked for tense and her overregularization rate (subtracted from 100%).

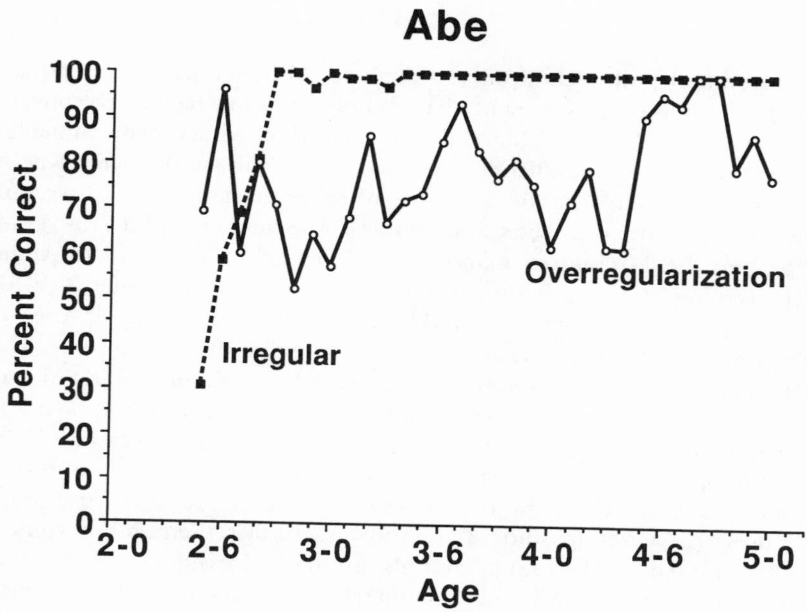

FIG. 39.—Proportion of Abe's irregular verbs in obligatory past tense contexts that were correctly marked for tense. Overregularizations do not enter into these data but are shown in the curve at the top (subtracted from 100%).

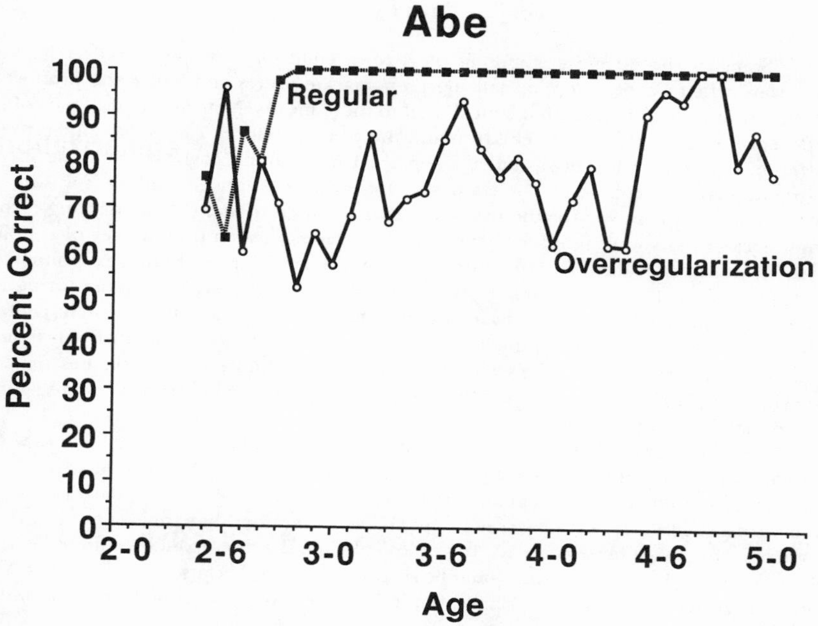

FIG. 40.—Proportion of Abe's regular verbs in obligatory past tense contexts that were correctly marked for tense and his overregularization rate (subtracted from 100%).

compared to the other children we examined. Although part of the explanation may lie in the nonrepresentative circumstances in which Abe's conversations were recorded (see Chap. IV, Sec. VII), this artifact seems unlikely to account for the entire difference. Also unusual about Abe and Kuczaj's cross-sectional sample is the high rate of tense marking of both irregular and regular verbs after Abe's first samples: Abe marked 97% of his regular verbs, and the 14 children marked 93.9% of theirs, compared to Adam's 72% marking of regulars during the period studied by Cazden in which he overregularized, Eve's 66%, and Sarah's 85%.[27] For example, Abe's observed overregularization rate is 24%. Imagine that this figure comes from his failing to retrieve the past form of an irregular verb on 24.7 out of every 100 occasions on which he tries to mark it for tense, and then applying the regular suffixation process to the stem on 97% of those occasions. What would happen if Abe suffixed verbs only as successfully as Adam did? He would have regularized the irregulars only 72% of the time, resulting in 17.8 overregularizations and 6.9 stem forms. (In fact, the number would be less because Adam overregularized his nonmarked irregulars in past tense contexts a smaller proportion of the time than he marked his regular verbs.) We would measure his overregularization rate as 17.8/(17.8 + 75.3), or 19.1%, 5 percentage points closer to the rest of the children.[28]

[27] Some of the differences among the Brown children may simply reflect how old they were when Cazden stopped tallying their marking rates and hence the proportion of early transitional samples that contributed to these means. Note as well that part of the difference between the Brown children and the Kuczaj children can be attributed to the different methods that Kuczaj and Cazden used in counting correct past tense forms. Cazden apparently counted a correct past tense form as "supplied" only if it was in one of the obligatory contexts for the past tense that she used to identify no-marking errors; other correct pasts were ignored (hence the difference between the number of supplied irregular forms she tallied and the number of correct irregulars we found, as summarized in App. Tables A1–A3). Kuczaj appeared to have counted all overt past tense forms as if their very appearance was prima facie evidence that each one was obligatory in its context. This difference in method is unlikely to be responsible for much of the difference, however, because, for most of Abe's months and Kuczaj's children, the estimates of tense marking were 100% or close to it; therefore, subtracting some correct past tense forms would make little or no difference.

[28] Another way of replacing Abe's rate of successful regularization with Adam's would be to use their rates of regularizing an irregular verb when the correct irregular past form was not produced (i.e., overregularizations as a proportion of overregularizations plus stem forms in past tense contexts; see Chap. IV, Sec. VI) rather than their rates of suffixing regular verbs in past tense contexts. In that calculation, the discrepancy would be reduced almost entirely. The comparison would be suspect, however, because the estimate of Abe's rate of regularizing irregular tokens is not independent of his overall overregularization rate, the figure we would be adjusting.

II. THE DEVELOPMENT OF IRREGULAR TENSE MARKING AND OVERREGULARIZATION

So far, we have examined evidence on the relation between overregularization and the marking of regular verbs in obligatory contexts. The data suggest that by the time overregularization first appears, children are already marking *irregular* verbs more often than not in obligatory past tense contexts (see Table 7 and Figs. 33–37 and 39; Abe's first month may be a counterexample). Presumably, these early relatively high rates of irregular marking reflect partial acquisition of the syntactic requirement in English that verbs be marked for tense in main clauses (see Stromswold, 1990), together with knowledge of the semantics of the past tense itself. Given a general motive to mark past tense on irregular verbs, the regular affixation process, once it is acquired, can serve as the means to do so when retrieval fails. Indeed, once the Brown children began to overregularize, they never did so at a rate higher than their rate of nonmarking of irregular verbs in obligatory contexts prior to overregularization. That is, when overregularizations appear, they occupy some of the space in children's past tense conversations formerly occupied by bare stems. This is consistent with the hypothesis that overregularization steps in when retrieval fails; if overregularizations occurred at much higher rates than immediately preceding nonmarking rates, they would seem to represent some radical "reorganization" or global "regression," but they do not. In Kuczaj's subjects, we do not have estimates of the rate of irregular marking prior to the onset of overregularization, but even in the samples available we see that the rates of nonmarking in the youngest-age samples are far higher than overregularization rates thereafter. Indeed, acquisition of regular affixation seems to top off the reservoir of obligatory past tense contexts; as Kuczaj (1977a, p. 593) notes, "Apparently once the child has gained stable control of the regular past tense rule, he will not allow a generic verb form to express 'pastness,' which eliminates errors such as *go, eat* and *find,* but results in errors like *goed, eated,* and *finded.*"

Although the reliable marking of tense on irregular verbs accompanies overregularization, it does not appear to be tightly linked in time to its onset or level.[29] In individual months, children can use irregular verbs correctly in obligatory contexts more often than not without overregularizing (e.g., Adam and Sarah) and can overregularize while leaving irregulars unmarked

[29] Note that this is a modification of a conclusion stated in an earlier draft of this *Monograph* circulated as a technical report, which was based on the ages at which Brown's 90% for 6 hours requirement had been met, before Cazden's full data set was made available to us.

more often than not (Abe's first month). Moreover, although the rate of irregular marking in obligatory contexts tends to correlate over months with overregularization rates in all children, the correlations were always lower than the corresponding ones between overregularization and the rate of regular marking. Nor is this entirely surprising. Although marking past tense reliably should increase the *number* of overregularization errors (and hence could correlate with the appearance of such errors for sampling reasons if the total number of irregular past forms were low, which it is not for Adam and Sarah), it does not necessarily increase the *rate* of overregularization calculated over all irregular verbs marked for past tense. That is because if a child neglected to mark irregular verbs for tense, we would see both few overregularizations and few correct irregular past tense forms (with unmarked stems taking their place), all things being equal.

Nonetheless, we can speculate on two conceivable reasons why past tense overregularization does tend to occur in the presence of high rates of irregular past tense marking. One is that the acquisition of the obligatory tense requirement in English might be an impetus for the acquisition of the regular suffixation process itself, which is a means for the tense requirement to be satisfied for all verbs, memorized or not. (We return to this possibility in Chap. VIII, Sec. I*C*, where we consider how a regular rule might be learned.) Second, because tense is stored as part of the lexical entry of irregular verbs, they might tend to be activated by normal lexical retrieval processes driven by the intent to communicate certain kinds of semantic content. In comparison, activation of the regular operation, a grammatical process, might be invoked more often for grammatical reasons (to satisfy the tense requirement). That is, *broke* automatically comes to mind when one is thinking simultaneously of breaking and of pastness, whereas thinking of fixing and pastness summons only the word *fix,* plus a call to the regular tense-marking operation. If lexical retrieval is more automatic or reliable than on-line application of regular marking, then once a child's language system is driven by the grammatical requirement to mark tense, there is a motive to apply regular marking when retrieval of an irregular fails, and overregularizations will result. In contrast, without the requirement, tense might be marked only when the irregular form was lexically activated for semantic reasons. Whether these speculations can be supported by independent data, or whether they are necessary at all, we leave as a question for future research.

III. SUMMARY

It appears that acquisition of the regular suffixation process of English is the proximal trigger for overregularization errors: overregularizations first appear during a window in which the child goes from leaving most regular verbs unmarked in past tense contexts to marking them more often than not, and at rates comparable to those for irregular verbs. An overall tendency to mark past tense on irregular verbs, combined with imperfect retrieval of irregular forms from memory and with a regular process that is capable of applying to any stem, even if closely tied to an irregular past, sets the stage for overregularization errors.

VII. FACTORS CAUSING DIFFERENCES IN OVERREGULARIZATION RATES AMONG VERBS

Although overregularization rates are low in general, not all verbs are overregularized at the same rate, and some verbs are overregularized by some children at some stages more often than they are produced correctly. By examining what it is about a verb that makes it more or less likely to be overregularized, one can test many hypotheses about the psychology of overregularization.

In this chapter, we correlate a variety of lexical factors with overregularization rates across a large set of irregular verbs. To minimize averaging artifacts, we calculated these correlations for each of the 19 ChiLDES children with individual transcripts that overregularized at least once. When we report averages for these correlations and tests of the average against a null hypothesis of zero, we first transformed each child's correlation coefficient (r) to Fisher's z; the reported mean correlations were obtained by averaging the z scores and transforming the mean z back to a correlation coefficient.

In addition, when suitable, we computed a single measure that aggregates overregularization tendencies for verbs across all 25 children. Pooling tokens across children is inappropriate, as the children with the largest samples would dominate the means. However, averaging together each child's overregularization rate for a given verb is also not appropriate because such means are in danger of being artifactually influenced by individual children with extreme values and idiosyncratic subsets of verbs. For example, if a child who is fond of using the verb *hear* also happened to be a high overregularizer across the board, then the mean overregularization rate of *hear* across children would be artifactually high. This problem is accentuated for small samples of a given verb for a given child, which can contribute extreme high or low overregularization rates to the mean across children. To minimize these artifacts, for each child we considered only verbs that he or she used at least 10 times in the past tense. Furthermore we standardized each child's set of overregularization rates for different verbs (i.e., for each child we converted the overregularization rate for each verb to a z score, using the mean and standard deviation of the overregularization rates for different verbs used by that child). The z scores for a given verb were then averaged across children. These scores, representing the relative overregularization rate for each verb in the aggregate sample, are summarized in Appendix Table A9. For the convenience of the reader we have also linearly rescaled these mean z scores back to proportions that can be more intuitively interpreted as "average overregularization rates." For each verb, we multiplied its z score by the mean across children of the standard deviations that had been used to calculate the z scores (i.e., the mean of the 25 standard deviations, one for each child, of the overregularization rates for that child's different verbs), added it to the mean overregularization rate for that verb (including zeros from the children who never overregularized), and added an additional constant of .02 to raise the least-overregularized verb from a negative value to zero. Note that these figures are primarily for ease of comparing relative overregularization rates among verbs and do not literally correspond to a mean across children.

I. FREQUENCY

As we discussed in Chapter II, if overregularization results from a failure to retrieve a listed past tense form, forms with greater memory strength should be more resistant to overregularization (MacWhinney, 1978; Pinker, 1984; Slobin, 1971). The more often a parent uses a past tense form, the stronger the memory trace for that form should be, and the stronger the association between it and the corresponding stem form. Thus, the adult frequency of an irregular verb in its past tense form should be negatively correlated with its overregularization rate for children. Bybee and Slobin (1982a) found a significant negative rank-order correlation over verbs between their preschool children's overregularization rates and the frequencies of the verbs in the speech of the preschool children's caretakers. They found a similar effect for some subclasses of verbs for the past tense forms experimentally elicited from their third-grade subjects. MacWhinney (1978) documents similar findings in children acquiring other languages. We sought to replicate this effect with our larger sample of children and to examine it within individual children, to ensure that it is not an averaging artifact.

Three measures of adult frequency were used: (1) for each verb used in the past tense by a child, the frequency of the past tense form of that verb in the speech of the adults talking to that child; (2) an aggregate parental frequency measure computed by averaging the 19 sets of adult frequencies, one set from each child; and (3) the past tense counts from

Francis and Kucera's (1982) corpus of a million words of written text. (We include correlations with the Francis and Kucera data base because it is the most commonly used source of frequency information in psycholinguistics; it should predict children's behavior less well then parental frequency counts, of course, because it is from written English addressed to adults.) Frequencies and mean frequencies were converted to logs because the frequencies could range over several orders of magnitude (especially for Francis-Kucera figures) and because we expected that a frequency difference of 1 versus 10 would have a greater effect than a frequency difference of 1,001 versus 1,010. For the purpose of calculating correlations with these logs, frequencies and mean frequencies of zero were arbitrarily assigned the value zero.

Frequency had a very clear effect. The aggregate overregularization rates across 19 children significantly correlate with the aggregate parental frequency counts, $r(37) = -.37$, $p < .05$, and nonsignificantly correlate with Francis-Kucera frequencies, $r(37) = -.14$, $p > .10$. Of the 19 children, all had overregularization rates across verbs that correlated negatively with the log aggregate parental measure (range $-.12$ to $-.61$), 18 correlated negatively with the log frequency of their own parents, and 16 had negative correlations with log Francis-Kucera frequency. These sets of individual children's correlation coefficients have means that are significantly less than zero: mean $r = -.33$, $t(18) = 8.89$, $p < .001$, for the aggregate parental frequency; mean $r = -.34$, $t(18) = 6.80$, $p < .001$, for each child's own parents; mean $r = -.16$, $t(18) = 4.45$, $p < .001$, for Francis-Kucera frequency.

II. PHONOLOGICAL SIMILARITY BETWEEN STEM AND PAST

An important fact about irregular verbs is that their past tense forms, although unpredictable in other regards, generally preserve most of the phonological composition of their stems. *Go-went* and *be-was* are exceptions; for the other irregulars such as *come-came, feel-felt,* and *bring-brought,* the past and stem overlap to an extent that would be uncanny if the pair consisted of two arbitrary words linked only as memorized paired associates. Pinker and Prince (1988) point out that theories of irregular morphology should explain this fact, but that the Rumelhart-McClelland model failed to do so.

A. Number of Changes from the Stem Form to the Past Form

In some theories of generative grammar (e.g., Chomsky & Halle, 1968; Halle & Mohanan, 1985), irregular pasts are generated by applying to the stem one or more rules that replace a circumscribed substring of phonological segments. It is in the very nature of rules that any segment not changed by the rule is left untouched and hence will automatically appear in the past tense form. This is how the similarity between the members of an irregular pair is explained.

MacKay (1976) suggested that these rules are applied by speakers on line when they produce irregular past forms and that each application consumes a determinate portion of processing resources. When comparing the response times for adult subjects to produce past tense forms when given their stems, he found that verbs with "simple" vowel changes were produced most quickly, followed by regular verbs, followed by verbs with "complex" vowel changes, followed by verbs with both a vowel change and the *-t* suffix. If MacKay's hypothesis that the psychological complexity of irregulars is predicted by the number of rule applications in the grammatical derivation, as proposed by irregular-rule theories, such effects may also affect children's overregularizations. Irregulars with more changes require more rule applications and hence may be harder to produce; when the derivation breaks down, the regular rule steps in.

This hypothesis can be tested by correlating the number of phoneme changes that must be executed to derive the past from the stem with the overregularization rate for that stem. What counts as a "change" will of course depend on one's theory of possible phonological operations, but a reasonable if crude first approximation would be to count each single vowel substitution, consonant substitution, consonant addition, or consonant deletion as one change. For example, in *see-saw,* one phoneme, the vowel, must be replaced; in *sweep-swept,* a vowel must be replaced and a consonant suffixed, for a total of two. Hence, on average, a verb like *sweep* should be overregularized at a higher rate than a verb like *see.* In these calculations, we treated each diphthong as a single phoneme.

We did not find a consistent positive correlation between number of phonemes changed and overregularization rate: for the aggregate rates across the 19 children, $r(34) = -.10$.[30] For 14 of the 19 children, correlations were also negative, as was the mean of the correlations ($-.08$).

B. Degree of Phonological Overlap between Stem and Past Forms

It is possible that there really are no irregular rules, and that the commonalities between stem and past (a heterogeneous set of patterns that

[30] For Adam, Eve, and Sarah, no-change verbs were included; *have, be,* and *do* were excluded because it is not clear how irregular-rule theories would treat them (all three have irregular present tense forms, and *be* has two past forms, *was* and *were,* neither related to the infinitive).

range from simple vowel changes to such severe distortions as *bring-brought*) are to be accounted for by other means. For example, these pairs may have been generated in earlier stages of the language by genuine rules, now defunct; the pairs that were produced by these rules, because they shared phonological material, were easy for learners to memorize and have preferentially survived over the centuries in Darwinian fashion (see Bybee & Slobin, 1982a, 1982b; Lieber, 1980; Pinker & Prince, 1988).

One extreme mechanism by which stem-past similarity might operate is by affecting the likelihood with which children recognize that a stem form and its past tense counterpart are alternative versions of the same verb, as opposed to two independent verbs. In fact, it has been proposed that failure to unite two inflected forms within a single inflectional paradigm for a given verb is an important general cause of overregularization, accounting for why it takes place despite the blocking principle (Bybee & Slobin, 1982a; Clark, 1987, 1990; Kuczaj, 1981; Pinker, 1984; Pinker & Prince, 1988; see also n. 5 above). Two phenomena suggested this hypothesis. First, Kuczaj (1981) and Pinker and Prince (1988) noted that children productively inflect irregular stems: *ate, ated,* and *ating* coexist with *eat, eated,* and *eating,* as if they were two verbs. Second, Bybee and Slobin (1982a) noted that irregular verbs that end in a vowel that changes from stem to past (*fly-flew, see-saw, know-knew, blow-blew,* etc.) are particularly prone to being overregularized. If phonological overlap between stem and past is a critical cue for two forms to be lumped together as versions of the same verb, the meager common portion among verbs in this class (e.g., initial *s-* for *see* and *saw*) would make it harder for the child to recognize that they were forms of a single verb.

The hypothesis that a failure to unify two stems within a common verb paradigm is the major cause of overregularization appears to be too strong. Empirically, errors like *ating* and *thoughting* are uncommon, and tend to appear later in development than simple overregularizations (Kuczaj, 1977a, 1981). Theoretically, the cues that would tell the child that the two forms were versions of the same verb are present throughout development, leaving it a puzzle that the child takes so long to notice them. Moreover, the linguistically valid cues for common membership militate strongly against the child's ever considering the past stem to be an independent verb. Kuczaj (1981) notes that the child correctly treats the past stem as indicating pastness: *was wenting* occurs; *is wenting* does not. But according to cross-linguistic research in lexical semantics, tense is an extremely unnatural, perhaps nonexistent, inherent semantic component of verbs (Bybee, 1985; Pinker, 1989; Talmy, 1985). Languages do not like independent verbs that mean "do *X*" and "do *X* in the past." If children's hypotheses mesh with what is linguistically possible, they should not posit such verbs.

Weaker versions of the hypothesis are plausible, however. Perhaps phonological dissimilarity between stem and past does not have so large an effect that it prevents children from mentally linking them over the long term, accounting for the very existence of overregularization, but does have a smaller effect over the short term, causing slight delays in mentally unifying past and stem for verbs with dissimilar pasts compared to verbs with similar pasts. Moreover, if links between stem and past are not immediately acquired at full strength, stem-past similarity could have an influence on children's ability to retrieve the past form after some kind of link had been formed. This could come about if on some occasions the child retrieves the past only after first mentally activating the stem. Common phonological material between stem and past might improve the speed or probability with which a past form is activated, if, for example, both forms are linked via pointers to a common representation of their phonological constituents, or if they actually overlap in their underlying phonological representations at some level. That is, it might be easier to retrieve *strung* given *string* than *brought* given *bring*.

If phonological similarity has an effect on overregularization, it would be the degree of phonological overlap, not the degree of phonological change, that should be related to overregularization proneness. The degree of phonological overlap for irregular pairs was quantified as follows. We began by counting the number of phonemes preserved from stem to past. For example, *forget-forgot* has five phonemes preserved, whereas *catch-caught* has only one. Counting shared phonemes alone would be highly misleading, however, because speakers certainly represent words in a format that is more structured than a simple list of segments. In particular, the consonant-vowel (CV) skeleton underlying a form is thought to be a distinct level of representation in phonology (see Kaye, 1990), and this would saliently capture the relatedness of *see* and *saw* or *throw* and *threw* even if the sheer number of shared segments was slight—the lack of a consonant at the end of a verb is itself a feature of similarity. Thus, we also counted the segments that changed content but preserved their positions in the verb's CV skeleton (with half the weight of phonemes that preserved both their content and their skeleton position), so that *see* and *saw* were counted as more similar than *say* and *said*. Similarly, consonants that preserved their content but changed position in the CV skeleton were given a quarter as much weight as consonants that preserved both content and position, so that *l* was given less weight in *feel-felt* than in *steal-stole*. (As it turns out, nothing hinges on this particular way of measuring stem-past similarity; similar results occur if all phonemes are weighted equally or if shared phonological features, rather than shared phonemes, are counted.)

The prediction is that the amount of preserved phonological structure should correlate negatively with overregularization rates; that is, the more similar the stem and past, the less likely the child is to overregularize the verb. At first it might appear that the prediction has already been tested in the preceding section: every phoneme that is changed is a phoneme that is not preserved, so the number of phonemes changed (previously tested) should correlate negatively with the amount of overlapping phonological structure (to be tested here). However, the correlation is only −.55, leaving enough independent variance to test for a negative correlation with overregularization rates even though we just saw that the phonemes-changed measure had no effect. In fact, the correlation is positive for the aggregate overregularization rate (.10), for the mean correlation for these children (.07), and for 14 of the 19 children individually.

One might note that the irregular with the least phonological material preserved, *go-went,* is high in frequency. This suggests that any difficulty in learning more dissimilar past pairs might be compensated for by the higher frequency of such items, masking an effect of dissimilarity per se. Indeed, the correlation between aggregate parental frequency and phonological overlap is −.31 ($p < .005$). An effect of phonological overlap could be unmasked in a multiple regression analysis using frequency and phonological overlap as predictors. Such an analysis fails to reveal an effect of phonological overlap: the partial correlation, holding constant the child's own parental frequency, is in the nonpredicted direction for the aggregate measure over children and for 10 of the 19 individual children. (Similar noneffects are found when frequency is partialed out of the correlation between overregularization and the number of phonemes changed, which is not surprising because the correlation between the two predictors is only −.05.) In sum, we have failed to find clear evidence that the degree of stem-past similarity or dissimilarity affects the overregularization rate of irregular verbs.

The failure of any measure of relative stem-past similarity to explain differing overregularization rates is unexpected given the pervasiveness of such similarity in the English irregular verb system. Perhaps a modicum of phonological similarity, together with the obvious semantic similarity between stem and past, may be sufficient for children to recognize the relatedness of most verbs and their irregular pasts. Thereafter, irregular pasts are retrieved directly in response to a call to the entire lexical paradigm and the "past" feature, bypassing the stem form itself (as was suggested in Chap. IV, Secs. VII*A* and VIII).

III. PROTECTION BY FAMILIES OF SIMILAR IRREGULAR PAIRS

Not only are irregular verb stems similar to their past tense forms, but they also tend to be similar to other irregular verb stems that have comparable past tense forms. Irregular verbs fall into clusters such as *sting-stung, swing-swung, string-strung,* and so on. The minor rules posited by some theories of generative morphology (e.g., a rule changing *i* to ∧; see Halle & Mohanan, 1985) are meant to explain this second kind of similarity as well. The form of irregulars is by definition unpredictable on phonological grounds, so the rules must be tagged as applicable only to a fixed list of words, but if the number of rules is smaller than the number of words, the existence of similarity clusters is explained.

However, Pinker and Prince (1988) pointed out problems for such theories. The irregular clusters are held together by far more common features than just the segment changed by the putative rule: *string, sting,* and *swing* share not only an *i,* but also a velar nasal as their final consonant and an *s* as part of an initial consonant cluster. Trying to capture these *hypersimilarities* by adding them to the rule as context terms (e.g., "Change *i* to ∧ in the context C——*ng*") fails in both directions. It falsely includes many forms like *bring-brought* and *sing-sang,* and it fails to include verbs that are clearly related to the cluster by family resemblance, such as *stick* (final consonant velar but nonnasal) and *spin* (final consonant nasal but nonvelar; see also Bybee & Slobin, 1982a).

In some ways, the Rumelhart-McClelland model handles these imperfect partial similarities well: after being trained on 82 irregulars, some of the model's outputs for new irregulars that it had not previously encountered were correct, such as *wept, clung,* and *bid,* despite the complex and highly probabilistic nature of the patterns that such generalizations represent. Furthermore, the model proved to be highly sensitive to the subregularity that no-change verbs all end in a *t* or a *d,* overgeneralizing it to regulars and to other irregulars that end in *t* or *d.* This can be attributed to the fact that the model records the relative frequencies of many different mappings between substrings of stems and substrings of pasts, superimposing them across the different verbs that exemplified them.

Pinker and Prince (1988), while disagreeing with Rumelhart and McClelland's suggestion that both regular and irregular forms are generated in a single associative network, noted that their model might offer insights as to how irregular verbs are stored. If the traditional notion of rote memory for irregular storage is thought of not as an unstructured list of slots but as also involving some kind of associative network in which recurring similarities are recorded and superimposed, the hypersimilar family resemblance classes can be explained because they contain sets of verbs that are easier to memorize than unrelated singletons, and that are prone to occasional generalizations (e.g., *brung, bote*) by analogy. In this interpretation, Rumelhart and McClelland would be providing a better model of the irregular rote component of the inflectional system. Related suggestions had been made prior to Rumelhart and McClelland (1986) by Bybee and Slobin (1982a) and MacWhinney (1978). MacWhinney suggests that some children utter some productive forms by a mechanism distinct from both rote lexical storage and rule application, namely, rhyme-driven analogies. Bybee and Slobin suggested that speakers form *schemas* for recognizing typical phonological patterns of irregular past tense forms. Children learn to associate past forms with their stems more easily if they conform to a past tense schema, and they are more likely to select stored forms that conform to a schema when producing past tenses.

If belonging to a family of similar irregulars undergoing similar changes strengthens the memory trace of a given irregular form, it should be more resistant to overregularization than more isolated irregulars, holding frequency constant. The prediction that partial regularity blocks overregularization was first suggested by Slobin (1971) and has been further tested by Bybee and Slobin (1982a) and Kuczaj (1977a, 1978). The most robust effect is that verbs that end in *t* or *d* are less likely to have *-ed* added, and are more likely to be uttered in no-change form, than verbs without those endings. This is true for both no-change irregulars, leading to improved performance, and other kinds of irregulars, leading to no-change errors; both kinds are protected from overregularization (for reviews, see Pinker & Prince, 1988; and Rumelhart & McClelland, 1986). (We see the effect in our data as well: of the 11 verbs ending in *t* or *d* listed in App. Table A10, 10 of them were overregularized at aggregate rates lower than the mean across verbs.) As mentioned, the Rumelhart-McClelland model duplicated this phenomenon. However, Pinker and Prince (1988) point out that the effect is potentially so overdetermined that identifying the psychologically active cause or causes is nearly impossible. The no-change class is large (the largest among the irregular verbs), shows an exceptionless hypersimilarity (all its verbs end in *t* or *d*), involves a single kind of change (none), shares its verb-final consonant with the regulars, and when regularized results in a phonological pattern (adjacent identical stop consonants) that the phonology of English tries to avoid. Thus, the existence of an effect of family strength should be confirmed with other materials.

Bybee and Slobin also showed that children overregularized subclasses with different kinds of vowel changes at different rates. They attributed the differences to different degrees of stem-past similarity, as discussed in the preceding section. But as we have seen, the effects of stem-past similarity are difficult to demonstrate, if they exist at all. Furthermore, Pinker and Prince (1988) showed that stem-stem similarity may be the more relevant factor: the overregularization rates for the different vowel change classes correlate well with the number of English irregular verbs sharing the vowel changes that the class members undergo. They suggested that this explains why the Rumelhart-McClelland model mimicked the ranking of overregularization rates for these subclasses, at least in one stage. However, even here the existence of a stem family effect was not perfectly clear: Bybee and Slobin's subclasses, as interpreted by Rumelhart and McClelland, were heterogeneous and contained many possible contaminants, such as the inclusion of the unusual *go-went* in the *blow/grow/know* subclass (for discussion, see also Egedi & Sproat, 1991).

A better test of the family strength effect would eschew the necessarily imperfectly constructed subclasses in favor of a direct measure of the strength of the family members for each irregular verb. Because there are many different possible models of associative memory (differing in how widely their associations spread in phonological space), none of them simulated perfectly by any given family strength measure, we computed three different measures, of differing degrees of inclusiveness, all of them based on the principal dimensions of similarity within families of irregulars (Pinker & Prince, 1988). The first measure was based on rhymes: for each verb we summed the frequency (not the log frequency) of the past tense forms of each of the other irregular verbs whose stems and past tense forms rhyme with those of the verb in question. For example, for *sting-stung* we would add the frequencies of *clung, flung, swung,* and so on. The verb's own frequency was not included; although it surely affects the strength of the family it belongs to, we wanted to see if we could find independent support for a family strength effect, unconfounded by the frequency effect already documented. The second measure was based on the final consonant cluster: we summed the frequencies of the past tense forms of all the irregular verbs that shared the final consonant cluster with the verb stem in question and that underwent the same change from stem to past (vowel change, consonant change, consonant addition, and so on; see the subclasses in the appendix to Pinker & Prince, 1988). For example, for *stick-stuck* we would add the frequencies of *struck* and *snuck,* even though their stems, *strike* and *sneak,* do not rhyme with *stick.* The third and most inclusive measure added the frequencies of the irregular verbs that shared a final consonant with the verb stem in question and that underwent the same change from stem to past. For example, for *stick-stuck* we would add the frequencies not only of *struck* and *snuck* but also of *stunk* and *slunk.* Verbs ending in a vowel were treated as if they shared a final consonant.

Because many irregular neighbors like *slunk* would be far-fetched candidates for children's lexicons, we actually selected members of irregular word families, and took their frequencies, from the adults' speech in the transcripts of the child in question, using the 19 children with individual transcripts that overregularized at least once. The independent variables took on very different values for each child, so aggregate measures are not appropriate.

The prediction we are testing is as follows. The higher the frequencies of an irregular verb's family members, the less likely the verb is to be overregularized. The prediction appears to be borne out. For the family of rhymes, the correlation coefficient between family strength and overregularization rate was negative for 17 of the 19 children. The mean of the correlations, $-.07$, is significantly different from zero, $t(18) = 2.23$, $p < .05$. For the family of verbs sharing a final consonant cluster and a past tense change, the correlation was negative for all 19 children, with a mean of $-.11$, $t(18) = 9.99$, $p < .001$. For the most inclusive family, sharing a final consonant and a past tense change, the correlations were also negative for all 19 children, with a mean of $-.11$, $t(18) = 10.03$, $p < .001$.

To ensure that this effect cannot be attributed to a confound with the frequency of each verb, we held the log parental frequency constant in a partial correlation analysis. For all three family sizes, 16 of the 19 children had negative partial correlation coefficients, and the mean partial correlation coefficient remained negative and significantly less than zero (for rhyme, mean $r = -.08$, $t[18] = 2.22$, $p < .05$; for final consonant cluster, mean $r = -.08$, $t[18] = 4.005$, $p = .001$; for final consonant, mean $r = -.08$, $t[18] = 4.01$, $p = .001$).

We conclude that there is a small, although reliable, effect whereby verbs are protected from overregularization to the extent that they are phonologically similar to other verbs (weighted by their frequencies) displaying the same irregular pattern.

IV. ATTRACTION TO FAMILIES OF SIMILAR REGULAR VERBS

The preceding analysis confirms the hypothesis of Slobin, Bybee, and Kuczaj that partial regularity blocks overregularization. It is consistent both with the Rumelhart-McClelland model and with Pinker and Prince's augmentation of the traditional rote-rule model in which the rote component has some associative-memory-like properties. A test that might distinguish the latter two models is whether families of similar *regular* verbs pull an irregular *toward* overregularization in the same way that families of similar irregulars pull it away. Since in the traditional rote-rule model regular past tense forms need not be stored because they can be generated by a rule, under the simplest hypothesis regular past tense forms should not attract irregulars. Of course, storage of regulars is possible within such theories—what could prevent it, given that it allows the learning of individual irregular items?—but such storage is not necessary except under certain circumstances in which the existence or form of the regular cannot be predicted, such as in the child before the regular rule is learned, and doublets such as *dived* and *dove* where both members must be stored. Thus, in general, we should not find strong effects of storage of regulars in a rule theory, and in no case should the ability to generalize to new forms depend on the previous storage of similar old ones. That this property does in fact distinguish rule-based theories from the Rumelhart-McClelland model was shown by the behavior of the model on newly presented regular verbs. At asymptote, the model erred on 33% of the regular verbs it was tested on, producing no output at all for six that were dissimilar from those in its training set, such as *jump* and *pump* (Pinker & Prince, 1988; Prasada & Pinker, in press). In contrast, adults easily regularize highly unusual sounding novel forms such as *ploamph* or *keelth* (Prasada & Pinker, in press), and between the ages of 2 and 5 Abe left virtually no regular verb in past tense contexts unmarked, including his own unusual inventions *eat lunched, bonked, borned, axed, fisted,* and *poonked* (Kuczaj, 1977a).

To test whether families of regular verbs pull similar irregulars toward overregularization, we first extracted the 1,826 regular verbs rhyming with the irregulars that were listed in an on-line version of *Webster's Seventh Collegiate Dictionary,* which contains phonological representations of 8,217 verbs. Just as for the irregular families, three different size nets were cast. In the first, the sum of the frequencies of the regulars in a parent's speech that rhymed with each of the child's irregulars was computed (e.g., *winked* would contribute to the regular attractor strength of *stink*). In the second, verbs with the same final consonant cluster were grouped, so that *yanked* and *honked* as well as *winked* join the family of *stink.* In the third, verbs with the same final consonant were grouped, so that *hiked* and *harked* would also belong to *stink*'s attracting family. Verbs that ended in a vowel were treated as if they had a common final consonant.

If families of regular verbs pull similar irregulars toward overregularization, correlations between regular family strength and overregularization rate should be positive. In none of our tests do we find statistically significant correlations in that direction. For families of rhymes, the correlation was positive for 7 of the 19 children, with a mean of $-.01$. For families sharing a final consonant cluster, correlation coefficients were positive for 11 of the 19 children, with a mean of .08, not significantly different from zero, $t(18) = 1.14$, $p > .10$. For families sharing a final consonant, the correlation was positive for 11 of the 19 children, with a mean (.06) not significantly different from zero, $t < 1$. When the verb's own frequency is partialed out, the correlations with the smallest family strength measure (rhymes) are positive for only 8 of the 19 children, and the mean correlation across children was negative. For the middle-sized family (shared final consonant cluster), the correlations were positive for 12 of the children; the mean correlation was .09, not significantly different from zero, $t(18) = 1.45$, $p > .10$. For the largest (final consonant) family, the correlations with family strength were positive for 12 of the 19 children, with a mean of .06, not significantly different from zero, $t(18) = 1.11$, $p > .10$. Furthermore, it is not the case that the negative correlations come from children with smaller (hence noisier) samples; of the seven children who went in the nonpredicted direction, six were among the 14 children whose samples contained more than 100 irregular past tense tokens, and one of them was Abe, who had the richest data base of overregularizations.

Each of these measures was computed a second time, excluding polysyllabic verbs. Pinker and Prince (1988) point out that all irregulars are monosyllabic except for forms like *forget, understand,* and *overthrow* that contain a prefixed monosyllabic irregular. Therefore, if a verb is nonprefixed and polysyllabic, it is guaranteed to be regular. If a child became sensitive to this contingency, he or she could sequester such verbs from the mechanism giving rise to family strength effects, and our including them in our estimates could dilute our estimates of such effects. But the results were virtually identical in all cases.

V. SUMMARY

Correlations between children's overregularization rates and various properties of different irregular verbs yield the following conclusions. As expected, irregular verbs with lower-frequency past tense forms are more likely to be overregularized, underscoring the important role of the memory strength of the irregular past tense form in the overregularization process. The degree of phonological similarity or dissimilarity between a stem and its past tense form appears to have no influence on overregularization, suggesting that the errors are not primarily caused by difficulties in executing phonological changes in generating irregular forms or in uniting stems and pasts as part of a single verb paradigm during learning. We found evidence that irregular verbs are protected from overregularization by families of similar irregulars, although we failed to find evidence that they are drawn toward overregularization by families of similar regulars. This supports Rumelhart and McClelland's assumption that irregular patterns are stored in an associative memory, but fails to support their assumption that the regular pattern is stored in the same system.

VIII. SUMMARY AND CONCLUSIONS

The facts of overregularization can be summed up simply. After a period in which all the child's past tense forms of irregular verbs are correct, the child begins to overregularize. Overregularization then occurs at a low rate throughout the preschool and early school years, affecting all irregular verbs, to an extent that depends on the verb's rarity in parental speech. Its overall rate appears to be independent of changes in the mixture of regular and irregular verbs in the child's speech, the child's parents' speech, or the child's vocabulary. Instead, it seems to depend on the acquisition of the tense-marking system as a whole: development of the ability to mark regular verbs reliably for tense appears to be the immediate harbinger of overregularization, and reliable marking of irregular verbs for tense accompanies it. Aside from frequency, verbs' proneness to overregularization depends to a small extent on the strength of the verb's phonological neighborhood: clusters of similar irregular verbs protect one another from overregularization. In contrast, clusters of similar regular verbs do not appear to pull an irregular toward overregularization.

These facts can be accounted for by a simple theory. The child stores irregular past tense forms in a rote memory system, in which the strength of a memory trace is monotonically related to the frequency with which it is encountered. In addition, this memory system has some of the properties of an associative network: stem-past pairs displaying similar relations reinforce each other. (This same property occasionally leads to irregular generalizations such as *brang* and *wope*.) Regular past tense forms, in contrast, are generated by a mental concatenation operation that attaches a suffix to a stem. Because this rule can always be applied on line, regularly inflected forms need not, in general, be stored (although they can be under certain circumstances, such as before children have learned the rule). And because it simply adds an affix to the end of a stem with unspecified properties, the similarity of a given stem to previously encountered ones plays no role.[31] The two systems interact in a simple way: the retrieval of a stored irregular entry blocks the application of the regular rule.

The fact that overregularizations are a small minority of irregular past tense utterances at all stages shows that the blocking process is active in the child as soon as there is evidence for two modes of inflection at all. When overregularizations do occur, they are straightforwardly explained as a failure to retrieve the irregular past form (or, for past + *ed* errors, its "past" feature) in real time. This tendency is related to the frequency of the form in an obvious way that is an immediate consequence of the logic of irregularity and the fallibility of human memory. In the extreme case, an irregular form that has been attended to with zero frequency (e.g., *shend* for adults and many irregular verbs for young children) will have no memory trace; hence, it will be retrieved from memory with zero probability and will always be overregularized if the form is to be tense marked at all. An irregular form that has been heard once has a weak memory trace and hence a probability of being retrieved that is greater than zero but less than one. Irregulars that have been heard more times have correspondingly stronger memory traces and lesser overregularization probabilities; irregulars that have been heard thousands of times will be successfully retrieved virtually always. The learnability problem of recovering from errors is solved by a blocking principle that operates throughout development, fed by irregular forms whose potency increases with increasing exposures during development.

Of course there are aspects of overregularization that remain to be explained. There is considerable unexplained variance in exactly which verbs are overregularized at which rates and ages, and among different children's overregularization rates, and the temporal relation between obligatory tense marking and overregularization is as yet unclear. At present, we believe that we have run up against the limitations of the available data. Just as prior characterizations of overregularization were unclear or misleading owing to the limitations of paper-based diaries and transcript samples, current computer data bases of CHILDES size, although they have enabled tremendous progress, are still not up to the enormous task facing us in trying to understand details of language development. An hour of speech a week is still a paltry sampling of the richness of the language acquisition process, especially in the critical third year of life. We suspect that child language data bases with sampling frequencies of an order of magnitude

[31] The variation in the phonetic form of the regular affix, whereby *d* surfaces as *t* following unvoiced consonants and *id* following coronal stops, can be attributed to general phonological processes operating throughout English, not to the regular process itself (see Pinker & Prince, 1988).

greater than current ones would resolve many of the uncertainties in the current conclusions.

I. OBSERVATIONS ON THE NATURE AND LEARNABILITY OF THE TENSE-MARKING SYSTEM

Our suggested explanation of the overregularization process has three parts: decision to mark tense, imperfect memory retrieval, and possession of a regular process with universal applicability. Although the second postulate reflects a possibly uninteresting memory limitation of the child, the other two reflect quite remarkable linguistic accomplishments.

A. Observations on Tense Marking

As Pinker (1982, 1984) and Slobin (1982) point out, obligatory grammatical constraints pose difficult learning problems for the child. The fact that an inflection is obligatory means that there are no pragmatic cues to the semantic features that the inflection is encoding; parents must express the pastness of a past event, regardless of how relevant it is in the conversational context. Moreover, once the child has somehow figured out that past tense inflection encodes past tense, if he or she mistakenly assumes that it is optional, no parental input short of negative evidence can contradict the assumption. Pinker and Slobin thus suggest that the child is innately prepared to consider obligatory inflectional tense marking as a possible constraint in the language to be acquired; such a hypothesis is easily disconfirmed in systems where inflection for tense is in fact optional or not available. Our seemingly homely explanation for overregularization in terms of retrieval failure depends on the child having solved these daunting learnability problems (for an explicit hypothesis as to how the child solves them, see Pinker, 1984; and for evidence that children solve them quickly, see Stromswold, 1990; the problems are of course finessed in network simulations that are fed correct stem-past pairs in isolation). If the 2–3-year-old child did not consider tense marking to be obligatory, the failure to retrieve an irregular past in a past tense context would not automatically lead to overregularization; the child could simply leave the verb unmarked.

B. Observations on Regular Rules

A second noteworthy linguistic achievement of the late 2-year-old is possession of a process that is capable of yielding an inflected output form for any verb, no matter how strongly linked with an idiosyncratic irregular form, and regardless of whether a family of similar regular forms is available to serve as an analogy-supporting model. As Pinker and Prince (1988) point out, a rule that simply concatenates an affix with a stem, characterized in terms of a variable standing for any stem rather than particular patterns of the typical phonological contents of stems, easily provides this capability. A set of associations between stem phonology and past tense phonology is tied in varying degrees to the patterns it has been trained on. While such models could, in principle, approximate the unlimited applicability of a rule by training it on a set of regular stems that span enough of the phonological space of English to cover all cases, in practice this ability is compromised by the necessity of curbing links to the regular ending in order to avoid application to the irregulars. Presumably, it is for this reason that the Rumelhart-McClelland model failed to display the appropriate generalization abilities for novel regulars (Prasada & Pinker, in press). In managing to come out with a past tense form close to 100% of the time when called for, despite less than perfect memory retrieval, the children we have studied (most notably Abe) clearly have mastered an inflectional process of very wide applicability. If this regular process were not capable of applying to arbitrary irregular stems (and, in fact, 90% of Abe's irregulars were regularized at least once, together with many unusual creative forms like *poonked*), or if it depended on the existence of similar high-frequency regulars (which it does not seem to), then when faced with irregular retrieval failure, the child would be left with no choice but to utter the stem, even if his or her language system had called for a past tense form.

We envision regular rules as mental symbol concatenation operations, similar in operation to the core rules of syntax (see Pinker, 1991; Pinker & Prince, 1988, 1991; Prince & Pinker, 1988). This hypothesis is about a kind of mental machinery available to all language learners but put to use in different ways in different language systems. In English, it is used in a condition-free rule within a component of inflectional morphology that takes inputs from the rest of the morphological system and delivers its output to the syntactic component. This computational characterization may differ from many properties of rules informally called "regular" in traditional descriptive grammars. First, a regular rule in our sense need not be the only productive morphological phenomenon in a language; analogizing of irregular patterns (e.g., *brung*) can add new forms as well. Second, it need not apply to the majority of words in a given part-of-speech category; there is nothing in our characterization of regularity that directly pertains to the relative number of words involved, except that, as a fully productive and general process, a regular rule is potentially applicable to an unlimited number of stems whereas irregular analogizing becomes less and less probable as one departs from a subclass prototype. As such, a regular rule may be the only available device for borrowings, neologisms, conversions, onomatopoeia, and other forms that cannot be analogized to existing irregulars (see Kim, Pinker, et al., 1991; Prasada & Pinker, in press). Thus, a regular pattern is liable to assume majority status if such forms enter a language in large numbers, as has happened in English since the Middle English period (Pyles & Algeo, 1982). Third, a regular rule need not be totally insensitive to properties of the stem it affixes to: multiple rules may exist, each affixing an allomorph that applies to stems with a different property, although the conditions would be well defined (e.g., ending in a vowel vs. a consonant) and applicability to a stem within the class would be all or none, not proportional to the stem's global similarity to previously encountered stems. The most common hallmark of a regular process in our sense is *default status,* the ability to apply freely to any word not already linked to an irregular form, regardless of whether it is covered by memorization or analogy (e.g., *We rhumba'd all night*). The computational nature of the rule, as concatenation of an affix to a variable standing for the stem, renders it uniquely capable of playing this default role.

C. How Might a Regular Rule Be Learned?

We have said nothing about how any particular regular rule, such as the English past tense rule, is acquired. Extraction of the suffixation pattern itself can be achieved by examining the phonological differences between forms like *walk* and *walked,* which can be accomplished by a variety of pattern extraction algorithms (see, e.g., MacWhinney, 1978; Pinker, 1984; Pinker & Prince, 1988; Rumelhart & McClelland, 1986). A greater challenge is to show how the child decides whether to internalize a pattern as a regular rule or as a list of (possibly analogy-supporting) individual items such as *bend-bent.* How might this be done? Given the results of Chapter V, children do not appear to depend on a regular pattern applying to a majority of tokens or to be influenced by either the relative or the absolute number of types. Indeed, children begin to overregularize with something on the order of 100 verbs in their vocabularies, and they mark few or none of them for past tense before they begin to overregularize the irregulars, raising the possibility that the child does not need to process large amounts of input data to seize on the regular pattern. We lack evidence that would allow us to identify which cues children actually use to acquire a regular rule, but we can list several logical possibilities, each one a visible consequence of the regular nature of a rule and hence a potential cue to regularity (for further discussion, see Pinker & Prince, 1991). We can also check to see if any of these cues is clearly ruled out by existing evidence on the linguistic input available to children.

First, Pinker and Prince (1988) suggested that the crucial cue might be the ability of a morphological process to apply successfully to several kinds of stem, each belonging to a different competing irregular pattern. For example, *need-needed* exists despite *bleed-bled* and *feed-fed; blink-blinked* exists despite *drink-drank* and *sink-sank; seep-seeped* exists despite *sleep-slept* and *sweep-swept.* Indeed, *all* the rhymes of irregular patterns in English (except perhaps for verbs ending in *-ing*) can also be found in verb roots that are regular. This property is diagnostic of the fact that the regular rule does not carve out a set of phonological territories in the interstices of those claimed by irregular families but can apply to anything at all. The phonological omnipotence of the regular rule is even more apparent in regular-irregular homophones, such as *lie-lay* (recline) and *lie-lied* (fib), *fit-fit* (intransitive) and *fit-fitted* (transitive), and *meet-met* and *mete-meted.* (Of course, the homophones themselves are surely too rare to be the cues used by children.)

Second, the mere heterogeneity of the stem patterns that are heard to be regularly inflected (regardless of whether the inflection trumps some competing irregular pattern characteristic of such stems) may tell the child that the inflection is the product of a rule with either well-defined conditions or none at all. The Rumelhart-McClelland model is driven by a process roughly of this ilk because the applicability of the regular suffix in the model depends on the variety of input patterns that are linked to the output nodes representing that suffix, and these links are strengthened with exposure to the relevant patterns. But the learning process we consider here is somewhat different. As mentioned, the range of generalization of the regular pattern in the Rumelhart-McClelland model is computed over the same representation that is used to represent the words to begin with. This representation has to have enough information to distinguish regulars from any irregular and for the full phonetic form of the past tense form to be reconstructed. This allows the potential conditions for the regular pattern to be sliced too finely; the regular pattern can be tied to highly specific combinations of stem patterns, with no across-the-board generalization to all nonirregular stems. If, instead, the phonological content of words is represented in one, detailed kind of representation, but a small number of candidate conditions of a rule are represented in a separate, much sparser one, then a morphological pattern can be recognized as fully applicable as soon as it is seen to appear with every one of the stem conditions in this smaller, better-defined set (for discussion, see Pinker, 1984; Pinker & Prince, 1988, 1991; and Prasada & Pinker, in press).

Third, a very reliable cue for regularity is the ability of a process to apply to verbs that are derived from other categories such as nouns, adjectives, and names. These verbs do not have verb roots and hence have no base lexical entry to which an irregular memorized form can be attached; only a fully general regular rule can apply to them, acting as a default (see Kim, Marcus, et al., 1991; Kim, Pinker, et al., 1991; Kiparsky, 1982; Pinker

& Prince, 1988). For example, *ring the city* (i.e., "form a ring around") has the past tense form *ringed,* not *rang,* because this sense of *to ring* has a noun root, not a verb that could be collapsed with the one underlying *ring-rang.* Hearing such forms could, in principle, tell a learner that the *-ed* affix is not stored with verb roots and hence must be a regular operation.

Fourth, even a single word with a highly unusual sound pattern, such as *out-Gorbachev'd* or *rhumba'd,* provides information about the generality and possible default status of a morphological pattern.

Fifth, the syntactic requirement that tense be marked *obligatorily* may impel the child's learning mechanism to seek a pattern that can provide the needed form under a wide range of circumstances. The fact that Adam, Eve, Sarah, and Abe were marking irregular verbs for tense a majority of the time near the period in which they were first controlling the regular suffix lends some credence to this suggestion. Of course obligatoriness itself cannot distinguish between regular rule and irregular storage plus analogy, but it might cause the child to promote the most general process to rule status.

Finally, aspects of the phonological properties of regular inflection might provide cues about its regularity. For example, the English past tense inflectional process consists of a suffixation, which is the same kind of process used for the third person singular inflection (*-s*), the progressive inflection (*-ing*), the plural, and the possessive. This could signal to the learner that, in English, suffixation is the process used quite generally for regular inflection whereas the mutations seen in irregular verbs do not belong to any larger system (see Wurzel, 1989). Moreover, a suffix that exerts no change on a stem, or some change that is consistent across all stems, might be classified as regular because it would suggest a process that treats the verb as an opaque variable rather than in terms of its phonological content (Kiparsky, 1982). In English, these properties hold of regular inflection, and of course are confounded: adding a *-d* suffix leaves virtually all verbs unchanged (the exceptions are the irregular verbs *flee, say, hear, sell, tell,* and *do*).

As mentioned, this is a list of hypothetical cues, which we provide to allay possible suspicions that regularity in our sense is unlearnable or learnable only from input sequences that our data already rule out. To decide which of these cues are in fact used by the child's learning mechanisms, it is necessary to determine which of them reliably accompany regular rules across different languages, which are in fact available in parental speech to children of the relevant ages, and which ones are controlled by children simultaneously with their treatment of the pattern as a regular process.

The actual set of regular verbs that children use to induce regular past tense inflection is, of course, difficult to determine from transcript data, which record a small fraction of the speech heard by children and provide no information about what portion of that speech is actually used by the child. In Appendix Table A11, we attempt to bracket the true list by providing one list that is likely to be too big and another that is likely to be too small. The maximal list contains all the regular verbs used at least once in the entire set of transcripts, in any tense, by Adam, Eve, Sarah, or the adults conversing with them. This list approximates the pool of verbs potentially occurring in past tense forms in parental speech to which the children might be attending before they deploy the regular inflection productively. We do not know, however, that each child heard each verb in this list, or that each child heard each verb before acquiring the regular inflection, or that each child had actually attended to the verbs he or she did hear. Thus, we also provide a more conservative estimate, consisting only of the regular verbs that each child actually used (in any tense) in his or her transcripts preceding the first transcript with an overregularization.

The maximal list is consistent with several of the possibilities for cues to regularity entertained in this section. It contains many verbs that rhyme with irregulars (e.g., *ache, blind, blink, call, care, cheat, claw, cry, dare, die, end, exercise, fold, fry, guide, hatch, heat, invite, hand, kick, kid, land, lick, leak, like, live, mind, pee, peel, peep, pick, pin, play, pray, pretend, rake, reach, row, remind, repair, scare, scoot, sew, ski, smell, sneeze, snow, spell, spray, squeeze, stare, stay, steam, surprise, sway, tease, tick, tie, trick, trim, trust, turn, use, wet, yell*). Indeed, most of the irregular clusters of rhymes have regular counterparts in the list. In addition, there are a number of likely denominal verbs (including *bomb, bubble, chain, clip, color, comb, dust, end, fan, fish, glue, hammer, iron, lock, mail, paint, paste, pee, pump, rope, sail, screw, shovel, skate, ski, smoke, stamp, staple, steam, tape, thread, unbuckle, unbutton, unchain, unplug, unscrew,* and *wee-wee*) and onomatopoeic verbs (including *bang, bark, bash, blast, bop, burp, clap, crack, crash, fizz, growl, howl, jabber, meow, pop, smash, swish, zip,* and *zoom*), which may have the same status as denominals (see Pinker & Prince, 1988). Verbs with noncanonical and complex phonologies (especially verbs that do not conform to canonical pattern for English basic words, namely, monosyllables or polysyllables with initial stress) are represented by *allow, attach, belong, decorate, disappear, disturb, erase, excuse, meow, organize, prepare, pretend, recognize, remember,* and *urinate,* among others.

Interestingly, even the minimal lists (regular verbs used by each child before overregularizing) exemplify most of these potential cues. The reader can confirm that each child controlled many verbs rhyming with a variety of irregulars. Adam and Sarah had acquired several denominal verbs (*fish, paint, plug, rain, rope,* and *screw* and *comb, paint, rain, smoke,* and *wee-wee,* respectively) and onomatopoeic verbs (*crack, growl, knock, squeal,* and *squeak* and *knock* and *bump,* respectively). Adam and Sarah also had phonologically noncanonical verbs (*attach, exercise,* and *remember* for Adam; *organize* for Sarah). Even Eve, whose minimal list comes from only four transcripts, used eight verbs rhyming with six kinds of irregulars (*cry, kick, lick, pick, play, show, turn, use*), one likely deadjectival verb (*empty*), and an onomatopoeic form (*crack*). Thus, the data suggest that each of the possible cues to regularity entertained in this section is available to children; whether they are used, necessary, or sufficient, however, remains unknown.

II. RELEVANCE TO HISTORICAL CHANGE

Children regularize irregular verbs, especially the lower-frequency ones, and the English language, over the centuries, has been regularizing irregular verbs, especially the lower-frequency ones (Bybee, 1985). There must be some connection. Perhaps anticipating a trend, *Newsweek* (Gelman, 1986) attributed to Jill de Villiers the half-joke, "Leave children alone and they'd tidy up the English language."

But the remark can be turned around. Children, in fact, *are* left alone (Brown & Hanlon, 1970; Marcus, 1992; Morgan & Travis, 1989), but it does not really matter whether they are or not, for time is on their side. All they have to do is wait, and they will be adults in full custody of the language that is passed on to the next generation. If children really had a distaste for irregular verbs, nothing could have stopped them from tidying up the English language long ago, yet we still have over 100 irregular verbs, most quite secure, some of them transmitted as irregulars in a generation-to-generation chain of successful memorizations linking us to prehistoric peoples thousands of years in the past (Pyles & Algeo, 1982). Clearly, children are not the relentless rule engines of earlier accounts but are quite happy to learn irregulars, and why not? If one has the mental tools to acquire on the order of 50,000 words, each representing an arbitrary sound-meaning pairing, and the ability to link abstract features like tense to words with special markings, memorizing and retaining another few hundred words with the features built in should be no strain. And blocking their regularized counterparts is simply a consequence of the fact that stem and irregular are part of an organized grammatical system, with designated slots for each feature-marked variant of a word.

As Bybee and Slobin (1982b) point out, it is adults who bear most of the blame for the permanent regularization of irregulars in a language. They note that one cannot attribute historical change to children's overregularization errors unless children prefer these errors and continue to do so into adulthood, which, for virtually all irregular verbs in a given generation, they do not. Given what we know about overregularization in children and adults (e.g., Ullman & Pinker, 1990, 1992), the following scenario seems more plausible. A weak irregular memory entry in adults can lead to occasional blocking failures, hence regularizations, for the same reason that children overregularize. Presumably, this reduces the frequency of the irregular past tense form in the parent generation's speech further, and combined with an overall decline in all tense forms for the verb, it may erode to the point where one generation of children rarely hears it and hence never ceases to overregularize it, at which point it has changed to a regular.

III. RELEVANCE TO CONNECTIONIST MODELING OF LANGUAGE ACQUISITION

Although some of the questions treated in this *Monograph* were first raised in Pinker and Prince's (1988) analysis of Rumelhart and McClelland's connectionist simulation of language acquisition, this *Monograph* is not intended as an extension of their critique, and the points we make here are meant to shed light on the nature and causes of overregularization in general. They are not intended either to support or to refute the entire set of connectionist models, or the entire set of models based on grammatical rules, but pertain to many issues that are independent of that distinction, such as the relevant rarity of overregularization, its dependence on the frequency of irregular past forms, and its relation to tense marking in general.

In only three places did we explicitly test predictions of the Rumelhart-McClelland model. The first examined their suggestion that children's U-shaped development could be explained without a distinction between early rote storage of lexical items and later deployment of a productive morphological process. Rather, they suggested, a single pattern associator could display that transition given the assumption that irregulars are higher in frequency than regulars and that the child undergoes a vocabulary explosion causing the sudden acquisition of a large number of regulars and a concomitant change in the number of regular items submitted to the past tense learning device. Our results fail to find evidence either for a change in the input to the past tense system or for a vocabulary explosion at the right point in development that was assumed to cause it. In contrast, the data suggest that children use correct irregulars before overregularizing because they lack the productive mechanism generating regular forms altogether. These discoveries remove one of the more dramatic phenomena that had been adduced as evidence for the Rumelhart-McClelland model (e.g., Sampson, 1987; Smolensky, 1988). Of our other two tests, one supported the Rumelhart-McClelland model's prediction that irregular verbs are stored in a memory system that records patterns of mapping between stems and pasts and applies them in graded fashion to similar stems. The other test failed to support the model's prediction that the patterns shown by regular verbs are stored and generalized in this way.

A natural question arises. Do the incorrect predictions of the Rumelhart-McClelland model apply to connectionist models of the acquisition of inflection in general or only to their particular implementation? Theorists arguing for connectionism as a general solution to problems in cognitive science have, virtually unanimously, provided one answer: the problems are specific to the Rumelhart-McClelland model, and are primarily technological. The Rumelhart-McClelland model, an early effort in the recent revival of neural net modeling, was a feedforward network without a hidden layer; that is, each input node was connected directly to each output node, and activation passed from input to output in a single step. Gasser and Lee (1991), MacWhinney and Leinbach (1991), McClelland (1988), and Plunkett and Marchman (1991, 1990) have claimed that most of its problems are eliminated when higher-tech connectionist machinery is substituted. The usual suggested replacement is a feedforward network with one hidden layer of nodes separating input and output (e.g., MacWhinney & Leinbach, 1991; Plunkett & Marchman, 1991), its connection weights modified by the error back-propagation learning algorithm (Rumelhart, Hinton, & Williams, 1986).

The claim that addition of a hidden layer is sufficient to remedy the Rumelhart-McClelland model's problems, especially its failed predictions about the dependence of overregularization on vocabulary balance, has never been demonstrated, however, and it is probably wrong. Egedi and Sproat (1991) have tested a parallel distributed processing (PDP) model that was trained on a sequence of English verbs similar to that fed to the Rumelhart-McClelland model, and they submitted their model to similar kinds of evaluation. The model enjoyed the advantages of a hidden layer whose weights were trained by the back-propagation algorithm, a more realistic phonological representation, and a more powerful mechanism converting the output node activations to pronounceable words. Nonetheless, the behavior of the Egedi-Sproat model was virtually identical in the relevant respects to that of the Rumelhart-McClelland model. It displayed U-shaped development in its acquisition of irregulars at a point at which it was suddenly flooded with regulars, but it showed no such trend with a constant input mixture. And it failed to produce a coherent output form for large numbers of new regular verbs on which it had been tested if those verbs differed phonologically from the common patterns in the training set.

Plunkett and Marchman (1991, 1990) claimed that their hidden-layer model, trained on a variety of schedules with artificial verbs, showed U-shaped development with a constant mixture of regular and irregular verbs as input. But they examined no psychological data and defined "U-shaped development" as any wiggle in a developmental curve rather than the extended initial period of correct performance in children that psychologists had pointed to and that we confirmed quantitatively. Even this claim was abandoned in a subsequently written paper (Plunkett & Marchman, 1990), which relied on a changing vocabulary balance as much as the Rumelhart-McClelland model did; moreover, in that paper, they switched to a third and a fourth definition of "U-shaped development" (alternation between correct and irregular tokens, and immunity of early learned irregulars from overregularization; see Chap. IV, Sec. II*A*), again leaving the original phenomenon unexplained within their framework.

It is not surprising that the mere technological improvement of adding a hidden layer does not change the psychological fidelity of models with the basic design of the Rumelhart-McClelland model. The main point of Pinker and Prince (1988) was not that connectionist models are incapable of modeling psychological phenomena but that many of the key theoretical commitments in explaining such phenomena have little to do with whether a model is implemented in one or another kind of computational hardware but involve more basic questions of representation and organization, such as, What is the format of representation for words? How many subsystems are used to map from stem to past? What kind of computation does each one do? What are its inputs and outputs? The problem with many connectionist models, they argued, was inherent, not in connectionist machinery itself, but in the attempts of connectionist theorists to bypass these issues and attempt to use a single, all-purpose learning device for all linguistic and cognitive functions. In particular, Pinker and Prince questioned Rumelhart and McClelland's commitment (also adopted by most subsequent connectionist modelers) to a system that lacked distinct representations for words, that did not distinguish between regular rules and irregular storage but computed both within a single device, and that fed only phonological (and possibly semantic) information into the past tense system, ignoring morphological and syntactic structure. Obviously, adding a hidden layer of nodes to the Rumelhart-McClelland model has nothing to do with these issues.

The modeling efforts of MacWhinney and Leinbach (1991) demonstrate this point nicely. The authors do not attempt to model children's U-shaped development; they attribute it to a dissociation between rote storage of lexical entries and pattern extraction, as in the more traditional accounts of MacWhinney (1978), Pinker (1984), and Pinker and Prince (1988), and consider the lexical entries to belong to a separate system that they do not attempt to model. But they fail to acknowledge that the commitment to traditional linguistic distinctions exemplified in their model runs even deeper. MacWhinney and Leinbach's representation for the phonological content of the stem has a separate subset of hardware nodes for each position in a word, rather than representing order implicitly in a pattern of activation across a large set of context-sensitive nodes, as in the Rumelhart-McClelland model. More important, the architecture of their model, which they arrived at after a period of trial and error, is clearly tailored to a qualitative architectural distinction between irregular storage and a stem-independent regular suffixation process. The main route of their model is a four-layer (two-hidden-layer) pattern associator with 200 nodes in each hidden layer, sufficient for memorizing the 180 irregular verbs in English (perhaps even by using some of the hidden nodes as "grandmother"cells, a direct implementation of the traditional notion of "rote memory"; see Scalettar & Zee, 1988). But they supplemented this conventional connectionist pattern associator with a distinct second route, which connected each input node directly with the output node coding the same phoneme and position, with an innate weight of 1.0 (the maximum), bypassing the intermediate layers and omitting all connections between one segment in the input and segments with different positions or different contents in the output. The bypass route is a second, innate, nonassociative copying mechanism, tailor made for regular verbs because the regular map simply copies the stem without internal modification and regardless of its content. Without calling attention to it, MacWhinney and Leinbach have designed a model with two distinct, innate pathways, one suited for irregular storage and analogy, the other for regular suffixation of the stem (for further discussion, see Prasada & Pinker, in press).

In sum, we see no evidence that adding a hidden layer to a model with the basic design of the Rumelhart-McClelland model alleviates its empirical problems, in particular, the two that we examined in this *Monograph.* At this point, the models that leave its basic design untouched inherit its problems, and another model with better overall performance abandoned the radical assumption of a single associative map and adopted the traditional tenet of separate mechanisms for lexical entries, irregular links, and a nonassociative copying process ideal for the regulars.

Although we have shown that existing connectionist models restricted to a single associative network do not account for the facts of children's level, onset, and lexical distribution of overregularization, we are not claiming that no connectionist model is capable of doing so. The set of possible connectionist models encompasses a wide variety of relative propensities for rote memory versus generalization and includes models in which the balance between these tendencies changes during a training run. These tendencies are influenced by a variety of design parameters left open to the network creator, such as the coding scheme for the input features, their degree of probabilistic blurring, the topology of the network (e.g., the number of hidden layers and the number of nodes in each one), the learning rate, the momentum factor, the temperature, the training schedule, and others. Conceivably, someone might find a combination of design parameters that allows some unitary connectionist network to display childlike rote and regularization modes of behavior at different points in a realistic training sequence.

But even if such behavioral mimicry were achieved, this hypothetical model would still have to be evaluated against the full set of data relevant to the psychology of morphology (see Pinker, 1991; Pinker & Prince, 1991), and it is unlikely that a generic model tweaked with just the right parameter settings to display past tense overregularization would be consistent with the larger picture. For example, the English plural has very different vocabulary statistics from the past tense (only a few of the high-frequency English nouns are irregular, so irregular forms cannot plausibly dominate early vocabulary), but it appears to develop with the same U-shaped sequence and low overregularization rate and submits to the same grammatical treatment in terms of lexical storage and a default regular rule (Cazden, 1968; Kim, Marcus, et al., 1991; Marcus, in preparation; Pinker & Prince, 1988). Moreover, there is a family of facts of a very different kind that independently favors a dual-mechanism (rule-rote) model over any unitary network, no matter how well it is designed to display rulelike and rotelike modes. These facts are summarized in the final section.

IV. EVIDENCE THAT CHILDREN RESPECT QUALITATIVE DISTINCTIONS BETWEEN REGULAR AND IRREGULAR PROCESSES

Linguistic research has shown that regular and irregular inflected forms differ *qualitatively,* in terms of their sensitivity to qualitative grammatical distinctions and their relation to other grammatical processes. In at least three cases, children have been shown to be sensitive to these distinctions in their patterns of regularization and overregularization.

First, Gordon (1985) noted that English compounds can contain irregular plurals (e.g., *mice-infested*) but not regular plurals (e.g., **rats-infested*). The phenomenon has been explained in terms of Kiparsky's (1982) level-ordering theory of morphology, but the kernel of the explanation can be captured simply: the process forming such compounds takes as input stems stored in the lexicon, not complex forms created by an inflectional rule; if irregulars are stored in the lexicon, as we have suggested, they automatically can feed compounding. In an elicitation experiment, Gordon found that children produced novel compounds containing irregular plurals (*mice-eater*) but never novel compounds containing regular plurals (**rats-eater*). Nor did they form compounds out of their own overregularizations—children who said *mouses* would nonetheless avoid saying **mouses-eater*.

Second, Stromswold (1990) looked at the three irregular verbs that are morphologically identical to auxiliaries: *do* (as in *do something* or *do it*), possessional *have,* and copula *be.* Each of these verbs is identical to an auxiliary not only in the stem form but in every single one of its irregularly inflected versions. *Do,* whether used as a main verb or as the auxiliary in negations, inversions, and emphatics, has the irregular forms *does* and *did.* The perfect auxiliary *have,* like possessional *have,* maps onto the irregular forms *has* and *had. Be,* whether serving as a copula verb, a progressive auxiliary, or a passive auxiliary, has the irregular forms *am, is, are, was, were,* and *been.* Moreover, the semantic relations are the same in all cases: the relation between *have a book* and *had a book* is the same as the relation between *have eaten* and *had eaten; I am tired* is to *I was tired* as *I am resting* is to *I was resting.* Clearly, there are too many of these parallelisms to be coincidental, and a parsimonious assumption is that the irregular forms of the main verb and of the auxiliary versions are stored in the same mechanism because, if they were not, at least one divergence among these 10 comparisons would be expected. But their susceptibility to overregularization is qualitatively different: in a sample of 40,000 child sentences containing these verbs, Stromswold found that the main verb versions are overregularized at rates comparable to those we have found here, whereas the auxiliary versions of the same verbs were *never* overregularized. This extreme conservatism was predicted, on the grounds of learnability considerations and other developmental data, by the theory in Pinker (1984), according to which the child's language acquisition mechanisms recognize auxiliary verbs as belonging to a distinguished set of elements because of certain semantic and phonological properties, and as a result sequester their lexical representations from regular morphological operations. In other words, children appear to be capable of treating two verb forms identically in terms of irregular inflectional patterns but qualitatively differently in terms of regular inflectional patterns.

Third, Kim, Marcus, et al. (1991) tested children's sensitivity to the constraint mentioned in Section I*C* of Chapter VIII that verbs derived from nouns and adjectives are regular, even if homophonous to an irregular verb. For example, *to high-stick* (i.e., "hit with a stick held high") has the past tense *high-sticked,* not *high-stuck.* Recall that the effect is a consequence of the fact that possessing an irregular past tense form is a property that holds of verb *roots,* not verbs in general (unless they have an irregular verb root as their head); verbs formed from nouns have a noun as their head, not an irregular verb root; hence, there is no source for an irregular form, and the default regular rule reliably applies. So in order to predict a verb's past tense form, its phonological properties do not suffice (nor do its semantic features; see Kim, Pinker, et al., 1991); its morphological structure must be input to the relevant mechanisms. The effect has been demonstrated to be extremely robust in naive adults faced with inflecting novel denominal verbs (Kim, Pinker, et al., 1991), and Kim, Marcus, et al. (1991) showed it to hold in 3–8-year-old children as well: children regularize denominal verbs homophonous with irregulars, such as *to fly* in the sense of "to cover a piece of paper with flies," more often than they overregularize the irregular verb itself, even when the irregular verb is used with nonstandard meanings and hence is equally unfamiliar.

These three phenomena suggest that it is necessary to attribute children's regularizations (including overregularizations) to a different mechanism than their irregulars, on the basis of the qualitatively different inputs and outputs the two patterns implicate: the production of irregulars but not overregularizations feeds compound formation; the production of irregulars but not overregularizations is fed by auxiliary verbs; the production of regularizations of verbs but not their irregular forms is fed by verbs derived from nouns. We have shown that exactly this kind of distinction between memory and rule mechanisms provides a simple account for a huge variety of facts about the rate, onset, and lexical properties of overregularization.

APPENDIX

TABLE A1

Adam's Rates of Overregularization and Past Tense Marking

Age	Corr Irreg (1)	Overrg Stem + *ed* (2)	Overrg Past + *ed* (3)	Overrg Rate (4)	Irreg Corr Oblig Cntexts (5)	Irreg Stems Oblig Cntexts (6)	Irreg Mark Rate (7)	Reg Corr Oblig Cntexts (8)	Reg Stems Oblig Cntexts (9)	Reg Mark Rate (10)
2-3	40	0	0	.00	15	15	.50	0	5	0
2-4	14	0	0	.00	4	11	.27	4	24	.14
2-5	51	0	0	.00	38	12	.76	1	27	.04
2-6	90	0	0	.00	54	8	.87	1	16	.06
2-7	58	0	0	.00	60	11	.85	0	11	0
2-8	61	0	0	.00	44	16	.73	4	13	.24
2-9	31	0	0	.00	26	21	.55	0	12	0
2-10	36	0	0	.00	31	3	.91	0	5	0
2-11	39	2	0	.05	31	6	.84	9	11	.45
3-0	74	0	0	.00	47	18	.72	16	11	.59
3-1	115	0	0	.00	64	2	.97	8	0	1.00
3-2	103	0	0	.00	51	10	.84	5	7	.42
3-3	181	0	0	.00	108	10	.92	51	10	.84
3-4	132	3	0	.02	80	6	.93	15	7	.68
3-5	124	3	0	.02	95	1	.99	14	2	.88
3-6	108	1	0	.01	60	0	1.00	14	0	1.00
3-7	93	1	1	.02						
3-8	133	2	0	.01						
3-9	85	3	0	.03						
3-10	31	1	0	.03						
3-11	76	1	0	.01						
4-0	57	0	0	.00						
4-1	43	1	0	.02						
4-2	59	1	0	.02						
4-3	42	1	0	.02						
4-4	79	4	0	.05						
4-5	47	1	0	.02						
4-7	151	10	1	.07						
4-8	40	2	0	.05						
4-9	55	3	0	.05						
4-10	68	1	2	.04						
4-11	79	0	0	.00						
5-2	51	3	0	.06						

NOTE.—The columns correspond to (1) number of correct irregular past tense tokens; (2) number of stem + *ed* (e.g., *breaked*) overregularization tokens; (3) number of past + *ed* (e.g., *broked*) overregularization tokens; (4) rate of overregularization (proportion of irregular past tense form tokens that are overregularizations); (5) number of correct irregular past tense forms in obligatory past tense contexts; (6) number of stem forms of irregular verbs in obligatory past tense contexts; (7) irregular past marking rate (proportion of obligatory past tense contexts, not including overregularizations, where an irregular verb was supplied in the past tense); (8) number of correct regular past tense forms in obligatory past tense contexts; (9) number of stem forms of regular verbs in obligatory past tense contexts; and (10) regular past marking rate (proportion of obligatory past tense contexts where a regular verb was supplied in the past tense). The last six columns are based on unpublished data provided by Courtney Cazden, described in Cazden (1966, 1968) and Brown (1973).

TABLE A2

Eve's Rates of Overregularization and Past Tense Marking

Age	Corr Irreg (1)	Overrg Stem +*ed* (2)	Overrg Past +*ed* (3)	Overrg Rate (4)	Irreg Corr Oblig Cntexts (5)	Irreg Stems Oblig Cntexts (6)	Irreg Mark Rate (7)	Reg Corr Oblig Cntexts (8)	Reg Stems Oblig Cntexts (9)	Reg Mark Rate (10)
1-6	2	0	0	0	1	5	.17	2	2	.50
1-7	5	0	0	0	1	4	.20	0	15	.00
1-8	13	1	1	.13	13	1	.93	2	8	.20
1-9	52	0	0	.00	15	13	.54	4	12	.25
1-10	24	3	0	.11	15	12	.56	7	5	.58
1-11	34	2	0	.06	25	18	.58	6	5	.55
2-0	25	0	0	.00	12	19	.39	12	6	.67
2-1	30	9	0	.23	20	24	.45	25	2	.93
2-2	60	7	0	.10	51	7	.88	20	1	.95
2-3	40	1	0	.02	10	4	.71	2	1	.67

Note.—For descriptions of columns and data, see the note to Table A1.

TABLE A3

Sarah's Rates of Overregularization and Past Tense Marking

Age	Corr Irreg (1)	Overrg Stem +*ed* (2)	Overrg Past +*ed* (3)	Overrg Rate (4)	Irreg Corr Oblig Cntexts (5)	Irreg Stems Oblig Cntexts (6)	Irreg Mark Rate (7)	Reg Corr Oblig Cntexts (8)	Reg Stems Oblig Cntexts (9)	Reg Mark Rate (10)
2-3	8	0	0	0	1.5	0	1	0	.5	0
2-4	19	0	0	0	4.5	8	.36	0	2	0
2-5	21	0	0	0	8.5	3	.74	1	0	1.00
2-6	26	0	0	0	16	14	.53	2	1.5	.57
2-7	57	0	0	0	20.5	13	.61	0	4.5	0
2-8	20	0	0	0	10	2	.83	0	.5	0
2-9	80	0	0	0	24	6	.80	9	6	.60
2-10	25	1	0	.04	7	3	.70	10	4	.71
2-11	27	0	0	0	10	3.5	.74	1.5	.5	.75
3-0	46	0	0	0	12	5.5	.69	3.5	1	.78
3-1	34	0	0	0	35	0	1	4	2.5	.62
3-2	52	0	0	0	24	2	.92	3.5	2	.64
3-3	39	1	0	.02	24.5	2	.92	2.5	2	.56
3-4	20	0	0	0	19.5	1	.95	1	1	.5
3-5	44	1	0	.02	17	6	.74	3	0	1.00
3-6	35	1	0	.03	16.5	4.5	.79	2.5	1	.71
3-7	61	0	0	0	34	4	.89	5.5	.5	.92
3-8	63	1	0	.02	38.5	4.5	.90	8	2.5	.76
3-9	27	0	0	0	23.5	0	1	2.5	0	1.00
3-10	64	3	0	.04	45.5	1	.98	21.5	1	.96
3-11	67	2	0	.03	42.5	5.5	.89	6	0	1.00
4-0	30	0	1	.03	21.5	4.5	.83	4	1	.80
4-1	67	1	0	.01	45	1	.98	13	1	.93
4-2	122	9	1	.08	50	4	.93	22	0	1.00
4-3	41	1	0	.02						
4-4	76	1	0	.01						
4-5	54	2	0	.04						
4-6	70	0	0	0						
4-7	71	5	1	.08						
4-8	64	12	0	.16						
4-9	59	7	1	.12						
4-10	56	4	0	.07						
4-11	78	4	0	.05						
5-0	58	2	0	.03						
5-1	36	3	0	.08						

Note.—For descriptions of columns and data, see the note to Table A1.

TABLE A4

ABE'S RATES OF OVERREGULARIZATION AND PAST TENSE MARKING

Age	Corr Irreg (1)	Overrg Stem + *ed* (2)	Overrg Past + *ed* (3)	Overrg Rate (4)	Irreg Mark Rate (5)	Reg Mark Rate (6)
2-5	9	2	2	.31	.31	.76
2-6	24	1	0	.04	.58	.63
2-7	27	16	2	.40	.69	.87
2-8	52	12	1	.20	.81	.80
2-9	102	36	6	.29	1	.98
2-10	44	34	6	.48	1	1
2-11	76	31	11	.36	.96	1
3-0	24	16	2	.43	1	1
3-1	64	19	11	.32	.99	1
3-2	82	8	5	.14	.99	1
3-3	91	36	9	.33	.97	1
3-4	107	38	4	.28	1	1
3-5	89	31	1	.26	1	1
3-6	74	12	1	.15	1	1
3-7	58	4	0	.06	1	1
3-8	88	16	2	.17	1	1
3-9	80	22	2	.23	1	1
3-10	69	14	2	.19	1	1
3-11	75	21	3	.24	1	1
4-0	13	2	6	.38	1	1
4-1	67	19	7	.28	1	1
4-2	42	7	4	.21	1	1
4-3	39	14	10	.38	1	1
4-4	16	10	0	.38	1	1
4-5	29	3	0	.09	1	1
4-6	68	3	0	.04	1	1
4-7	59	3	1	.06	1	1
4-8	38	0	0	0	1	1
4-9	26	0	0	0	1	1
4-10	62	16	0	.21	1	1
4-11	47	6	1	.13	1	1
5-0	45	13	0	.22	1	1

NOTE.—The columns correspond to (1) number of correct irregular past tense tokens; (2) number of stem + *ed* (e.g., *breaked*) overregularization tokens; (3) number of past + *ed* (e.g., *broked*) overregularization tokens; (4) rate of overregularization (proportion of irregular past tense form tokens that are overregularizations); (5) irregular past marking rate (correct irregular pasts as a proportion of the sum of correct irregular pasts and stem forms in obligatory past tense contexts); and (6) regular past marking rate (correct regular pasts as a proportion of the sum of correct regular pasts and stem forms in obligatory contexts). The last two columns are taken from the appendices to Kuczaj (1976; see also Kuczaj, 1977a).

TABLE A5

Adam's Irregular Verbs

Verb	Correct	Stem +*ed*	Past +*ed*	Overreg Rate	Verb	Correct	Stem +*ed*	Past +*ed*	Overreg Rate
be	137	0	0	0	*light*	0	0	0	. . .
beat	1	2	0	.67	*lose*	50	0	0	0
bend	1	0	0	0	*make*	141	7	0	.05
bite	12	0	0	0	*mean*	0	0	0	. . .
bleed	0	0	0	. . .	*meet*	1	0	0	0
blow	0	1	0	1	*put*	69	0	0	0
break	97	0	0	0	*read*[a]				
bring	17	0	0	0	*rend*	0	0	0	. . .
build	0	0	0	. . .	*ride*	5	0	0	0
buy	10	0	0	0	*ring*	0	0	0	. . .
catch	73	2	0	.03	*rise*	0	0	0	. . .
choose	0	0	0	. . .	*run*	9	0	1	.10
come	51	1	0	.01	*say*	129	0	0	0
cut	11	1	0	.08	*see*	104	0	0	0
dig	0	0	0	. . .	*send*	0	0	0	. . .
do	93	1	0	.01	*shake*	0	0	0	. . .
draw	1	4	0	.80	*shoot*	35	0	0	0
drink	0	0	0	. . .	*shrink*	0	0	0	. . .
drive	1	1	0	.50	*shut*	0	0	0	. . .
eat	21	0	0	0	*sing*	0	0	0	. . .
fall	182	2	0	.02	*sit*	1	0	0	0
feed	0	0	0	. . .	*sleep*	0	1	0	1
feel	0	3	0	1	*slide*	0	0	0	. . .
fight	0	0	0	. . .	*spend*	0	0	0	. . .
find	60	0	0	0	*spin*	0	0	0	. . .
fly	1	0	0	0	*spit*	0	0	0	. . .
forget	27	0	0	0	*stand*	0	1	0	1
freeze	0	0	0	. . .	*steal*	4	0	2	.33
get	586	0	0	0	*stick*	2	4	0	.67
give	19	0	0	0	*strike*	0	0	0	. . .
go	125	0	0	0	*string*	0	0	0	. . .
grind	0	0	0	. . .	*sweep*	0	0	0	. . .
grow	1	2	0	.67	*swim*	0	0	0	. . .
hang	0	0	0	. . .	*swing*	0	0	0	. . .
have	56	0	0	0	*take*	62	1	1	.03
hear	53	0	0	0	*teach*	0	1	0	1
hide	0	0	0	. . .	*tear*	1	0	0	0
hit	35	0	0	0	*tell*	59	0	0	0
hold	0	1	0	1	*think*	33	0	0	0
hurt	28	0	0	0	*throw*	3	3	0	.50
keep	0	0	0	. . .	*wake*	1	1	0	.50
know	1	0	0	0	*wear*	0	0	0	. . .
leave	15	0	0	0	*win*	0	4	0	1
lend	0	0	0	. . .	*wind*	0	0	0	. . .
let	3	0	0	0	*write*	17	0	0	0
lie	0	0	0	. . .					

[a] Analyzed only for Abe.

TABLE A6

Eve's Irregular Verbs

Verb	Correct	Stem + *ed*	Past + *ed*	Overreg Rate
be	22	0	0	0
beat	0	0	0	. . .
bend	0	0	0	. . .
bite	7	0	0	0
bleed	0	0	0	. . .
blow	0	0	0	. . .
break	15	0	0	0
bring	2	0	0	0
build	0	0	0	. . .
buy	3	0	0	0
catch	6	0	0	0
choose	0	0	0	. . .
come	23	4	0	.15
cut	0	0	0	. . .
dig	0	0	0	. . .
do	7	2	0	.22
draw	0	0	0	. . .
drink	0	1	0	1
drive	0	0	0	. . .
eat	0	0	0	. . .
fall	2	8	0	.80
feed	0	0	0	. . .
feel	0	0	0	. . .
fight	0	0	0	. . .
find	1	0	0	0
fly	0	0	0	. . .
forget	18	0	0	0
freeze	0	0	0	. . .
get	55	0	0	0
give	3	0	0	0
go	20	5	0	.20
grind	0	0	0	. . .
grow	0	0	0	. . .
hang	0	0	0	. . .
have	20	0	0	0
hear	0	0	0	. . .
hide	0	0	0	. . .
hit	1	0	0	0
hold	0	0	0	. . .
hurt	5	0	0	0
keep	0	0	0	. . .
know	0	0	0	. . .
leave	1	0	0	0
lend	0	0	0	. . .
let	0	0	0	. . .
lie	0	0	0	. . .
light	0	0	0	. . .
lose	3	0	0	0
make	7	0	0	0
mean	0	0	0	. . .
meet	0	0	0	. . .
put	38	0	0	0
read[a]				
rend	0	0	0	. . .
ride	0	0	0	. . .
ring	0	0	0	. . .
rise	0	0	0	. . .
run	0	0	0	. . .
say	10	0	0	0
see	3	1	0	.25
send	1	0	0	0
shake	0	0	0	. . .
shoot	0	0	0	. . .
shrink	0	0	0	. . .
shut	1	0	0	0
sing	0	0	0	. . .
sit	4	0	0	0
sleep	0	0	0	. . .
slide	0	0	0	. . .
spend	0	0	0	. . .
spin	0	0	0	. . .
spit	0	0	0	. . .
stand	0	0	0	. . .
steal	0	0	0	. . .
stick	1	0	0	0
strike	0	0	0	. . .
string	0	0	0	. . .
sweep	0	0	0	. . .
swim	0	0	0	. . .
swing	0	0	0	. . .
take	0	0	0	. . .
teach	0	0	0	. . .
tear	0	0	1	1
tell	2	0	0	0
think	1	0	0	0
throw	0	1	0	1
wake	0	0	0	. . .
wear	0	1	0	1
win	0	0	0	. . .
wind	0	0	0	. . .
write	1	0	0	0

[a] Analyzed only for Abe.

TABLE A7

Sarah's Irregular Verbs

Verb	Correct	Stem +*ed*	Past +*ed*	Overreg Rate	Verb	Correct	Stem +*ed*	Past +*ed*	Overreg Rate
be	182	0	0	0	*light*	2	0	0	0
beat	0	0	0	. . .	*lose*	19	1	0	.05
bend	0	1	0	1	*make*	52	8	0	.13
bite	11	0	0	0	*mean*	1	0	0	0
bleed	0	0	0	. . .	*meet*	2	0	0	0
blow	1	0	0	0	*put*	55	1	0	.02
break	96	0	0	0	*read*[a]				
bring	9	0	0	0	*rend*	0	0	0	. . .
build	0	0	0	. . .	*ride*	0	0	0	. . .
buy	18	3	0	.14	*ring*	0	0	0	. . .
catch	31	1	1	.06	*rise*	0	0	0	. . .
choose	0	0	0	. . .	*run*	4	2	0	.33
come	15	3	1	.21	*say*	101	0	0	0
cut	6	0	0	0	*see*	59	0	0	0
dig	0	0	0	. . .	*send*	0	0	0	. . .
do	127	0	0	0	*shake*	2	0	0	0
draw	0	0	0	. . .	*shoot*	0	0	0	. . .
drink	4	0	0	0	*shrink*	1	0	0	0
drive	0	0	0	. . .	*shut*	3	0	0	0
eat	14	0	0	0	*sing*	1	0	0	0
fall	10	1	0	.09	*sit*	0	1	0	1
feed	0	0	0	. . .	*sleep*	2	0	0	0
feel	0	0	0	. . .	*slide*	0	3	0	1
fight	0	2	0	1	*spend*	0	0	0	. . .
find	27	0	0	0	*spin*	2	0	0	0
fly	2	1	2	.6	*spit*	0	0	0	. . .
forget	30	0	0	0	*stand*	0	0	0	. . .
freeze	1	0	0	0	*steal*	0	2	0	1
get	434	0	0	0	*stick*	1	0	0	0
give	33	0	0	0	*strike*	3	0	0	0
go	66	6	0	.08	*string*	0	0	0	. . .
grind	0	0	0	. . .	*sweep*	0	0	0	. . .
grow	1	1	0	.50	*swim*	0	1	0	1
hang	0	1	0	1	*swing*	0	0	0	. . .
have	137	0	0	0	*take*	35	2	0	.05
hear	10	5	0	.29	*teach*	5	0	0	0
hide	2	1	0	.33	*tear*	0	0	0	. . .
hit	27	0	0	0	*tell*	25	1	0	.04
hold	0	0	0	. . .	*think*	10	0	0	0
hurt	9	1	0	.10	*throw*	3	7	0	.70
keep	1	0	0	0	*wake*	3	2	0	.40
know	5	0	0	0	*wear*	1	0	0	0
leave	8	0	0	0	*win*	4	3	0	.43
lend	1	0	0	0	*wind*	1	0	0	0
let	1	0	0	0	*write*	1	0	0	0
lie	0	0	0	. . .					

[a] Analyzed only for Abe.

TABLE A8

Abe's Irregular Verbs

Verb	Correct	Stem + *ed*	Past + *ed*	Overreg Rate
be[a]				
beat	0	0	0	. . .
bend	1	1	0	.50
bite	3	4	0	.57
bleed	0	0	0	. . .
blow	4	9	0	.69
break	38	4	12	.30
bring	2	5	1	.75
build	1	8	0	.89
buy	7	5	0	.42
catch	22	5	1	.21
choose	1	1	0	.50
come	20	52	4	.74
cut	15	12	0	.44
dig	2	3	0	.60
do[a]				
draw	1	6	0	.86
drink	5	5	0	.50
drive	0	2	0	1
eat	82	18	2	.20
fall	72	54	3	.44
feed	0	1	0	1
feel	5	11	0	.69
fight	1	2	0	.67
find	143	1	2	.02
fly	5	4	0	.44
forget	67	0	0	0
freeze	1	0	0	0
get	194	4	50	.22
give	5	2	0	.29
go	117	60	4	.35
grind	0	0	0	. . .
grow	2	6	0	.75
hang	0	4	0	1
have[a]				
hear	13	27	0	.68
hide	2	0	0	0
hit	16	8	0	.33
hold	0	4	0	1
hurt	16	2	0	.11
keep	1	0	0	0
know	11	6	0	.35
leave	13	2	0	.13
lend	0	0	0	. . .
let	0	0	0	. . .
lie	0	0	0	. . .

Verb	Correct	Stem + *ed*	Past + *ed*	Overreg Rate
light	0	0	0	. . .
lose	8	1	0	.11
make	150	24	3	.15
mean	3	1	0	.25
meet	0	0	0	. . .
put	77	11	0	.12
read	1	1	0	.50
rend	0	0	0	. . .
ride	2	1	0	.33
ring	0	0	0	. . .
rise	0	0	0	. . .
run	4	6	0	.60
say	282	3	0	.01
see	166	4	3	.04
send	8	1	0	.11
shake	2	0	0	0
shoot	10	2	1	.23
shrink	0	0	0	. . .
shut	0	0	0	. . .
sing	2	1	0	.33
sit	1	1	0	.50
sleep	1	2	0	.67
slide	0	0	0	. . .
spend	0	1	0	1
spin	0	0	0	. . .
spit	0	2	1	1
stand	1	2	0	.67
steal	3	0	0	0
stick	1	1	0	.50
strike	0	0	0	. . .
string	0	1	0	1
sweep	0	2	0	1
swim	0	2	0	1
swing	0	3	0	1
take	21	6	3	.30
teach	3	0	0	0
tear	0	0	0	. . .
tell	52	7	0	.12
think	75	9	9	.19
throw	5	12	0	.71
wake	3	1	0	.25
wear	0	3	0	1
win	16	9	0	.36
wind	0	0	0	. . .
write	1	7	0	.88

[a] Analyzed only for Adam, Eve, and Sarah.

TABLE A9

Other Children's Overregularization Rates

Verb	ANC	Allsn	April	BOM	BRD	CHJ	DED	GAT	JOB	JUB	KIF	MAA	MIM	Naomi	Nat	Nthnl	Peter	TOS	TRH	VOH	ZOR
be[a]																					
beat[a]																					
bend	...	...	...	...	...	...	...	0	...	...	...	...	0	.33	...	...	...	...	...	...	...
bite	...	1	0	0	0	0	0	0	0	.12	0	0	0	0	...	0	0	0	0	...	...
bleed	...	...	...	...	...	...	...	...	...	...	...	...	...	...	...	...	...	...	...	...	...
blow	0	...	...	...	0	...	0	0	...	...	...	...	0	...	...	0	0	...	...	...	...
break	0	0	0	0	0	0	0	0	0	...	...	0	...	0	0	.29	.075	...	0	0	0
bring	...	...	...	...	...	...	0	0	0	...	...	0	0	0	0	...	0	...	...	...	...
build	0	...	...	...	...	0	...	...	...	...	...	...	...	...	...	...	...	...	...	...	...
buy	...	...	1	...	...	0	0	0	0	0	0	...	0	0	0	0	0	0	...	...	0
catch	...	...	...	1	0	.67	0	0	...	...	...	1	...	0	0	.25	0	0	...	...	...
choose	...	...	...	...	...	...	...	...	...	...	...	...	...	...	...	...	...	...	...	...	...
come	0	0	.67	0	0	0	1	0	0	0	...	0	0	0	0	0	0	0	0	0	0
cut[a]																					
dig	...	...	...	...	...	...	...	...	...	...	...	...	...	...	...	...	...	...	...	...	...
do[a]																					
draw	1	...	...	0	...	...	...	1	...	...	...	0	...	1	0	...	0	...	1	...	...
drink	...	...	...	0	...	...	...	...	0	...	...	...	...	0	...	1	1	0	...	...	...
drive	...	...	1	...	...	...	...	...	...	...	...	...	...	...	...	0	0	...	...	...	...
eat	0	0	0	0	0	0	0	0	0	0	0	...	...	0	...	.25	0	0	0	0	0
fall	1	0	.43	0	0	0	...	0	0	...	0	0	...	.04	0	0	.10	0	1	...	...
feed	...	...	...	...	...	...	...	...	...	...	...	...	...	...	...	...	...	...	0	...	...
feel	...	...	...	0	...	0	...	0	...	...	...	...	...	...	...	...	...	0	...	...	...
fight	...	...	...	...	...	...	...	...	...	...	...	...	...	...	...	...	...	...	.5	...	...
find	0	...	0	0	0	0	0	0	0	0	0	0	...	.2	...	0	0	...	...	...	0
fly	...	...	...	...	...	0	...	1	...	...	...	0	...	.75	...	...	...	...	0	...	...
forget	0	...	0	0	0	0	0	0	0	...	0	...	0	0	...	0	0	0	...	...	0
freeze	...	...	...	...	...	...	...	...	...	...	...	...	...	...	...	...	...	...	0	...	...
get	0	0	0	0	0	0	0	0	0	0	0	0	0	.01	0	0	0	0	...	0	0
give	...	0	0	0	...	0	0	0	0	0	0	0	0	0	0	0	.12	0	0	...	0
go	0	0	0	...	...	...	...	0	0	0	...	0	...	.05	0	.15	.07	0	...	0	0
grind	...	...	...	0	0	...	...	0	0	0	...	...	...	...	...	...	...	...	...	...	0
grow	...	...	...	...	.67	...	...	...	...	0	...	0	...	...	...	...	...	...	...	1	...
hang	...	...	...	...	...	...	...	...	...	...	...	...	...	...	...	...	...	...	...	...	...

have[a]																					
hear	0	...	...	0	0	0	0	0	0	0	0	0	0	0	...	...	0	0	...	0	...
hide	...	...	...	...	...	...	...	...	...	...	...	...	...	...	...	...	...	...	0	...	...
hit[a]																					
hold	...	...	...	0	...	...	...	0	...	...	...	...	...	1	...	...	...	...	...	...	...
hurt[a]																					
keep	...	...	...	...	...	...	0	1	...	...	...	...	...	...	...	...	...	...	...	...	...
know	0	...	...	0	...	...	0	...	...	0	...	...	0	0	...	...	...	...	0	...	...
leave	...	0	...	0	0	0	0	0	...	...	...	...	0	...	...	0	0	0	...	...	0
lend	...	...	...	...	...	...	...	...	...	...	...	...	...	...	...	...	...	...	0	...	...
let[a]																					
lie	...	...	...	...	0	0	...	0	...	...	...	...	...	...	...	...	...	...	...	...	...
light	...	...	...	...	...	...	...	...	...	...	...	...	...	...	...	...	...	...	...	...	...
lose	...	0	...	0	0	...	...	0	0	...	...	0	0	0	0	0	0	0	...	...	0
make	...	0	0	0	0	0	0	.1	0	0	0	0	0	.17	...	0	0	0	0	...	0
mean	0	...	...	...	...	0	...	...	0	...	...	...	...	...	...	...	...	...	0	...	...
meet	...	...	...	...	...	...	...	...	...	0	0	...	...	...	...	...	...	...	...	...	...
put[a]																					
read[a]																					
rend	...	...	...	...	...	...	0	...	...	...	...	...	...	...	...	...	...	...	...	...	...
ride	...	...	...	...	...	...	...	0	...	1	...	...	...	1	...	0	0	...	...	...	...
ring	...	...	...	...	...	...	...	1	...	...	...	...	...	...	...	...	...	...	...	...	...
rise	...	...	...	...	...	...	...	...	...	0	...	...	...	...	...	...	...	...	...	...	...
run	...	...	...	...	...	.4	.5	...	...	0	...	...	...	0	...	0	...	...	...	0	0
say	0	0	0	0	...	0	0	0	0	0	0	0	...	0	...	0	0	0	...	0	0
see	0	...	0	0	...	0	0	0	0	0	0	0	...	.29	0	0	0	0	...	0	...
send	...	...	...	0	...	...	1	...	0	0	...	...	...	...	...	...	...	...	...	...	...
shake	...	...	...	...	...	...	...	1	...	...	...	...	...	...	...	...	...	...	...	...	...
shoot	...	...	...	...	...	...	...	0	...	1	0	...	...	0	...	...	...	...	...	...	0
shrink	...	...	...	...	...	...	...	0	...	...	...	...	...	...	...	...	...	...	...	...	...
shut[a]																					
sing	...	...	...	...	...	...	...	...	...	...	...	...	...	0	...	...	...	...	...	...	...
sit	...	...	...	...	...	...	...	...	...	...	0	...	...	0	...	0	0	...	...	...	...
sleep	...	...	...	...	...	...	...	...	...	...	...	...	...	...	...	0	...	...	...	...	...
slide	...	...	...	...	...	...	...	...	...	...	...	...	...	...	...	...	...	...	...	...	...
spend	...	...	...	...	...	...	...	...	...	...	...	...	...	...	...	...	...	...	...	...	...
spin	...	...	...	...	...	...	...	...	...	...	...	...	...	...	...	...	...	...	...	...	...
spit	...	...	...	...	...	...	...	...	...	...	...	...	...	...	...	...	...	...	...	...	...
stand	...	...	...	...	...	...	...	...	...	...	...	...	...	0	...	...	...	...	...	...	...
steal	...	...	...	...	...	...	...	...	...	1	...	...	...	...	...	1	...	0	...	...	...

TABLE A9 (*Continued*)

Verb	ANC	Allsn	April	BOM	BRD	CHJ	DED	GAT	JOB	JUB	KIF	MAA	MIM	Naomi	Nat	Nthnl	Peter	TOS	TRH	VOH	ZOR
stick	0	0	...	...	...	...	...	...	...	...	...	.25	...	.08	...	0	0	0	...	...	0
strike	...	...	...	...	...	...	...	...	0	...	...	...	...	...	...	...	...	...	...	...	...
string	...	...	...	...	...	...	...	...	...	...	...	...	...	...	...	...	...	...	...	...	...
sweep	...	...	...	...	...	...	...	...	...	...	...	...	...	0	...	...	...	...	...	...	...
swim	...	...	0	...	...	...	...	...	...	...	...	...	...	0	...	...	...	...	...	...	...
swing	...	...	...	...	...	...	...	...	...	...	...	...	...	...	...	...	...	...	...	...	...
take	...	...	0	...	...	...	...	...	0	0	...	...	...	0	0	0	.13	0	...	0	0
teach	...	...	...	...	...	...	...	0	...	...	...	...	...	...	...	...	0	...	...	0	...
tear	...	...	...	...	...	...	...	...	...	...	...	...	...	...	...	...	...	...	...	...	...
tell	0	...	...	...	...	...	...	...	0	0	...	0	...	0	...	0	.33	0	...	0	0
think	0	...	...	...	...	...	...	0	...	0	...	0	...	0	...	...	0	0	...	0	0
throw	...	1	...	...	...	...	...	0	...	0	...	0	...	.44	...	.50	0	...	...	...	...
wake	...	...	...	...	...	...	...	...	...	...	...	0	...	0	...	...	.60	...	...	...	...
wear	...	...	...	...	...	...	...	...	...	...	...	...	...	...	...	...	...	...	...	...	...
win	...	...	...	...	...	...	...	...	0	...	...	...	...	...	0	...	0	...	...	0	0
wind	...	...	...	...	...	...	...	0	...	...	...	...	...	...	...	...	...	...	...	...	...
write	...	...	...	...	...	...	...	...	0	1	...	...	...	1	...	...	0	...	...	...	0

[a] Analyzed only for Adam, Eve, Sarah, and/or Abe.

TABLE A10

Aggregate Measures of Verbs' Overregularization Rates and Frequencies in Parental Speech

Verb	Mean Standardized Overregularization Rate (*z* score)	Mean *z* Converted Back to Overregularization Rate	Log Mean Parental Frequency	Verb	Mean Standardized Overregularization Rate (*z* score)	Mean *z* Converted Back to Overregularization Rate	Log Mean Parental Frequency
be	−.48	.03	5.81	*light*	. . .	. . .	0
beat	. . .	. . .	.70	*lose*	−.40	.04	2.39
bend	. . .	. . .	.34	*make*	.30	.16	3.26
bite	−.55	.01	3.10	*mean*	. . .	. . .	1.45
bleed	. . .	. . .	. . .	*meet*	. . .	. . .	1.39
blow	1.66	.40	1.20	*put*	−.55	.01	6.27
break	.20	.14	2.32	*read*	. . .	. . .	4.08
bring	−.43	.03	2.11	*rend*	. . .	. . .	. . .
build	. . .	. . .	.29	*ride*	. . .	. . .	.45
buy	.16	.14	2.19	*ring*	. . .	. . .	. . .
catch	.04	.12	1.58	*rise*	. . .	. . .	0
choose	. . .	. . .	. . .	*run*	2.51	.54	2.08
come	.35	.17	2.88	*say*	−.31	.06	3.95
cut	1.81	.42	4.09	*see*	−.56	.01	3.11
dig	. . .	. . .	. . .	*send*	. . .	. . .	.92
do	−.25	.07	6.39	*shake*	. . .	. . .	.92
draw	. . .	. . .	.75	*shoot*	−.42	.04	1.28
drink	.80	.25	1.10	*shrink*	. . .	. . .	. . .
drive	. . .	. . .	1.34	*shut*	. . .	. . .	3.02
eat	−.50	.02	2.24	*sing*	. . .	. . .	.51
fall	.70	.23	2.65	*sit*	. . .	. . .	1.58
feed	. . .	. . .	0	*sleep*	. . .	. . .	.92
feel	1.64	.39	.61	*slide*	. . .	. . .	0
fight	. . .	. . .	1.25	*spend*	. . .	. . .	1.10
find	−.20	.07	2.25	*spin*	. . .	. . .	. . .
fly	. . .	. . .	.62	*spit*	. . .	. . .	. . .
forget	−.60	.01	2.30	*stand*	. . .	. . .	−1.10
freeze	. . .	. . .	0	*steal*	. . .	. . .	.59
get	−.19	.08	4.80	*stick*	−.06	.10	2.32
give	−.47	.03	2.70	*strike*	. . .	. . .	. . .
go	.27	.16	3.69	*string*	. . .	. . .	. . .
grind	. . .	. . .	. . .	*sweep*	. . .	. . .	−.69
grow	. . .	. . .	0	*swim*	. . .	. . .	−1.39
hang	. . .	. . .	1.39	*swing*	. . .	. . .	. . .
have	−.48	.03	5.10	*take*	.30	.16	3.08
hear	.66	.22	2.15	*teach*	. . .	. . .	1.16
hide	. . .	. . .	.69	*tear*	. . .	. . .	.92
hit	−.30	.06	3.93	*tell*	−.58	.01	2.97
hold	. . .	. . .	.59	*think*	−.51	.02	3.60
hurt	−.40	.04	4.07	*throw*	3.06	.64	1.44
keep	. . .	. . .	1.22	*wake*	. . .	. . .	1.10
know	.14	.13	2.14	*wear*	. . .	. . .	.85
leave	−.63	.00	2.75	*win*	.17	.14	1.64
lend	. . .	. . .	. . .	*wind*	. . .	. . .	0
let	. . .	. . .	5.19	*write*	−.43	.03	1.23
lie	. . .	. . .	.98				

TABLE A11

Regular Verbs Available to Children

A. Regular Verbs Used at Least Once by Adam, Eve, Sarah, or the Adults Conversing with Them

ache, act, add, aim, allow, answer, ask, attach, back, bake, balance, bang, bark, bash, believe, belong, blast, bless, blind, blink, bob, boil, bomb, bop, borrow, bother, bounce, bow, bowl, box, breathe, brush, bubble, bump, burn, burp, bury, bust, call, camp, care, carry, carve, chain, change, chase, cheat, check, chew, chirp, choke, chop, clap, claw, clean, climb, clip, close, color, comb, cook, cool, copy, cough, count, cover, crack, crash, crawl, criss-cross, cross, crush, cry, curl, dance, dare, dash, decorate, dial, die, dip, dirty, disappear, disturb, dodge, drag, dress, dribble, drill, drip, drool, drop, drown, dry, dump, dust, empty, end, erase, excuse, exercise, faint, fan, fasten, fetch, file, fill, finish, fish, fix, fizz, flash, flip, float, fold, follow, fool, frighten, fry, glue, grab, growl, guess, guide, hammer, hand, handle, happen, hatch, hate, heat, help, holler, hook, hop, hope, howl, hug, hunt, hurry, hush, invite, iron, itch, jabber, joke, juggle, jump, kick, kid, kill, kiss, knock, land, last, laugh, leak, lean, learn, lick, lift, like, listen, live, load, lock, look, love, mail, manage, march, marry, mash, match, matter, measure, melt, meow, mess, mind, miss, mix, mock, move, murder, name, nap, need, obey, open, organize, own, pack, paint, pardon, park, pass, paste, pat, pay, pee, pee-pee, peek, peel, peep, perch, pick, pin, pinch, place, plant, play, plug, point, poke, polish, pop, pour, pout, practice, pray, prepare, press, pretend, print, promise, pull, pump, punch, punish, push, race, rain, raise, rake, reach, reattach, recognize, remember, remind, repair, rest, rinse, rip, rock, roll, rope, row, rub, ruin, rustle, sail, salute, save, scare, scoop, scoot, score, scratch, scream, screw, scribble, seem, serve, sew, share, sharp, sharpen, shave, shop, shout, shove, shovel, show, shrug, sigh, sip, skate, ski, skip, slap, slip, smack, smart, smash, smell, smile, smoke, smooth, snap, sneeze, sniff, snow, snuggle, soak, sound, spank, spell, spill, splash, spoil, spray, squash, squeak, squeal, squeeze, squirt, squish, squoosh, stab, stamp, staple, stare, start, starve, stay, steam, steer, step, stir, stop, straighten, stretch, study, suck, surprise, swallow, sway, swish, switch, talk, tangle, tape, taste, tease, thank, thread, tick, tickle, tie, tighten, tip, touch, trap, trick, trim, trip, trust, try, tuck, turn, twist, type, unbuckle, unbutton, unchain, unplug, unscrew, untangle, untie, urinate, use, visit, wag, wait, walk, want, wash, watch, wave, wee-wee, weigh, wet, whirl, whisper, whistle, wiggle, wink, wipe, wish, wobble, wonder, work, worry, wrap, wreck, yawn, yell, zip, zoom

B. Regular Verbs Used by Adam in the Transcripts Preceding His First Overregularization

ask, attach, bake, belong, bless, bow, burn, call, care, carry, change, check, chew, climb, close, cook, copy, count, crack, crawl, cross, cry, dance, drip, drop, dry, dump, excuse, exercise, fasten, finish, fish, fix, fold, frighten, growl, hand, happen, help, hop, hug, hurry, jabber, jump, kick, kiss, knock, laugh, like, listen, live, look, love, march, mess, miss, mix, move, need, open, pack, paint, park, pay, peek, pick, pinch, play, plug, point, pour, press, pretend, pull, push, rain, reach, remember, rock, roll, rope, save, screw, shine, shop, show, skip, slip, smoke, snow, spank, spill, squeal, squeak, squeeze, stay, step, stir, stop, talk, taste, thank, tickle, tie, touch, try, turn, use, wait, walk, want, wash, watch, whisper, wipe, wonder, work

C. Regular Verbs Used by Eve in the Transcripts Preceding Her First Overregularization

answer, bang, change, climb, crack, cry, dance, drop, empty, fix, happen, help, jump, kick, lick, like, look, move, open, pardon, pick, play, show, spill, step, taste, thank, touch, turn, use, wait, want, watch, wipe

D. Regular Verbs Used by Sarah in the Transcripts Preceding Her First Overregularization

bounce, bump, call, clean, close, comb, count, cover, cross, cry, dance, die, dress, dump, fix, happen, help, hug, jump, knock, laugh, lift, like, look, love, need, open, organize, paint, park, pat, peek, pick, pinch, play, poke, pour, pray, press, pull, push, rain, rip, rock, roll, shop, show, smoke, spank, stay, step, stop, talk, taste, tease, thank, tie, touch, turn, use, wait, walk, want, wash, watch, wee-wee, work, yawn

REFERENCES

Adams, S. (1938). Analysis of verb forms in the speech of young children, and their relation to the language learning process. *Journal of Experimental Education,* **7,** 141–144.

Anderson, J. R. (1983). *The architecture of cognition.* Cambridge, MA: Harvard University Press.

Anisfeld, M., Barlow, J., & Frail, C. M. (1968). Distinctive features in the pluralization rules of English speakers. *Language and Speech,* **11,** 31–37.

Anisfeld, M., & Gordon, M. (1968). On the psychophonological structure of English inflectional rules. *Journal of Verbal Learning and Verbal Behavior,* **7,** 973–979.

Anisfeld, M., & Tucker, G. R. (1967). The English pluralization rules of six-year-old children. *Child Development,* **38,** 1201–1217.

Aronoff, M. (1976). *Word formation in generative grammar.* Cambridge, MA: MIT Press.

Bateman, W. G. (1916). The language status of three children at the same ages. *Pedagogical Seminary,* **23,** 211–240.

Berko, J. (1958). The child's learning of English morphology. *Word,* **14,** 150–177.

Bever, T. G. (1975). Psychologically real grammar emerges because of its role in language acquisition. In D. Dato (Ed.), *Developmental psycholinguistics: Theory and applications* (Georgetown University Round Table on Languages and Linguistics). Washington, DC: Georgetown University Press.

Bever, T. G. (Ed.). (1982). *Regression in mental development: Basic processes and mechanisms.* Hillsdale, NJ: Erlbaum.

Bloom, L. (1973). *One word at a time: The use of single word utterances before syntax.* The Hague: Mouton.

Bohannon, J. N., & Marquis, A. L. (1977). Children's control of adult speech. *Child Development,* **48,** 1002–1008.

Bowerman, M. (1982a). Reorganizational processes in lexical and syntactic development. In E. Wanner & L. R. Gleitman (Eds.), *Language acquisition: The state of the art.* New York: Cambridge University Press.

Bowerman, M. (1982b). Starting to talk worse: Clues to language acquisition from children's late errors. In S. Strauss (Ed.), *U-shaped behavioral growth.* New York: Academic.

Bowerman, M. (1987). Commentary: Mechanisms of language acquisition. In B. MacWhinney (Ed.), *Mechanisms of language acquisition.* Hillsdale, NJ: Erlbaum.

Brown, R. (1973). *A first language: The early stages.* Cambridge, MA: Harvard University Press.

Brown, R. (n.d.). *Grammars for Adam, Eve and Sarah at Stages I–V.* Unpublished manuscripts, Harvard University, Department of Psychology.

Brown, R., & Bellugi, U. (1964). Three processes in the child's acquisition of syntax. In E. Lenneberg (Ed.), *New directions in the study of language.* Cambridge, MA: MIT Press.

Brown, R., Cazden, C., & de Villiers, J. (1971). *Directions for scoring fourteen English morphemes obligatory in some contexts.* Unpublished manuscript, Harvard University, Department of Psychology.

Brown, R., & Hanlon, C. (1970). Derivational complexity and order of acquisition in child speech. In J. R. Hayes (Ed.), *Cognition and the development of language.* New York: Wiley.

Brown, R., & McNeill, D. (1966). The "tip of the tongue" phenomenon. *Journal of Verbal Learning and Verbal Behavior,* **5,** 325–337.

Bryant, B., & Anisfeld, M. (1969). Feedback versus no-feedback in testing children's knowledge of English pluralization rules. *Journal of Experimental Child Psychology,* **8,** 250–255.

Burnham, K. P., & Overton, W. S. (1978). Estimation of the size of a closed population when capture probabilities vary among animals. *Biometrika,* **65,** 625–633.

Burnham, K. P., & Overton, W. S. (1979). Robust estimation of population size when capture probabilities vary among animals. *Ecology,* **60,** 927–936.

Bybee, J. L. (1985). *Morphology: A study of the relation between meaning and form.* Philadelphia: Benjamins.

Bybee, J. L., & Slobin, D. I. (1982a). Rules and schemes in the development and use of the English past tense. *Language,* **58,** 265–289.

Bybee, J. L., & Slobin, D. I. (1982b). Why small children cannot change language on their own: Suggestions from the English past tense. In A. Ahlqvist (Ed.), *Papers from the 5th International Conference on Historical Linguistics* (Current Issues in Linguistic Theory, Vol. **21,** Amsterdam Studies in the Theory and History of Linguistic Science IV). Philadelphia: Benjamins.

Carlton, L. E. (1947). Anomalous preterite and past participle forms in the oral language of average fourth grade children. *American Speech,* **22,** 40–45.

Carroll, J. B. (1961). Language development in children. In S. Saporta (Ed.), *Psycholinguistics: A book of readings.* New York: Holt, Rinehart & Winston.

Carstairs, A. (1987). *Allomorphy in inflexion.* London: Croom Helm.

Cazden, C. B. (1966). *Verb inflections.* Unpublished manuscript, Harvard University, Graduate School of Education.

Cazden, C. B. (1968). The acquisition of noun and verb inflections. *Child Development,* **39,** 433–448.

Cazden, C. B. (1972). *Child language and education.* New York: Holt, Rinehart & Winston.

Chamberlain, A. F. (1906). Preterite forms, etc., in the language of English-speaking children. *Modern Language Notes,* **21,** 42–44.

Chao, A. (1987). Estimating the population size for capture-recapture data with unequal capturability. *Biometrics,* **43,** 783–791.

Chomsky, N. (1959). A review of B. F. Skinner's *Verbal behavior. Language,* **3,** 26–58.

Chomsky, N., & Halle, M. (1968). *The sound pattern of English.* New York: Harper & Row.

Clark, E. V. (1982). The young word maker: A case study of innovation in the child's lexicon. In E. Wanner & L. R. Gleitman (Eds.), *Language acquisition: The state of the art.* New York: Cambridge University Press.

Clark, E. V. (1987). The principle of contrast: A constraint on language acquisition. In B. MacWhinney (Ed.), *Mechanisms of language acquisition.* Hillsdale, NJ: Erlbaum.

Clark, E. V. (1988). On the logic of contrast. *Journal of Child Language,* **15,** 317–335.

Clark, E. V. (1990). On the pragmatics of contrast. *Journal of Child Language,* **17,** 417–431.

Coltheart, M., Patterson, K. E., & Marshall, J. C. (Eds.). (1980). *Deep dyslexia.* London: Routledge & Kegan Paul.

Cox, M. V. (1989). Children's over-regularization of nouns and verbs. *Journal of Child Language,* **16,** 203–206.

Derwing, B., & Baker, W. (1979). Recent research on the acquisition of English morphology. In P. Fletcher & M. Garman (Eds.), *Language acquisition.* New York: Cambridge University Press.

de Villiers, J. G., & de Villiers, P. A. (1973). A cross-sectional study of the acquisition of grammatical morphemes in child speech. *Journal of Psycholinguistic Research,* **2,** 267–278.

Edwards, M. L. (1970). An annotated bibliography on the acquisition of English verbal morphology. *Ohio State University Working Papers in Linguistics,* **4,** 149–164.

Egedi, D. M., & Sproat, R. W. (1991). Connectionist networks and natural language morphology. Unpublished manuscript, AT&T Bell Laboratories, Linguistics Research Department, Murray Hill, NJ.

Ervin, S. M. (1964). Imitation and structural change in children's language. In E. H. Lenneberg (Ed.), *New directions in the study of language.* Cambridge, MA: MIT Press.

Ervin, S. M., & Miller, W. R. (1963). Language development. In H. W. Stevenson (Ed.), *Child psychology: The sixty-second yearbook of the National Society for the Study of Education* (Pt. 1). Chicago: University of Chicago Press.

Fowler, C. A., Napps, S. E., & Feldman, L. (1985). Relations among regular and irregular morphologically related words in the lexicon as related by repetition priming. *Memory and Cognition,* **13,** 241–255.

Francis, N., & Kucera, H. (1982). *Frequency analysis of English usage: Lexicon and grammar.* Boston: Houghton Mifflin.

Gasser, M., & Lee, C.-D. (1991). A short-term memory architecture for the learning of morphophonemic rules. In R. Lippmann, J. Moody, & D. Touretzky (Eds.), *Advances in neural information processing systems 3.* San Mateo, CA: Morgan Kaufmann.

Gathercole, V. (1979). *Birdies like birdseed the bester than buns: A study of relational comparatives and their acquisition.* Unpublished doctoral dissertation, University of Kansas.

Gathercole, V. (1987). The contrastive hypothesis for the acquisition of word meaning: A reconsideration of the theory. *Journal of Child Language,* **14,** 493–531.

Gathercole, V. (1989). Contrast: A semantic constraint? *Journal of Child Language,* **16,** 685–702.

Gelman, D. (1986, December 15). The mouths of babes. *Newsweek,* pp. 84–86.

Gleason, J. B. (1980). The acquisition of social speech and politeness formulae. In H. A. R. Giles (Ed.), *Language: Social psychological perspectives.* Oxford: Pergamon.

Gold, E. M. (1967). Language identification in the limit. *Information and Control,* **16,** 447–474.

Gordon, P. (1985). Level-ordering in lexical development. *Cognition,* **21,** 73–93.

Gordon, P. (1990). Learnability and feedback. *Developmental Psychology,* **26,** 217–220.

Grimshaw, J., & Pinker, S. (1989). Positive and negative evidence in language acquisition [Commentary on D. Lightfoot's "The child's trigger experience: 'Degree-0' learnability"]. *Behavioral and Brain Sciences,* **12,** 341.

Grimshaw, J., & Rosen, S. T. (1990). Knowledge and obedience: The developmental status of the binding theory. *Linguistic Inquiry,* **21,** 187–222.

Grudin, J., & Norman, D. A. (1991). Language evolution and human-computer interaction. *Proceedings of the 1991 annual meeting of the Cognitive Science Society.* Hillsdale, NJ: Erlbaum.

Guillaume, P. (1927). Le développement des éléments formels dans le langage de l'enfant. *Journal de Psychologie,* **24,** 203–229. (Translated as "The development of formal elements in the child's speech." In C. A. Ferguson & D. I. Slobin [Eds.], *Studies of child language development.* New York: Holt, Rinehart & Winston, 1983)

Hall, W. S., Nagy, W. E., & Linn, R. (1984). *Spoken words.* Hillsdale, NJ: Erlbaum.

Halle, M., & Mohanan, K. P. (1985). Segmental phonology of modern English. *Linguistic Inquiry,* **16,** 57–116.

Hart, J. T. (1965). Memory and the feeling-of-knowing experience. *Journal of Educational Psychology,* **56,** 208–216.

Higginson, R. (1985). *Fixing-assimilation in language acquisition.* Unpublished doctoral dissertation, Washington State University, Department of Anthropology.

Horn, E. (1925). Appropriate materials for instruction in reading. In G. M. Whipple (Ed.), *Twenty-fourth yearbook of the National Society for the Study of Education* (Pt. 1) (Report of the National Committee on Reading). Bloomington, IL: Public School Publishing Co.

Horn, M. D. (1927). The thousand and three words most frequently used by kindergarten children. *Childhood Education,* **3,** 118–122.

Ingram, D. (1989). *First language acquisition: Method, description, and explanation.* New York: Cambridge University Press.

Jacobs, R. A., Jordan, M. I., & Barto, A. G. (1991). Task decomposition through competition in a modular connectionist architecture: The what and where vision tasks. *Cognitive Science,* **15,** 219–250.

Karmiloff-Smith, A., & Inhelder, B. (1974–1975). If you want to get ahead, get a theory. *Cognition,* **3,** 195–212.

Kaye, J. (1990). *Phonology: A cognitive view.* Hillsdale, NJ: Erlbaum.

Kim, J. J., Marcus, G. F., Hollander, M., & Pinker, S. (1991). Children's inflection is sensitive to morphological structure. *Papers and Reports in Child Language,* **30,** 39–46.

Kim, J. J., Pinker, S., Prince, A., & Prasada, S. (1991). Why no mere mortal has ever flown out to center field. *Cognitive Science,* **15,** 173–218.

Kiparsky, P. (1982). *Explanation in phonology.* Dordrecht: Foris.

Kruschke, J. K. (1990). ALCOVE: A connectionist model of category learning. Research Report No. 19. Bloomington: Cognitive Science Program, Indiana University.

Kucera, H., & Francis, N. (1967). *Computational analysis of present-day American English.* Providence, RI: Brown University Press.

Kuczaj, S. A. (1976). *"-ing," "-s," & "-ed": A study of the acquisition of certain verb inflections.* Unpublished doctoral dissertation, University of Minnesota, Department of Psychology.

Kuczaj, S. A. (1977a). The acquisition of regular and irregular past tense forms. *Journal of Verbal Learning and Verbal Behavior,* **16,** 589–600.

Kuczaj, S. A. (1977b, March). *Old and new forms, old and new meanings: The form-function hypothesis revisited.* Paper presented at the biennial meeting of the Society for Research in Child Development, New Orleans.

Kuczaj, S. A. (1978). Children's judgments of grammatical and ungrammatical irregular past tense verbs. *Child Development,* **49,** 319–326.

Kuczaj, S. A. (1981). More on children's initial failure to relate specific acquisitions. *Journal of Child Language,* **8,** 485–487.

Lachter, J., & Bever, T. G. (1988). The relation between linguistic structure and associative theories of language learning—a constructive critique of some connectionist learning models. *Cognition,* **28,** 195–247.

Lenneberg, E. H. (1964). A biological perspective on language. In E. H. Lenneberg (Ed.), *New directions in the study of language.* Cambridge, MA: MIT Press.

Lieber, R. (1980). *On the organization of the lexicon.* Unpublished doctoral dissertation, Massachusetts Institute of Technology, Department of Linguistics and Philosophy.

Lorge, I., & Chall, J. (1963). Estimating the size of vocabularies of children and adults: An analysis of methodological issues. *Journal of Experimental Education,* **32,** 147–157.

MacKay, D. (1976). On the retrieval and lexical structure of verbs. *Journal of Verbal Learning and Verbal Behavior,* **15,** 169–182.

MacWhinney, B. (1978). Processing a first language: The acquisition of morphophonology. *Monographs of the Society for Research in Child Development,* **43**(1–2, Serial No. 174).
MacWhinney, B. (1987). The competition model. In B. MacWhinney (Ed.), *Mechanisms of language acquisition.* Hillsdale, NJ: Erlbaum.
MacWhinney, B. (1990). *The CHILDES Project: Computational Tools for Analyzing Talk (Version 0.88).* Pittsburgh, PA: Carnegie-Mellon University, Department of Psychology.
MacWhinney, B., & Leinbach, J. (1991). Implementations are not conceptualizations: Revising the verb learning model. *Cognition,* **40,** 121–157.
MacWhinney, B., & Snow, C. E. (1985). The Child Language Data Exchange System. *Journal of Child Language,* **12,** 271–296.
MacWhinney, B., & Snow, C. (1990). The Child Language Data Exchange System: An update. *Journal of Child Language,* **17,** 457–472.
Maratsos, M. P. (1983). Some current issues in the study of the acquisition of grammar. In J. H. Flavell & E. M. Markman (Eds.), P. H. Mussen (Series Ed.), *Handbook of child psychology: Vol. 3. Cognitive development.* New York: Wiley.
Maratsos, M. P. (1987, January 2). Gift of tongues. *Times Literary Supplement,* p. 19.
Marchman, V. (1988). Rules and regularities in the acquisition of the English past tense. *Center for Research on Language Newsletter* (University of California, San Diego), **2**(4).
Marchman, V., & Bates, E. (1991). *Vocabulary size and composition as predictors of morphological development* (Tech. Rep. No. 9103). San Diego: University of California, Center for Research in Language.
Marcus, G. F. (1992). *Negative evidence in language acquisition.* Manuscript submitted for publication.
Marcus, G. F. (in preparation). *Children's overregularization of English plurals: A quantitative analysis.*
McClelland, J. L. (1988). Connectionist models and psychological evidence. *Journal of Memory and Language,* **27,** 107–123.
McClelland, J. L., Rumelhart, D. E., & Hinton, G. E. (1986). The appeal of parallel distributed processing. In D. E. Rumelhart, J. L. McClelland, & the PDP Research Group, *Parallel distributed processing: Explorations in the microstructure of cognition: Vol. 1. Foundations.* Cambridge, MA: Bradford Books/MIT Press.
McNeill, D. (1966). Developmental psycholinguistics. In F. Smith & G. Miller (Eds.), *The genesis of language.* Cambridge, MA: MIT Press.
Menyuk, P. (1963). A preliminary evaluation of grammatical capacity in children. *Journal of Verbal Learning and Verbal Behavior,* **2,** 429–439.
Miller, G. A. (1977). *Spontaneous apprentices—children and language.* New York: Seabury.
Miller, W. R., & Ervin, S. M. (1964). The development of grammar in child language. In U. Bellugi & R. Brown (Eds.), *The acquisition of language. Monographs of the Society for Research in Child Development,* **29**(1, Serial No. 92).
Moe, A. J., Hopkins, C. J., & Rush, R. T. (1982). *The vocabulary of first-grade children.* Springfield, IL: Thomas.
Morgan, J. L., & Travis, L. L. (1989). Limits on negative information in language learning. *Journal of Child Language,* **16,** 531–552.
Osherson, D. N., Stob, M., & Weinstein, S. (1985). *Systems that learn.* Cambridge, MA: MIT Press.
Otis, D. L., Burnham, K. P., White, G. C., & Anderson, D. R. (1978). Statistical inference from capture data on closed animal populations. *Wildlife Monographs,* **63,** 1–135.
Patel, V. L., & Groen, G. J. (1991). The general and specific nature of medical expertise: A critical look. In A. Ericsson & J. Smith (Eds.), *Toward a general theory of expertise: Prospects and limits.* New York: Cambridge University Press.
Pinker, S. (1979). Formal models of language learning. *Cognition,* **7,** 217–283.

Pinker, S. (1982). A theory of the acquisition of lexical interpretive grammars. In J. Bresnan (Ed.), *The mental representation of grammatical relations.* Cambridge, MA: MIT Press.

Pinker, S. (1984). *Language learnability and language development.* Cambridge, MA: Harvard University Press.

Pinker, S. (1989). *Learnability and cognition: The acquisition of argument structure.* Cambridge, MA: MIT Press.

Pinker, S. (1991). Rules of language. *Science,* **253,** 530–535.

Pinker, S., Lebeaux, D. S., & Frost, L. A. (1987). Productivity and constraints in the acquisition of the passive. *Cognition,* **26,** 195–267.

Pinker, S., & Prince, A. (1988). On language and connectionism: Analysis of a parallel distributed processing model of language acquisition. *Cognition,* **28,** 73–193.

Pinker, S., & Prince, A. (1991). Regular and irregular morphology and the psychological status of rules of grammar. In *Proceedings of the 17th annual meeting of the Berkeley Linguistics Society.* Berkeley, CA: Berkeley Linguistics Society.

Plunkett, K., & Marchman, V. (1990). *From rote learning to system building* (Tech. Rep. No. 9020). San Diego: University of California, Center for Research in Language.

Plunkett, K., & Marchman, V. (1991). U-shaped learning and frequency effects in a multi-layered perceptron: Implications for child language acquisition. *Cognition,* **38,** 43–102.

Prasada, S., & Pinker, S. (in press). Generalizations of regular and irregular morphological patterns. *Language and Cognitive Processes.*

Prasada, S., Pinker, S., & Snyder, W. (1990, November). *Some evidence that irregular forms are retrieved from memory but regular forms are rule-generated.* Paper presented at the annual meeting of the Psychonomic Society, New Orleans.

Prince, A., & Pinker, S. (1988). Rules and connections in human language. *Trends in Neuroscience,* **11,** 195–202.

Pyles, T., & Algeo, J. (1982). *The origins and development of the English language* (3d ed.). New York: Harcourt Brace Jovanovich.

Reich, P. A. (1986). *Language development.* Englewood Cliffs, NJ: Prentice-Hall.

Rosenthal, R. (1984). *Meta-analytic procedures for social research.* Newbury Park, CA: Sage.

Rumelhart, D. E., Hinton, G. E., & Williams, D. (1986). Learning internal representations by error propagation. In D. E. Rumelhart, J. L. McClelland, & the PDP Research Group, *Parallel distributed processing: Explorations in the microstructure of cognition: Vol. 1. Foundations.* Cambridge, MA: Bradford Books/MIT Press.

Rumelhart, D. E., & McClelland, J. L. (1986). On learning the past tenses of English verbs. In J. L. McClelland, D. E. Rumelhart, & the PDP Research Group, *Parallel distributed processing: Explorations in the microstructure of cognition: Vol.* **2.** *Psychological and biological models.* Cambridge, MA: Bradford Books/MIT Press.

Rumelhart, D. E., & McClelland, J. L. (1987). Learning the past tenses of English verbs: Implicit rules or parallel distributed processing? In B. MacWhinney (Ed.), *Mechanisms of language acquisition.* Hillsdale, NJ: Erlbaum.

Sachs, J. (1983). Talking about there and then: The emergence of displaced reference in parent-child discourse. In K. E. Nelson (Ed.), *Children's language* (Vol. **4**). Hillsdale, NJ: Erlbaum.

Sampson, G. (1987, June 12). A turning point in linguistics. *Times Literary Supplement,* p. 643.

Scalettar, R., & Zee, A. (1988). Emergence of grandmother memory in feed forward networks: Learning with noise and forgetfulness. In D. Waltz & J. A. Feldman (Eds.), *Connectionist models and their implications: Readings from cognitive science.* Norwood, NJ: Ablex.

Seashore, R. H., & Eckerson, L. D. (1940). The measurement of individual differences in general English vocabularies. *Journal of Educational Psychology,* **31,** 14–38.

Seber, G. A. F. (1986). A review of estimating animal abundance. *Biometrics,* **42,** 267–292.

Slamecka, N. J. (1969). Testing for associative storage in multitrial free recall. *Journal of Experimental Psychology,* **81,** 557–560.

Slobin, D. I. (1971). On the learning of morphological rules: A reply to Palermo and Eberhart. In D. I. Slobin (Ed.), *The ontogenesis of grammar: A theoretical symposium.* New York: Academic.

Slobin, D. I. (1973). Cognitive prerequisites for the development of grammar. In C. Ferguson & D. I. Slobin (Eds.), *Studies of child language development.* New York: Holt, Rinehart & Winston.

Slobin, D. I. (1978). A case study of early language awareness. In A. Sinclair, R. J. Jarvella, & W. J. M. Levelt (Eds.), *The child's conception of language.* New York: Springer.

Slobin, D. I. (1982). Universal and particular in the acquisition of language. In E. Wanner & L. R. Gleitman (Eds.), *Language acquisition: The state of the art.* Cambridge: Cambridge University Press.

Smith, E. E., Langston, C., & Nisbett, R. E. (in press). The case for rules in reasoning. *Cognitive Science.*

Smith, M. E. (1933). Grammatical errors in the speech of preschool children. *Child Development,* **4,** 183–190.

Smith, M. E. (1935). A study of some factors influencing the development of the sentence in preschool children. *Journal of Genetic Psychology,* **46,** 182–212.

Smolensky, P. (1988). The proper treatment of connectionism. *Behavioral and Brain Sciences,* **11,** 1–74.

Stanners, R. F., Neiser, J. J., Hernon, W. P., & Hall, R. (1979). Memory representation for morphologically related words. *Journal of Verbal Learning and Verbal Behavior,* **18,** 399–413.

Stemberger, J. P. (1982). Syntactic errors in speech. *Journal of Psycholinguistic Research,* **11,** 313–345.

Stemberger, J. P. (1989). *The acquisition of morphology: Analysis of a symbolic model of language acquisition.* Unpublished manuscript, University of Minnesota, Department of Linguistics.

Stemberger, J. P., & MacWhinney, B. (1986). Frequency and the lexical storage of regularly inflected forms. *Memory and Cognition,* **14,** 17–26.

Strauss, S. (Ed.). (1982). *U-shaped behavioral growth.* New York: Academic.

Stromswold, K. J. (1990). *Learnability and the acquisition of auxiliaries.* Unpublished doctoral dissertation, Massachusetts Institute of Technology, Department of Brain and Cognitive Sciences.

Talmy, L. (1985). Lexicalization patterns: Semantic structure in lexical forms. In T. Shopen (Ed.), *Language typology and syntactic description: Vol. 3. Grammatical categories and the lexicon.* New York: Cambridge University Press.

Templin, M. (1957). *Certain language skills in children.* Minneapolis: University of Minnesota Press.

Ullman, M., & Pinker, S. (1990, October). *Why do some verbs not have a single past tense form?* Paper presented at the fifteenth annual Boston University Conference on Language Development.

Ullman, M., & Pinker, S. (1992). *The English past tense system: Native speaker judgments of regular and irregular forms and the effects of frequency and similarity.* Unpublished manuscript, Massachusetts Institute of Technology, Department of Brain and Cognitive Sciences.

Valian, V. (1991). Syntactic subjects in the early speech of American and Italian children. *Cognition,* **40,** 21–81.

Warren-Leubecker, A. (1982). Sex differences in speech to children. Unpublished master's thesis, Georgia Institute of Technology.

Wexler, K., & Culicover, P. (1980). *Formal principles of language acquisition.* Cambridge, MA: MIT Press.

Wurzel, W. U. (1989). *Inflectional morphology and naturalness.* Dordrecht: Kluwer.

Zwicky, A. (1970). A double regularity in the acquisition of English verb morphology. *Papers in Linguistics,* **3,** 411–418.

ACKNOWLEDGMENTS

We thank John J. Kim, Sandeep Prasada, Alan Prince, and Karin Stromswold for many helpful discussions and suggestions; Joan Bybee, Eve Clark, Michael Maratsos, and Joseph Stemberger for comments on an earlier draft; Roger Brown, Courtney Cazden, Jill de Villiers, Beth Levin, Michael Maratsos, Dan Slobin, Joseph Stemberger, Karin Stromswold, and Virginia Valian for sharing data and other information; and Elena D'Agustino, Marie Coppola, Hartley Kuhn, and Elliza McGrand for assistance with coding, manuscript preparation, and figures. Parts of this *Monograph* were presented at the 1989 and 1990 Boston University Conference on Language Development. Supported by National Institutes of Health grant HD 18381 and National Science Foundation grant BNS 91-09766 to Pinker and by a grant from the Alfred P. Sloan Foundation to the Massachusetts Institute of Technology Center for Cognitive Science. Marcus and Ullman are supported by National Defense Science and Engineering graduate fellowships. Xu was supported by a Dana Foundation award from Smith College. Correspondence should be sent to Marcus (gary@psyche.mit.edu) at E10-109, MIT, Cambridge MA 02139, or Pinker (steve@psyche.mit.edu) at E10-016, MIT, Cambridge MA 02139.

COMMENTARY

OVERREGULARIZATION IN THE ACQUISITION OF INFLECTIONAL MORPHOLOGY: A COMPARISON OF ENGLISH AND GERMAN

Harald Clahsen

In this Commentary, I will summarize results of studies of two inflectional subsystems of German, noun plurals and the formation of participles, and compare the results with those of Marcus et al. on English past tense formation. It will be argued that the evidence from both languages converges on one major point: that children's inflectional systems involve qualitative differences between regular and irregular morphology. Moreover, analysis of German indicates that this distinction cannot be reduced to frequency differences.

The main discovery of Marcus et al. is, I think, that overregularization errors such as **go-ed* are much less frequent than previously thought—that at all ages such errors account for only a small minority of children's irregular verbs (2.5%). Marcus et al.'s findings are based on sophisticated statistical and linguistic analyses of a massive amount of data. Adopting the dual-mechanism model from Pinker and Prince (1992), they propose a straightforward explanation of overregularization in language acquisition. Children (like adults) possess two distinct psychological mechanisms for inflection, a symbol-manipulating rule system and an associative memory system. Only when the child fails to retrieve an irregular form from his or her memory is the regular rule applied, resulting in occasional errors.

However, there is a problem with this conclusion. Marcus et al. make

The research reported here is supported by a grant from the German Science Foundation (grant Cl97/5-1). Correspondence should be addressed to Harald Clahsen, Allgemeine Sprachwissenschaft, Universität Düsseldorf, Universitätsstr. 1, 4000 Düsseldorf 1, FRG; e-mail: clahsen@ze8.rz.uni-duesseldorf.de.

general claims about the occurrence and distribution of overregularizations in language acquisition, but their sole evidence comes from past tense formation in English child language. Thus, it is unclear whether their results also hold for other inflectional systems and for languages other than English.

English inflection has a number of peculiarities. Relative to other languages, it is inflectionally poor. For example, it has only one productive noun plural (*-s*) and a single productive past tense inflection (*-ed*), whereas some languages can have several different noun plurals or tense affixes. Moreover, there are inflectional systems with far greater irregularity. For example, Bybee (1991) argued that the German plural system has no regular default. Finally, the regular-versus-irregular distinction is confounded with frequency in English: the regular past tense ending applies to the vast majority of verbs, including virtually all the lower-frequency Latinate vocabulary. Thus, the affix *-ed* may occur in overregularizations, not because of a unique psychological process, but simply because children have heard it used with so many different English verbs. Similarly, the plural affix *-s* is used with nearly all nouns in English, and it is therefore not surprising that English-speaking children use *-s* in overregularizations (e.g., **mouse-s, *ox-es,* etc.; cf. Gordon, 1985). Again, Bybee (1991) argued that there are no *qualitative* differences between regular and irregular morphology, that the observed differences are due instead to type frequency, that is, the number of distinct lexical items involved. This view is opposed to Marcus et al.'s explanation of overregularizations. Evidence from languages with different vocabulary statistics than English is necessary to decide this controversy. The data on German provide such evidence.

The Acquisition of English Past Tense Formation

The research reported in this *Monograph* is part of a larger ongoing project carried out by Steven Pinker and his colleagues at the Massachusetts Institute of Technology and other places. In this project, one subsystem of human language, inflectional morphology, is studied in detail from the perspectives of a variety of disciplines.

The main body of this *Monograph* presents a detailed description of the development of overregularizations in English child language. Overregularization errors are shown to be rare at all ages, and their occurrence is correlated over time with obligatory past tense marking of regular verbs; that is, overregularizations appear when the child ceases using bare stems to refer to past events. For months beforehand, all overtly marked irregular past forms are correct. Second, Marcus et al. found a *frequency effect* in the distribution of overregularizations: children make these errors more often for verbs that their parents use in the past tense less frequently. Third, Marcus et al. observed *effects of similarity* in the distribution of overregularizations: children make fewer overregularization errors for verbs that fall into families with more numerous and higher-frequency members (see also Bybee & Slobin, 1982).

Concerning the distribution of errors, it is striking that, of the various types of potential errors in past tense formation, only one type is productive in the data reported by Marcus et al.: overapplications of the regular past tense affix *-ed* to irregular stems (**go-ed*, etc.). In contrast, overapplications of irregular patterns are extremely rare. In the data from Adam, Eve, and Sarah, for example, there were only four instances in which irregular patterns are applied to inappropriate irregular verbs (*beat-*bate, beat-*bet, hit-*heet, bite-*bat*). Overextensions of irregular patterns to regular verbs are even rarer; Marcus et al. found only one instance of such an irregularization error, *trick-*truck* from Adam.[1]

Fletcher (1991) reported data from a case study of a British child showing that the distribution of past-time forms contrasts in an interesting way to the one found by Marcus et al. for American children. Fletcher observed that the British child has two different types of affixes to refer to past-time events, *-ed* (like the American children) and *-en* forms, as in **maden, *broughten, *getten*, etc. These *-en* forms appear without auxiliaries and, frequently (about 15%–20%), over an extended period of time (roughly from age 2-5 to age 3-5). Fletcher also noted that there was no identifiable difference in meaning between the past tense forms and the *-en* forms. He proposed a rather complicated phonological conditioning of the occurrences of *-en*. However, the list of verbs to which *-en* is assigned suggests that a morphological explanation might be more appropriate: *-en* may be affixed to irregular verbs but not to regular ones. Thus, forms such as **builden, *cutten, *putten*, etc. are documented in the data reported by Fletcher, but forms such as **walken, *loven*, and **saven* are not. It will be shown below that a similar distinction is made by German-speaking children.

Summarizing briefly, I think that there is evidence that both American and British children distinguish between regular and irregular inflection. Marcus et al.'s data indicate that the child has two qualitatively different types of past tense forms: (i) irregular forms that are not productively overextended and (ii) the affix *-ed*, which may occur both with regular and (inappropriately) with irregular verbs. Fletcher's data suggest that British children have a separate affix that is restricted to irregular verbs.

[1] Marcus et al. do not systematically investigate overapplications of irregular patterns. However, Marcus (personal communication) noted that, in a follow-up investigation, he and his colleagues found that such errors are indeed far rarer than overregularization errors.

Marcus et al. argue that two different psychological mechanisms underlie the observed regular-irregular distinctions: rule-based processes allowing productive on-line concatenation of affixes to stems and memory-based retrieval of stored items. They also convincingly argue that both mechanisms are involved in children's past tense formations in English. Irregular verb forms can be memorized from parental speech as soon as words of any kind can be learned—thus the correct irregulars in early development. The occurrence of overregularizations, however, must await the abstraction of the English rule from a set of word pairs. Once older children possess the rule, they apply it in past tense sentences whenever they fail to retrieve the irregular, resulting in occasional errors. Given that irregular forms are memorized items, they should be affected by properties of associative memory such as frequency and similarity, whereas regular forms should not be so affected. The frequency and similarity effects observed in the distribution of overregularization errors support these predictions.

However, it could be the case that the observed regular-irregular distinctions simply reflect peculiarities of past tense formation in English. In order to rule out this possibility, it is crucial that the findings regarding English be replicated in different languages and in different inflectional systems. In the following, I will therefore summarize the results of my and my colleagues' studies of the acquisition of two inflectional systems of German: noun plurals and participle formation.

Investigating German Inflectional Morphology

In our project of inflection in German, my colleagues and I are addressing questions similar to the ones Steven Pinker and his colleagues address with respect to English. Our major empirical goal is to discover regular-versus-irregular distinctions in nominal and verbal morphology of German. Like Pinker and his colleagues, we include a variety of data: (i) linguistic analyses of adult language; (ii) adult experimental data; and (iii) different kinds of language acquisition data, namely, language-unimpaired monolingual children (L1), specifically-language-impaired children (SLI), and adult second language learners (L2). Results from our project are presented in Clahsen, Rothweiler, Woest, and Marcus (1992), Rothweiler and Clahsen (1991), and Clahsen (1991). In the following, I will first briefly describe plural formation in German. Then I will summarize our results on the acquisition of noun plurals in German child language.

Noun Plurals in Adult German

There are five plural affixes in German, *-(e)n, -s, -e, -er,* and *-O,* three of which also allow a variant with an umlaut, for example, *der Apfel–die Äpfel* (the apple/apples), *die Kuh–die Kühe* (the cow/cows), and *der Wald–die Wälder* (the forest/forests). The use of these plural affixes (except *-s*) with specific nouns is highly arbitrary. There exist preferred combinations of nouns and plural allomorphs that are determined by gender and/or the morphophonological characteristics of the noun; however, the list of exceptions is quite long (cf., among others, Köpcke, 1988; Mugdan, 1977).

The plural *-s* is special in several ways. On the one hand, *-s* is extremely infrequent. It applies to fewer than 30 common nouns and is thus far less frequent than all the other plural inflections. On the other hand, there are various reasons suggesting that *-s* is the default plural affix in adult German. First, the use of *-s* is not restricted by properties of the stem/root to which it is assigned. Second, the plural *-s* is used for names (*die Müllers,* "the Mullers"), for newly created expressions such as clippings (*Sozis* [the clipped form of *Sozialisten*], "socialists"), for acronyms (*GmbHs* [the acronym meaning incorporation], "Inc."), and with borrowed and foreign words (*Kiosks,* "newsstands"). Third, the plural *-s* is the sole plural marker that does not occur inside compounds (**Autosberg,* "*cars heap"; **Sozistreffen* but *Sozialistentreffen* [clipped and full forms, respectively], "socialists' meeting").

In Clahsen et al. (1992), we proposed an analysis of German noun plurals in the framework of lexical morphology (Kiparsky, 1982, 1985). (In this model, differences between regular and irregular inflection are handled by assigning morphological [and phonological] rules to a set of ordered levels that operate successively in the derivation of an inflected word: irregular inflection takes place at level 1, compounding at level 2, and regular inflection at level 3.) We argued (in contrast to Bybee, 1991) that the German plural system has a regular (default) affix, namely, the plural *-s,* which, according to the level-ordering model, is assigned at level 3. This ensures that the plural affix *-s* occurs with nouns that do not yet have a marked lexical entry for plural. Moreover, because the default plural *-s* is on level 3, it is unavailable to rules of compounding that apply at level 2. The irregular plural allomorphs are on levels 1 or 2 and are therefore available for compound formation. In this way, the distribution of plurals inside compounds can be explained (for further details, see Clahsen et al., 1992).

Noun Plurals in German Child Language

Previous studies found that the plural is marked early and that, from age 3 on, plural markings are used in about 90% of the obligatory contexts (Park, 1978). It was also found that overregularizations are rare and that the plural *-n* is most often used in overregularizations (Schaner-Wolles, 1988; Veit, 1988). This tentatively suggests that German-speaking children develop a regular plural form. An additional criterion for distinguishing between regular and irregular plural forms in adult German is the distribution of plural markings inside compounds. With respect to child German, however, the use of plurals inside compounds has not been investigated in previous studies.

To fill this gap, Clahsen et al. (1992) analyzed plural formation and plurals inside compounds in the longitudinal data of 20 German-speaking monolingual children, 19 SLI children, and the extensive corpora from a language-unimpaired child, Simone. We found that, in the area of noun plurals, SLI children do not show any specific deficits. This contrasts with other areas of inflectional morphology, particularly subject-verb agreement, case marking, and gender, in which German-speaking SLI subjects are severely impaired (cf. Clahsen, 1991).

In our data, overregularizations of plural allomorphs are rare (3%–10%) throughout the whole period of observation. In overregularizations, the plural affixes *-n* and *-s* are used significantly more often than all other plural affixes: 17 children use *-n* in overregularizations and three children *-s*. The children's overregularizations of *-s* or *-n* are also qualitatively different from other errors in plural marking: *-s* or *-n* overregularizations are not sensitive to properties of the stems/roots at which they occur, and *-n* or *-s* may replace any other plural affix. Moreover, *-n* and *-s* are used in invented words. In contrast, the other plural allomorphs of German are not used productively in overregularizations. These observations indicate that the children have two kinds of plural markings: (i) irregular forms that are restricted in use and (ii) regular affixes that may replace any other plural allomorph. The allomorphs *-n* and, for three children, *-s* seem to be regular default plural forms.

With respect to the use of plural markers within compounds, we observed that the plural allomorphs *-e*, *-er*, and *-n* occur in nominal compounds (e.g., *bild-er-buch*, "picture book"; *hund-e-hütte*, "kennel") and that the plural *-s* does not occur within compounds (*auto-bahn*, "highway"; *oma-zeitung*, "grandmother newspaper"). Such compounds are correct adult-like forms.

The most important observation is that the plural *-n* can be left out inside compounds, even in cases in which it is required in German; consider the following examples:

(1a) **blume-vase* (= *blume-n-vase*, "vase"),
(1b) **bauer-hof* (= *bauer-n-hof*, "farm"),
(1c) **tanne-baum* (= *tanne-n-baum*, "Christmas tree").

Concerning the omissions of *-n* inside compounds, three observations are relevant. First, the only affix omitted from compounds is *-n*. Second, *-n* is left out only when it is a true plural marker; for example, in compounds such as *rasenmäher* (lawn mower) in which *-n* is the final consonant of the root *rasen, -n* is not left out by the children. Third, what is most striking is that the children who omitted the plural *-n* in compounds were generally the same children who overregularized with *-n*. We found a statistically significant correlation ($r = .69$, $p < .005$) between the rates at which different children overregularized *-n* and the rates at which those children omitted *-n* from compounds, indicating that, the more often children overregularized, the more often they omitted *-n* in compounds.

We suggested a morphological analysis (in terms of lexical morphology) to account for the observed correlation between plurals inside compounds and overregularizations: that the plural allomorphs *-n* and *-s* are regular affixes (i.e., on level 3) and that the other allomorphs are irregular (i.e., on level 1). This means that, in case the child does not find a plural entry on level 1 for a particular noun, that noun either will not be inflected for plural or will receive a plural marking on level 3 (i.e., with *-n* or *-s*). This accounts for the overregularizations of *-n* and *-s*. Because compounding takes place at level 2 and *-n* and *-s* are level 3 affixes, they are left out in compounds. (For details, see Clahsen et al., 1992.)

Our findings concerning the omission of *-n* in compounds provide an example where children make an "error" with respect to the adult language but the "error" conforms to subtle principles of grammatical organization (i.e., level ordering). In adult German, the *-n* plural occurs frequently in compounds. Thus, there is no adult model for omitting *-n* inside compounds, and the children go systematically against a well-established input pattern. However, in the level-ordering model, the "error" automatically follows from the children's misinterpreting *-n* as a default plural. This indicates that children not only absorb the properties of the adult language but at the same time construct their own grammars and in doing so obey general principles of grammatical organization.

A comparison of the results concerning German noun plurals with those concerning past tense and plural formation in English shows parallels with respect to the regular-irregular distinction. Similar to what Marcus et al. (among others) observed for past tense formation in English child language, we found that, in the noun plurals of German-speaking children, the default affix occurs in errors while the irregulars do not. Moreover, the default affix is omitted in nominal compounds, both in child and in adult German; this conforms to what Gordon (1985) found for English. In contrast to English, however, the default plural of German cannot be determined on the basis of frequency. Thus, the observed qualitative parallels between English and German are hard to explain in a unitary inflectional architecture influenced only by vocabulary statistics. On the other hand, morphological theory (e.g., the level-ordering model) can account for the regular-irregular distinctions observed in both languages.

Participle Formation in Adult German

In adult and in child German, simple past tense forms are rarely used in spoken discourse. Instead, events in the past are expressed through what is traditionally called the present perfect. This consists of a finite auxiliary (*haben,* "to have," or *sein,* "to be") and nonfinite past participle forms—a situation similar to that found in English. Therefore, the closest equivalent to English past tense formation is German participle formation.

As can be seen in the following examples, three patterns of participle inflection are distinguished in traditional grammars: (i) *weak* inflection, which involves *-t* affixation without stem/root changes (2a); (ii) *strong* inflection, that is, *-n* affixation plus stem changes (2b, 2d); and (iii) *mixed* inflection, or *-t* affixation plus stem changes (2c). In a manner similar to that in English, ablaut and other changes of the verbal root/stem in German occur in both simple past tense forms and past participles. Only "weak" verbs never involve root/stem changes (cf. [2a]). Finally, prefixation with *ge-* is prosodically determined: *ge-* occurs in participles when the verbal root/stem has stress on the first syllable. Because this is most often the case in German verbs, the *ge-* prefix is very frequent:

(2a) *káufen* = *gekauft*
to buy = bought

(2b) *vertréiben* = *vertrieb* = *vertrieben*
to expel = expelled = expelled

(2c) *rennen* = *rannte* = *gerannt*
to run = ran = run

(2d) *gehen* = *ging* = *gegangen*
to go = went = gone

Wunderlich (1991) proposed that the distribution of *-t* and *-n* in participles can be accounted for in terms of two rules:

(3a) *n*; ROOT[+PART] → [+PART];
(3b) *t*; ROOT[ ] → [+PART].

The *-n* affixation rule in (3a) is a property-specific rule because it applies only to roots that are lexically marked with the feature [+PART]. In contrast to (3a), the left-hand side of the *-t* affixation rule (3b) does not include any restrictions on possible roots. This means that (3b) can freely apply to any verbal root that is not yet linked to the feature [+PART]. Therefore, the rule in (3b) has default status.[2] In order to yield the correct distribution, the order in which the rules in (3) are applied has to be fixed. Otherwise, nothing would rule out participles such as **gegangt* in which the default affix has been (incorrectly) assigned to a strong verb. This order of application independently follows from the "elsewhere condition" of lexical morphology (Kiparsky, 1982, 1985). The elsewhere condition is a general constraint on morphological processes and ensures that property-specific rules have priority over default rules, which are applied "elsewhere." Thus, (3a) is applied on all stems/roots with the specific feature [+PART]; in the remaining cases, the general rule (3b) applies.

Participle formation of novel or invented verbs confirms the proposed distinction between (3a) and (3b). Consider, for example, the invented verb *faben*. There is only one grammatical way of forming a past participle out of such a novel verb, the regular *gefab-t;* stem/root changes (**gefub-t*) and *-n* affixation (**gefab-en*) are ungrammatical. This shows that, when idiosyncratic information on participle roots is not lexically specified as in the case of novel verbs, the default rule applies.

Crucially, the linguistic differences between *-t* and *-n* affixation in German past participle formation do not coincide with quantitative differences in vocabulary statistics. In German, verbs affixed with the participle affix *-t* do not outnumber the irregular verbs requiring the participle affix *-n*.[3] This is in contrast to past tense formation in English, where the default status of the *-ed* suffix is confounded with its high frequency.[4] With respect to acquisition, the comparison between the two languages may therefore allow the qualitative and quantitative differences between regular and irregular systems to be teased apart. Such a comparison will be made in the next section.

[2] For the small number of verbs in the so-called mixed class we require an additional specification to ensure that, in forming past participles, *-t* is assigned to the irregular past tense root. Otherwise, we would get ungrammatical participles such as **gerennt* instead of *gerannt*. It is not clear whether this has to be specified in a separate rule (cf. Wunderlich, 1991).

[3] According to Ruoff (1981), 1,000 verb types account for 96% of all verb tokens in German. The *token frequencies* are as follows: 47% strong verb tokens, 32% verb tokens of the mixed class, and 17% weak verb tokens. The *type frequencies* among these 1,000 verbs are as follows: 502 strong verb types, 50 verb types of the mixed class, and 448 weak verb types. Thus, in terms of type and token frequencies, verbs requiring the participle affix *-t* are similar to verbs requiring the participle affix *-n*. A second relevant source is Meier (1964), who counted the 8,000 most frequent word forms in German texts. Among the 1,200 most frequent word forms are 23 strong past participles with the *-n* affix, 3 participles of the mixed class with the *-t* affix, and 8 participles of weak verbs with the *-t* affix. Again, there is no frequency preference for the (regular) *-t* affix.

[4] In Francis & Kucera (1982), there are 26,201 past tense tokens and 2,347 types. Regular past tense forms make up 59% of the tokens and 91% of the types; irregular forms are then 41% of the tokens and 9% of the types. Thus, regular forms are clearly dominant in English, in both type and token frequency.

Participles in German Child Language

In her research summary of the early diary studies of the acquisition of German, Mills (1985) quoted some instances of overregularizations of *-t* in participles, but she provided little data.

More recently, Rothweiler and Clahsen (1991) investigated spontaneous speech samples from 22 monolingual German-speaking children studied longitudinally, 19 SLI and 3 language unimpaired. As with noun plurals, we found no qualitative differences between the SLI children and the normal controls in the area of participle inflection; that is, we found the same types of errors and similar overregularization rates.

Our most important finding is that only the default *-t* affixation rule is overregularized by the children, whereas the property-specific *-n* affixation rule is not overextended. The overregularization rates for the *-t* suffix range from 0 to 0.18 with a mean of 0.04 (and a standard deviation of 0.05) for the SLI children and a mean of 0.10 (and a standard deviation of 0.06) for the language-unimpaired children.[5] Notice that, with respect to English past tense formation, Marcus et al. found similar overregularization rates for the *-ed* suffix, ranging from 0 to 0.24, with a mean of 0.04. This is within the same distribution as the overregularization rates for the participle affix *-t* in German, suggesting that children use similar mechanisms to acquire the two inflectional systems.

The participle affix *-t* may occur on all kinds of verbs, on weak verbs and verbs of the mixed class as well as on strong verbs, yielding overregularization errors such as **genehmt* instead of *genommen* (taken) and **gegebt* instead of *gegeben* (given). In contrast to that, the participle affix *-n* is restricted to strong verbs yielding correct adult-like participles. In all the corpora from the language-unimpaired children, we found only one instance in which *-n* is (incorrectly) assigned to a weak verb (**geschlachten* instead of *geschlachtet,* "slaughtered"); in the data from the SLI children, three instances of this kind were found. Thus, although the irregular participle affix *-n* was not productively extended to regular verbs, the regular participle affix *-t* was (comparatively often) overapplied to strong verbs.

A parallel (asymmetrical) distribution can be observed in the stem errors. In the data from both the SLI children and the normal controls, there are no examples of a participle in which an irregular stem pattern has been extended to a weak verb. For example, in forming a participle of the regular verb *lieben* (to love), the child might produce **geloben* instead of the correct form *geliebt,* in analogy to similar-sounding strong verbs such as *fliegen-geflogen* (to fly–flown), *bieten-geboten* (to offer–offered), *fliehen-geflohen* (to

[5] We calculated overregularization rates as the number of cases with *-t* assigned to strong verbs divided by the total number of past participles of strong verbs.

flee–fled), etc. Such errors, however, do not occur in the data. The only kinds of stem errors we found were regular stems replacing irregular ones, for example, **gebind* instead of *gebunden* (bounded) and **gewinn* instead of *gewonnen* (won).

The observed asymmetries in the distribution of errors suggest that children qualitatively distinguish between regular and irregular inflection. Specifically, the German data indicate that only default rules such as the *-t* affixation rule are overregularized; in contrast, irregularizations, that is, overextensions of irregular patterns (the affix *-n* and irregular stems), to regular verbs are not productive. The same holds for the data on English past tense formation investigated by Marcus et al. Strikingly, these parallels between the results obtained from English and those obtained from German were found despite differences between the two languages in terms of vocabulary frequencies. This shows that the regular-irregular distinction cannot be reduced to frequency differences.

Conclusion

We found dissociations between regular and irregular inflectional processes in three areas of morphology: English past tense formation, German noun plurals, and participle formation in German. Regular patterns are overextended to irregulars in children's inflection errors, but not vice versa. Moreover, linguistic processes such as compounding are sensitive to the regular-irregular distinction. For example, English and German compounds may contain irregular plurals, but not regulars. The acquisition data on German and English indicate that this also holds for child language.

These observations have a straightforward *linguistic* explanation: children and adults employ two kinds of morphological processes: (i) specific processes that are applied only under restricted circumstances and (ii) default processes that can be applied with no restrictions. The default-specific distinction is represented in Kiparsky's model of lexical morphology in terms of different layers in the lexicon and in terms of different kinds of morphological rules. Specific processes can be restricted either to lexical items (i.e., suppletion rules) or to properties of stems/roots (e.g., *-n* affixation). Suppletion processes are specific to lexical items. Property-specific rules are sensitive to properties of the stems/roots to which they are assigned, for example, *-n* affixation in German participles (cf. [3a]). Typically, specific processes are not overapplied. Moreover, the results show that default processes are positioned strictly after all other processes. Thus, specifically marked forms (e.g., suppletives) do not undergo the default process, and default rules cannot enter into other processes, such as compounding.

In contrast to lexical morphology as well as other versions of morphological theory (cf. Anderson, 1985; Halle, 1990) in which default and specific inflectional processes are typically described in terms of symbolic rules, in the dual-mechanism model adopted by Marcus et al. the regular-irregular distinction is interpreted in terms of two qualitatively different *psychological* mechanisms: regular inflections are based on symbolic rules (like in lexical morphology), but irregular inflections are claimed to be rote-based retrieval processes of stored items. Marcus et al. provide evidence for the dual-mechanism approach from past tense formation in English child language, for example, frequency and similarity effects in irregulars but not in regulars.

In the German acquisition data, however, we do not (yet) have evidence that irregular inflection should be handled by a distinct associative memory system. We found that children (like adults) possess productive inflectional rules that do not crucially depend on vocabulary frequency, but the possibility that even irregular inflectional processes are based on symbolic rules cannot be excluded. Moreover, in its present form, the dual-mechanism approach leaves some theoretical questions open. For example, what is the status of property-specific processes such as *-n* affixation in German participles? Such processes differ from default rules because they apply only under restricted circumstances; on the other hand, *-n* affixation is clearly a productive concatenation of an affix to a stem rather than a rote-based process. Thus, the dual-mechanism model needs to distinguish between different types of symbolic rules, and it requires additional principles that ensure that the rules are applied in the right order. Marcus et al.'s blocking principle seems to be too narrow in this regard because it is restricted to idiosyncratic forms listed in the lexicon and thus would not apply to property-specific rules such as *-n* affixation. Kiparsky's elsewhere condition would be more appropriate.

In sum, there is strong evidence that grammatical inflection in the language of children and adults involves productive affixation rules. However, the additional claim of the dual-mechanism model that irregular inflection is governed by mechanisms of associative memory rather than symbolic rules requires further theoretical and empirical support before we can transfer it to other inflectional systems and to languages other than English.

References

Anderson, S. (1985). *Phonology in the twentieth century: Theories of rules and theories of representation.* Chicago: University of Chicago Press.

Bybee, J. (1991). Natural morphology: The organization of paradigms and language acquisition. In T. Huebner & C. Ferguson (Eds.), *Crosscurrents in second language acquisition and linguistic theories.* Amsterdam: Benjamins.

Bybee, J., & Slobin, D. I. (1982). Rules and schemas in the development and use of English past tense. *Language*, **58,** 265–289.

Clahsen, H. (1991). *Child language and developmental dysphasia: Linguistic studies of the acquisition of German*. Amsterdam: Benjamins.

Clahsen, H., Rothweiler, M., Woest, A., & Marcus, G. F. (1992). *Regular and irregular inflection in the acquisition of German noun plurals*. Manuscript submitted for publication.

Fletcher, P. (1991, September). *The significance for the cognition hypothesis of an unusual past time form in an English child*. Paper presented at the Symposium for Rick Cromer, Cambridge.

Francis, N., & Kucera, H. (1982). *Frequency analysis of English usage: Lexicon and grammar*. Boston: Houghton Mifflin.

Gordon, P. (1985). Level-ordering in lexical development. *Cognition*, **21,** 73–93.

Halle, M. (1990). An approach to morphology. *North-Eastern Linguistic Society*, **20,** 150–184.

Kiparsky, P. (1982). From cyclic phonology to lexical phonology. In H. V. D. Hulst & N. Smith (Eds.), *The structure of phonological representations* (Pt. 1). Dordrecht: Foris.

Kiparsky, P. (1985). Some consequences of lexical phonology. In C. Ewen & J. Anderson (Eds.), *Phonology yearbook* (Vol. **2**). Cambridge: Cambridge University Press.

Köpcke, K.-M. (1988). Schemas in German plural formation. *Lingua*, **74,** 303–335.

Meier, H. (1964). *Deutsche Sprachstatistik*. Hildesheim: Olms.

Mills, A. (1985). The acquisition of German. In D. Slobin (Ed.), *The cross-linguistic study of language acquisition*. Hillsdale, NJ: Erlbaum.

Mugdan, J. (1977). *Flexionsmorphologie und Psycholinguistik*. Tübingen: Narr.

Park, T.-Z. (1978). Plurals in child speech. *Journal of Child Language*, **5,** 237–250.

Pinker, S., & Prince, A. (1992). Regular and irregular morphology and the psychological status of rules of grammar. In *Proceedings of the 17th Annual Meeting of the Berkeley Linguistics Society*. Berkeley, CA: Berkeley Linguistics Society.

Rothweiler, M., & Clahsen, H. (1991, October). *Past participles in German child language: A comparative study of normal and disordered language development*. Paper presented at the Boston University Conference on Language Development.

Ruoff, A. (1981). *Häufigkeitswörterbuch gesprochener Sprache*. Tübingen: Niemeyer.

Schaner-Wolles, C. (1988). Plural vs. Komparativerwerb im Deutschen: Von der Diskrepanz zwischen konzeptueller und morphologischer Entwicklung. In H. Günter (Ed.), *Experimentelle Studien zur Flexionsmorphologie*. Hamburg: Buske.

Veit, S. (1988). Das Verständnis von Plural- und Komparativformen bei (entwicklungs) dysgrammatischen Kindern im Vorschulalter. In G. Kegel et al. (Eds.), *Sprechwissenschaft und Psycholinguistik*. Opladen: Westdeutscher.

Wunderlich, D. (1991). Eine Unterspezifikationsanalyse der deutschen Verbmorphologie. Unpublished manuscript, University of Düsseldorf.

CONTRIBUTORS

Gary F. Marcus (B.A. 1989, Hampshire College) is a doctoral candidate in cognitive science in the Department of Brain and Cognitive Sciences, Massachusetts Institute of Technology. His research interests center on the psychology of language.

Steven Pinker (Ph.D. 1979, Harvard University) is professor in the Department of Brain and Cognitive Sciences, Massachusetts Institute of Technology. His research interests include language acquisition, linguistics, and visual cognition. He is the author of *Language Learnability and Language Development* (1984) and *Learnability and Cognition: The Acquisition of Argument Structure* (1989) and is the editor of *Visual Cognition* (1985), *Connections and Symbols* (with Jacques Mehler, 1988), and *Lexical and Conceptual Semantics* (with Beth Levin, 1992).

Michael Ullman (B.A. 1988, Harvard University) is a doctoral candidate in cognitive science in the Department of Brain and Cognitive Sciences, Massachusetts Institute of Technology. His research interests center on the psychology of language and the use of neuroimaging techniques to study localization of language processing in the brain.

Michelle Hollander (B.A. 1987, Brandeis University) is currently a doctoral candidate in developmental psychology in the Department of Psychology, University of Michigan. She worked as a technical assistant in the Department of Brain and Cognitive Sciences, Massachusetts Institute of Technology, from 1987 to 1991 and is coauthor with Jess Gropen and Steven Pinker of three experimental papers in language acquisition. Her research interests are cognitive development and educational psychology.

T. John Rosen (Ph.D. 1972, University of Wisconsin—Madison) is currently at the Boston VA Aphasia Research Center and is an assistant research professor of psycholiguistics in the Department of Neurology at the Boston University School of Medicine. He was a research scientist in the Department of Brain and Cognitive Sciences, Massachusetts Institute of Technology, from 1984 to 1991. His research interests include methodology and statistics in cognitive neuroscience research and language in aging and dementia. He is the author of "Statistical Practice in Aging and Dementia Research," a chapter in the *Handbook of Neuropsychology,* edited by F. Boller and J. Grafman.

Fei Xu (B.A. 1991, Smith College) is a doctoral candidate in cognitive science in the Department of Brain and Cogitive Sciences, Massachusetts Institute of Technology. Her research interests include cognitive development and language development.

Harald Clahsen (*Habilitation* "postdoctoral thesis" 1987, University of Düsseldorf) is a senior lecturer in the Department of Linguistics, University of Düsseldorf. His research focuses on first language acquisition, language disorders, and second language development by adults. His interests also include the theory of syntax and the structure of pidgins and creoles. He is the author of *Child Language and Developmental Dysphasia* (1991).

STATEMENT OF EDITORIAL POLICY

The *Monographs* series is intended as an outlet for major reports of developmental research that generate authoritative new findings and use these to foster a fresh and/or better-integrated perspective on some conceptually significant issue or controversy. Submissions from programmatic research projects are particularly welcome; these may consist of individually or group-authored reports of findings from some single large-scale investigation or of a sequence of experiments centering on some particular question. Multiauthored sets of independent studies that center on the same underlying question can also be appropriate; a critical requirement in such instances is that the various authors address common issues and that the contribution arising from the set as a whole be both unique and substantial. In essence, irrespective of how it may be framed, any work that contributes significant data and/or extends developmental thinking will be taken under editorial consideration.

Submissions should contain a minimum of 80 manuscript pages (including tables and references); the upper limit of 150–175 pages is much more flexible (please submit four copies; a copy of every submission and associated correspondence is deposited eventually in the archives of the SRCD). Neither membership in the Society for Research in Child Development nor affiliation with the academic discipline of psychology are relevant; the significance of the work in extending developmental theory and in contributing new empirical information is by far the most crucial consideration. Because the aim of the series is not only to advance knowledge on specialized topics but also to enhance cross-fertilization among disciplines or subfields, it is important that the links between the specific issues under study and larger questions relating to developmental processes emerge as clearly to the general reader as to specialists on the given topic.

Potential authors who may be unsure whether the manuscript they are planning would make an appropriate submission are invited to draft an outline of what they propose and send it to the Editor for assessment.

This mechanism, as well as a more detailed description of all editorial policies, evaluation processes, and format requirements, is given in the "Guidelines for the Preparation of *Monographs* Submissions," which can be obtained by writing to Wanda C. Bronson, Institute of Human Development, 1203 Tolman Hall, University of California, Berkeley, CA 94720.